Pr...

CHRIS...

SELECTED MESSAGES

Book 1

SELECTED MESSAGES

From the Writings of
Ellen G. White

BOOK ONE

Significant and ever-timely counsels gathered from periodical articles, manuscript statements, and certain valuable pamphlets and tracts long out of print.

•

REVIEW *and* HERALD
PUBLISHING ASSOCIATION
WASHINGTON, D.C.

Contents

~~~~~~

PAGE

A Word to the Reader

~~~~~~

The presentation of books carrying the name of Ellen G. White on the title page, yet appearing decades after the death of the author, calls for a word of explanation. It will bring assurance to the reader to know that *Selected Messages* and other Spirit of prophecy works that have appeared since the author's death in 1915 are published in harmony with the express provisions of Mrs. E. G. White's will.

At the time of her death the messenger of the Lord left as an enduring treasure to the church an assemblage of more than 100,000 pages of material consisting of her current books, 4,500 articles in denominational periodicals, scores of tracts, pamphlets, out-of-print books, and her manuscripts, diaries, and letters.

A matter of great concern to Mrs. White during the last few years of her life was that of the future use and ever-widening publication of the prophetic messages entrusted to her. On February 9, 1912, in her last will and testament, she made definite provision for the continuing care of her literary works. Five men were chosen by her to serve for life as members of a self-perpetuating Board of Trustees responsible for the care of her writings.

For this important task, Mrs. White chose leading men of the denomination who were carrying large burdens in church administration. Those named by her to serve as trustees were: Arthur G. Daniells, then president of the General Conference; Francis M. Wilcox, then editor of the *Review and Herald;* Charles H. Jones, for many years manager of the Pacific Press; Clarence C. Crisler, one of her secretaries, who came to her employment from the General Conference, and who, after her death, was sent to the Far East to serve as division secretary; and William C. White, her son, who, after the death of Elder James White in 1881, traveled constantly with his mother and assisted her in the publishing of her writings, and in other ways.

Mrs. White's instruction to this board provided authorization for the continued publication of her books, for the ever-widening distribution of these volumes in other languages, and for "the printing of compilations from my manuscripts."

It was her expectation that as the church grew and faced new needs and entered upon new crises there would be a demand for compilations of her writings presenting various lines of instruction gathered from her manuscripts, pamphlets, and periodical articles.

Since Mrs. White's death the library of books from her pen has been enlarged to include the following works issued in this sequence:

> Fundamentals of Christian Education (1923)
> Counsels on Health (1923)
> Testimonies to Ministers and Gospel Workers (1923)
> Christian Service (1925)
> Messages to Young People (1930)
> Medical Ministry (1933)
> Counsels on Diet and Foods (1938)
> Counsels on Sabbath School Work (1938)

Counsels on Stewardship (1940)
Evangelism (1946)
Counsels to Writers and Editors (1946)
The Story of Redemption (1947)
Temperance (1949)
Welfare Ministry (1952)
The Adventist Home (1952)
My Life Today (1952)
The Colporteur Ministry (1953)
Child Guidance (1954)
Sons and Daughters of God (1955)

In addition to these books a supplement of Ellen G. White materials has been assembled for each of the seven volumes of *The Seventh-day Adventist Bible Commentary.*

Selected Messages is a unique type of compilation, in that it seeks to gather together and make permanently available not only valuable periodical articles and manuscript statements but also certain priceless old pamphlets and tracts now out of print. Included among the counsels here presented are her statements on inspiration written in the mid-and-late 1880's, her observations on the "two laws" penned at about the turn of the century, the pamphlet, "Should Christians Be Members of Secret Societies?" published in 1893, messages of comfort to those in affliction or facing death, and a sizable group of periodical articles dealing at length with key doctrinal points. Certain of these materials have been brought to the attention of the church through reprints of Mrs. White's articles in our journals and in leaflets, and in some cases through quotations in the books of other authors dealing with the Spirit of prophecy, but these sources cannot be included in the *Index to the Writings of Ellen G. White.*

Selected Messages, Books 1 and 2, include items that have been published in *Notebook Leaflets,* formerly known as *"Elmshaven" Leaflets.* These miscellaneous leaflets treating many subjects have been highly valued. Not a few of the documents from which these were drawn, however, were through subsequent years embodied in such books as *Medical Ministry, Evangelism,* and *The Adventist Home,* and in other cases paralleling statements appear in these books of more recent issue. Those portions that still have a unique place in presenting counsel and instruction have been included in *Selected Messages.* Hence it will not be necessary longer to keep the *Notebook Leaflets* in print. The issuance of these volumes also makes possible the presentation of small groups of choice materials not published before, but which will be greatly appreciated.

The several sections in these volumes are quite unrelated. An introductory statement will be found at the opening of each section, giving the background of the items that appear. Here and there through the text, notes of explanation will be found. These are not inserted for the purpose of interpreting the counsel, but to call attention to circumstances and special situations that may have a bearing on the points presented.

This work, *Selected Messages,* has been compiled in the offices of the Ellen G. White Publications under the direction of the Board of Trustees of the Ellen G. White Publications and by its staff. Introductory statements are signed by this board, and explanatory notes, approved by the trustees, are signed "Compilers."

Selected Messages is included in the new *Index to the Writings of Ellen G. White.* That these volumes published so many years after Mrs. White's death may bring to the church in permanent form instruction that will be of service in the accomplishment of our God-assigned task, is the sincere prayer and desire of the Publishers and

THE BOARD OF TRUSTEES OF THE
ELLEN G. WHITE PUBLICATIONS

The Light on Our Pathway

INTRODUCTION

~~~~~~~~~~~~~~~~~~~~~~~~~~~~~~~

Statements penned by Ellen G. White, regarding her work as the messenger of the Lord and concerning the processes by which God communicates His will to members of the human family, are always helpful and interesting. Such are presented in this opening section of *Selected Messages*.

Although the question of inspiration was touched on at intervals through her seventy years of ministry, the outstanding presentation is the author's Introduction to *The Great Controversy* (not appearing here) written in May, 1888. An earlier statement, "Objections to the Bible," penned in 1886, is published herein, and another, "The Inspiration of the Word of God," written in the autumn of 1888, is also presented here. A fourth major statement, "The Mysteries of the Bible a Proof of Its Inspiration," was published in 1889 and may be found in *Testimonies,* volume 5, pages 698-711.

Various explanations about her work, the republication of the 1913 tract "The Writing and Sending Out of the Testimonies to the Church," and Mrs. White's answers to certain questions and charges concerning her earlier writings round out the section devoted to "The Light on Our Pathway."—WHITE TRUSTEES.

1.

The Inspiration of the Prophetic Writers

~~~~~~~~~~~~~~~~

THE INSPIRATION OF THE WORD OF GOD

This is a time when the question with all propriety may be asked, "When the Son of man cometh, shall he find faith on the earth?" (Luke 18:8).

Spiritual darkness has covered the earth and gross darkness the people. There are in many churches skepticism and infidelity in the interpretation of the Scriptures. Many, very many, are questioning the verity and truth of the Scriptures. Human reasoning and the imaginings of the human heart are undermining the inspiration of the Word of God, and that which should be received as granted, is surrounded with a cloud of mysticism. Nothing stands out in clear and distinct lines, upon rock bottom. This is one of the marked signs of the last days.

This Holy Book has withstood the assaults of Satan, who has united with evil men to make everything of divine character shrouded in clouds and darkness. But the Lord has preserved this Holy Book by His own miraculous power in its present shape—a chart or guidebook to the human family to show them the way to heaven.

But the oracles of God have been so manifestly neglected that there are but few in our world, even of those who profess to explain it to others, who have the divine knowledge of the Scriptures. There are learned men who have a college education, but these shepherds do not feed the flock of God. They do not consider that the excellencies of the Scriptures will be continually unfolding their hidden treasures as precious jewels are discovered by digging for them.

There are men who strive to be original, who are wise above what is written; therefore, their wisdom is foolishness. They discover wonderful things in advance, ideas which reveal that they are far behind in the comprehension of the divine will and purposes of God. In seeking to make plain or to unravel mysteries hid from ages from mortal man, they are like a man floundering about in the mud, unable to extricate himself and yet telling others how to get out of the muddy sea they themselves are in. This is a fit representation of the men who set themselves to correct the errors of the Bible. No man can improve the Bible by suggesting what the Lord meant to say or ought to have said.

Some look to us gravely and say, "Don't you think there might have been some mistake in the copyist or in the translators?" This is all probable, and the mind that is so narrow that it will hesitate and stumble over this possibility or probability would be just as ready to stumble over the mysteries of the Inspired Word, because their feeble minds cannot see through the purposes of God. Yes, they would just as easily stumble over plain facts that the common mind will accept, and discern the Divine, and to which God's utterance is plain and beautiful, full of marrow and fatness. All the mistakes will not cause trouble to one soul, or cause any feet to stumble, that would not manufacture difficulties from the plainest revealed truth.

God committed the preparation of His divinely inspired Word to finite man. This Word, arranged into books, the Old and New Testaments, is the guidebook to the inhabitants of a fallen world, bequeathed to them that, by studying and obeying the directions, not one soul would lose its way to heaven.

Those who think to make the supposed difficulties of Scripture plain, in measuring by their finite rule that which is inspired and that which is not inspired, had better cover their faces, as Elijah when the still small voice spoke to him; for they are in the presence of God and holy angels, who for ages have communicated to men light and knowledge, telling them what to do and what not to do, unfolding before them scenes of thrilling interest, waymark by waymark in symbols and signs and illustrations.

And He [God] has not, while presenting the perils clustering about the last days, qualified any finite man to unravel hidden mysteries or inspired one man or any class of men to pronounce judgment as to that which is inspired or is not. When men, in their finite judgment, find it necessary to go into an examination of scriptures to define that which is inspired and that which is not, they have stepped before Jesus to show Him a better way than He has led us.

I take the Bible just as it is, as the Inspired Word. I believe its utterances in an entire Bible. Men arise who think they find something to criticize in God's Word. They lay it bare before others as evidence of superior wisdom. These men are, many of them, smart men, learned men, they have eloquence and talent, the whole lifework [of whom] is to unsettle minds in regard to the inspiration of the Scriptures. They influence many to see as they do. And the same work is passed on from one to another, just as Satan designed it should be, until we may see the full meaning of the words of Christ, "When the Son of man cometh, shall he find faith on the earth?" (Luke 18:8).

Brethren, let not a mind or hand be engaged in criticizing the Bible. It is a work that Satan delights to have any of you do, but it is not a work the Lord has pointed out for you to do.

Men should let God take care of His own Book, His living oracles, as He has done for ages. They begin to question some parts of revelation, and pick flaws in the apparent inconsistencies of this statement and that statement. Beginning at Genesis, they give up that which they deem questionable, and their minds lead on, for Satan will lead to any length they may follow in their criticism, and they see something to doubt in the whole Scriptures. Their faculties of criticism become sharpened by exercise, and they can rest on nothing with a certainty. You try to reason with these men, but your time is lost. They will exercise their power of ridicule even upon the Bible. They even become mockers, and they would be astonished if you put it to them in that light.

Brethren, cling to your Bible, as it reads, and stop your criticisms in regard to its validity, and obey the Word, and not one of you will be lost. The ingenuity of men has been exercised for ages to measure the Word of God by their finite minds and limited comprehension. If the Lord, the Author of the living oracles, would throw back the curtain and reveal His wisdom and His glory before them, they would shrink into nothingness and exclaim as did Isaiah, "I am a man of unclean lips, and I dwell in the midst of a people of unclean lips" (Isa. 6:5).

Simplicity and plain utterance are comprehended by the illiterate, by the peasant, and the child as well as by the full-grown man or the giant in intellect. If the individual is possessed of large talents of mental powers, he will find in the oracles of God treasures of truth, beautiful and valuable, which he can appropriate. He will also find difficulties, and secrets and wonders which will give him the highest satisfaction to study during a long lifetime, and yet there is an infinity beyond.

Men of humble acquirements, possessing but limited capabilities and opportunities to become conversant in the Scriptures, find in the living oracles comfort, guidance, counsel, and the plan of salvation as clear as a sunbeam. No one need be lost for want of knowledge, unless he is willfully blind.

We thank God that the Bible is prepared for the poor man as well as for the learned man. It is fitted for all ages and all classes.—Manuscript 16, 1888 (written at Minneapolis, Minn., in autumn of 1888).

Objections to the Bible

Human minds vary. The minds of different education and thought receive different impressions of the same words, and it is difficult for one mind to give to one of a different temperament, education, and habits of thought by language exactly the same idea as that which is clear and distinct in his own mind. Yet to honest men, right-minded men, he can be so simple and plain as to convey his meaning for all practical purposes. If the man he communicates with is not honest and will not want to see and understand the truth, he will turn his words and language in everything to suit his own purposes. He will misconstrue his words, play upon his imagination, wrest them from their true meaning, and then entrench himself in unbelief, claiming that the sentiments are all wrong.

This is the way my writings are treated by those who wish to misunderstand and pervert them. They turn the truth of God into a lie. In the very same way that they treat the writings in my published articles and in my books, so do skeptics and infidels treat the Bible. They read it according to their desire to pervert, to misapply, to willfully wrest the utterances from their true meaning. They declare that the Bible can prove anything and everything, that every sect proves their doctrines right, and that the most diverse doctrines are proved from the Bible.

The writers of the Bible had to express their ideas in human language. It was written by human men. These men were inspired of the Holy Spirit. Because of the imperfections of human understanding of language, or the perversity of the human mind, ingenious in evading truth, many read and understand the Bible to please themselves. It is not that the difficulty is in the Bible. Opposing politicians argue points of law in the statute book, and take opposite views in their application and in these laws.

The Scriptures were given to men, not in a continuous chain of unbroken utterances, but piece by piece through successive generations, as God in His providence saw a fitting opportunity to impress man at sundry times and divers places. Men wrote as they were moved upon by the Holy Ghost. There is "first the bud, then the blossom, and next the fruit," "first the blade, then the ear, after that the full corn in the ear." This is exactly what the Bible utterances are to us.

There is not always perfect order or apparent unity in the Scriptures. The miracles of Christ are not given in exact order, but are given just as the circumstances occurred, which called for this divine revealing of the power of Christ. The truths of the Bible are as pearls hidden. They must be searched, dug out by painstaking effort. Those who take only a surface view of the Scriptures will, with their superficial knowledge, which they think is very deep, talk of the contradictions of the Bible, and question the authority of the Scriptures. But those whose hearts are in harmony with truth and duty will search the Scriptures with a heart prepared to receive divine impressions. The illuminated soul sees a spiritual unity, one grand golden thread running through the whole, but it requires patience, thought, and prayer to trace out the precious golden thread. Sharp contentions over the Bible have led to investigation and revealed the precious jewels of truth. Many tears have been shed, many prayers offered, that the Lord would open the understanding to His Word.

The Bible is not given to us in grand superhuman language. Jesus, in order to reach man where he is, took humanity. The Bible must be given in the language of men. Everything that is human is imperfect. Different meanings are expressed by the same word; there is not one word for each distinct idea. The Bible was given for practical purposes.

The stamps of minds are different. All do not understand expressions and statements alike. Some understand the statements of the Scriptures to suit their own particular minds and cases. Prepossessions, prejudices, and passions have a strong influence to darken the understanding and confuse the mind even in reading the words of Holy Writ.

The disciples traveling to Emmaus needed to be disentangled in their interpretation of the Scriptures. Jesus walked with them disguised, and as a man He talked with them. Beginning at Moses and the prophets He taught them in all things concerning Himself, that His life, His mission, His sufferings, His death were just as the Word of God had foretold. He opened their understanding that they might understand the Scriptures. How quickly He straightened out the tangled ends and showed the unity and divine verity of the Scriptures. How much men in these times need their understanding opened.

The Bible is written by inspired men, but it is not God's mode of thought and expression. It is that of humanity. God, as a writer, is not represented. Men will often say such an expression is not like God. But God has not put Himself in words, in logic, in rhetoric, on trial in the Bible. The writers of the Bible were God's penmen, not His pen. Look at the different writers.

It is not the words of the Bible that are inspired, but the men that were inspired. Inspiration acts not on the man's words or his expressions but on the man himself, who, under the influence of the Holy Ghost, is imbued with thoughts. But the words receive the impress of the individual mind. The divine mind is diffused. The divine mind and will is combined with the human mind and will; thus the utterances of the man are the word of God.—Manuscript 24, 1886 (written in Europe in 1886).

UNITY IN DIVERSITY

There is variety in a tree, there are scarcely two leaves just alike. Yet this variety adds to the perfection of the tree as a whole.

• In our Bible, we might ask, Why need Matthew, Mark, Luke, and John in the Gospels, why need the Acts of the Apostles, and the variety of writers in the Epistles, go over the same thing?

The Lord gave His word in just the way He wanted it to come. He gave it through different writers, each having his own individuality, though going over the same history. Their testimonies are brought together in one Book, and are like the testimonies in a social meeting. They do not represent things in just the same style. Each has an experience of his own, and this diversity broadens and deepens the knowledge that is brought out to meet the necessities of varied minds. The thoughts expressed have not a set uniformity, as if cast in an iron mold, making the very hearing monotonous. In such uniformity there would be a loss of grace and distinctive beauty. . . .

The Creator of all ideas may impress different minds with the same thought, but each may express it in a different way, yet without contradiction. The fact that this difference exists should not perplex or confuse us. It is seldom that two persons will view and express truth in the very same way. Each dwells on particular points which his constitution and education have fitted him to appreciate. The sunlight falling upon the different objects gives those objects a different hue.

Through the inspiration of His Spirit the Lord gave His apostles truth, to be expressed according to the development of their minds by the Holy Spirit. But the mind is not cramped, as if forced into a certain mold.— Letter 53, 1900.

THE LORD SPEAKS IN IMPERFECT SPEECH

The Lord speaks to human beings in imperfect speech, in order that the degenerate senses, the dull, earthly perception, of earthly beings may comprehend His words. Thus is shown God's condescension. He meets fallen human beings where they are. The Bible, perfect as it is in its simplicity, does not answer to the great ideas of God; for infinite ideas cannot be perfectly embodied in finite vehicles of thought. Instead of the expressions of the Bible being exaggerated, as many people suppose, the strong expressions break down before the magnificence of the thought, though the penman selected the most expressive language through which to convey the truths of higher education. Sinful beings can only bear to look upon a shadow of the brightness of heaven's glory.—Letter 121, 1901.

No Man to Pronounce Judgment on God's Word

Both in the [Battle Creek] Tabernacle and in the college the subject of inspiration has been taught, and finite men have taken it upon themselves to say that some things in the Scriptures were inspired and some were not. I was shown that the Lord did not inspire the articles on inspiration published in the *Review*,* neither did He approve their endorsement before our youth in the college. When men venture to criticize the Word of God, they venture on sacred, holy ground, and had better fear and tremble and hide their wisdom as foolishness. God sets no man to pronounce judgment on His Word, selecting some things as inspired and discrediting others as uninspired. The testimonies have been treated in the same way; but God is not in this.—Letter 22, 1889.

---

* Reference here is to a series of articles the writer of which advocated that there were "differences in degrees" of inspiration. See *The Review and Herald*, Jan. 15, 1884.—COMPILERS.

2.

Ellen G. White and Her Writings

~~~~~~~~~~~~~~~~

A LETTER TO DR. PAULSON

St. Helena, California
June 14, 1906

DEAR BROTHER:

Your letter came to me while in southern California. For some weeks the consideration of matters connected with the development of our sanitarium work there, and the writing out of the views given me regarding the earthquake and its lessons, have taken my time and strength.

But now I must respond to the letters received from you and others. In your letter you speak of your early training to have implicit faith in the testimonies and say, "I was led to conclude and most firmly believe that *every* word that you ever spoke in public or private, that every letter you wrote under *any* and *all* circumstances, was as inspired as the Ten Commandments."

My brother, you have studied my writings diligently, and you have never found that I have made any such claims, neither will you find that the pioneers in our cause ever made such claims.

In my introduction to *The Great Controversy* you have no doubt read my statement regarding the Ten Commandments and the Bible, which should have helped you to a correct understanding of the matter under consideration. Here is the statement:

"The Bible points to God as its author; yet it was written by human hands; and in the varied style of its different books it presents the characteristics of the several writers. The truths revealed are all 'given by inspiration of God' (2 Tim. 3:16); yet they are expressed in the words of men. The Infinite One by His Holy Spirit has shed light into the minds and hearts of His servants. He has given dreams and visions, symbols and figures; and those to whom the truth was thus revealed, have themselves embodied the thought in human language.

"The Ten Commandments were spoken by God Himself, and were written by His own hand. They are of divine, and not human composition. But the Bible, with its God-given truths expressed in the language of men, presents a union of the divine and the human. Such a union existed in the nature of Christ, who was the Son of God and the Son of man. Thus it is true of the Bible, as it was of Christ, that 'the Word was made flesh, and dwelt among us' (John 1:14).

"Written in different ages, by men who differed widely in rank and occupation, and in mental and spiritual endowments, the books of the Bible present a wide contrast in style, as well as a diversity in the nature of the subjects unfolded. Different forms of expression are employed by different writers; often the same truth is more strikingly presented by one than by another. And as several writers present a subject under varied aspects and relations, there may appear, to the superficial, careless, or prejudiced reader, to be discrepancy or contradiction, where the thoughtful, reverent student, with clearer insight, discerns the underlying harmony.

"As presented through different individuals, the truth is brought out in its varied aspects. One writer is more strongly impressed with one phase of the subject; he grasps those points that harmonize with his experience or with his power of perception and appreciation; another seizes upon a different phase; and each, under the guidance of the Holy Spirit, presents what is most forcibly impressed upon his own mind—a different aspect of the truth in each, but a perfect harmony through all. And the truths thus revealed unite to form a perfect whole, adapted to meet the wants of men in all the circumstances and experiences of life.

"God has been pleased to communicate His truth to the world by human agencies, and He Himself, by His Holy Spirit, qualified men and enabled them to do His work. He guided the mind in the selection of what to speak and what to write. The treasure was entrusted to earthen vessels, yet it is, none the less, from Heaven. The testimony is conveyed through the imperfect expression of human language, yet it is the testimony of God; and the obedient, believing child of God beholds in it the glory of a divine power, full of grace and truth."

The Integrity of the Testimonies

In perfect harmony with this are my statements found in the article "The Testimonies Slighted," written June 20, 1882, and published in *Testimonies for the Church*, volume 5, No. 31, pages 62-84. From this I quote for your consideration, several paragraphs:

"Many are looking with self-complacency upon the long years during which they have advocated the truth. They now feel that they are entitled to a reward for their past trials and obedience. But this genuine experience in the things of God in the past, makes them more guilty before Him for not preserving their integrity and going forward to perfection. The faithfulness for the past year will never atone for the neglect of the present year. A man's truthfulness yesterday will not atone for his falsehood today.

"Many excused their disregard of the testimonies by saying, 'Sister White is influenced by her husband; the testimonies are molded by his spirit and judgment.' Others were seeking to gain something from me which they could construe to justify their course or to give them influence.

It was then I decided that nothing more should go from my pen until the converting power of God was seen in the church. But the Lord placed the burden upon my soul. I labored for you earnestly. How much this cost both my husband and myself, eternity will tell. Have I not a knowledge of the state of the church, when the Lord has presented their case before me again and again for years? Repeated warnings have been given, yet there has been no decided change. . . .

"Yet now when I send you a testimony of warning and reproof, many of you declare it to be merely the opinion of Sister White. You have thereby insulted the Spirit of God. You know how the Lord has manifested Himself through the Spirit of prophecy. Past, present, and future have passed before me. I have been shown faces that I had never seen, and years afterward I knew them when I saw them. I have been aroused from my sleep with a vivid sense of subjects previously presented to my mind and I have written, at midnight, letters that have gone across the continent, and arriving at a crisis, have saved great disaster to the cause of God. This has been my work for many years. A power has impelled me to reprove and rebuke wrongs that I had not thought of. Is this work of the last thirty-six years from above or from beneath? . . .

"When I went to Colorado I was so burdened for you that, in my weakness, I wrote many pages to be read at your camp meeting. Weak and trembling, I arose at three o'clock in the morning to write to you. God was speaking through clay. You might say that this communication was only a letter. Yes, it was a letter, but prompted by the Spirit of God, to bring before your minds things that had been shown me. In these letters which I write, in the testimonies I bear, I am presenting to you that which the Lord has presented to me. I do not write one article in the paper, expressing merely my own ideas. They are what God has opened before me in vision—the precious rays of light shining from the throne. . . .

"What voice will you acknowledge as the voice of God? What power has the Lord in reserve to correct your errors and show you your course as it is? What power to work in the church? If you refuse to believe until every shadow of uncertainty and every possibility of doubt is removed, you will never believe. The doubt that demands perfect knowledge will never yield to faith. Faith rests upon evidence, not demonstration. The Lord requires us to obey the voice of duty, when there are other voices all around us urging us to pursue an opposite course. It requires earnest attention from us to distinguish the voice which speaks from God. We must resist and conquer inclination, and obey the voice of conscience without parleying or compromise, lest its promptings cease, and will and impulse control.

"The word of the Lord comes to us all who have not resisted His Spirit by determining not to hear and obey. This voice is heard in warnings, in counsels, in reproof. It is the Lord's message of light to His people. If we wait for louder calls or better opportunities, the light may be withdrawn, and we left in darkness. . . .

"It pains me to say, my brethren, that your sinful neglect to walk in the light has enshrouded you in darkness. You may now be honest in not recognizing and obeying the light; the doubts you have entertained, your neglect to heed the requirements of God, have blinded your perception so that darkness is now to you light, and light is darkness. God has bidden you to go forward to perfection. Christianity is a religion of progress. Light from God is full and ample, waiting our demand upon it. Whatever blessings the Lord may give, He has an infinite supply beyond, an inexhaustible store from which we may draw. Skepticism may treat the sacred claims of the gospel with jests, scoffing, and denial. The spirit of worldliness may contaminate the many and control the few; the cause of God may hold its ground only by great exertion and continual sacrifice, yet it will triumph finally.

"The word is: Go forward; discharge your individual duty, and leave all consequences in the hands of God. If we move forward where Jesus leads the way we shall see His triumph, we shall share His joy. We must share the conflicts if we wear the crown of victory. Like Jesus, we must be made perfect through suffering. Had Christ's life been one of ease, then might we safely yield to sloth. Since His life was marked with continual self-denial, suffering, and self-sacrifice, we shall make no complaint if we are partakers with Him. We can walk safely in the darkest path if we have the Light of the world for our guide. . . .

"When the Lord last presented your case before me, and made known to me that you had not regarded the light which had been given you, I was bidden to speak to you plainly in His name, for His anger was kindled against you. These words were spoken to me: 'Your work is appointed you of God. Many will not hear you, for they refused to hear the Great Teacher; many will not be corrected, for their ways are right in their own eyes. Yet bear to them the reproofs and warnings I shall give you, whether they will hear or forbear.' ". . .

In connection with these quotations, study again the article "The Nature and Influence of the Testimonies," in *Testimonies,* volume 5, pages 654-691.

The statement which you quote from Testimony No. 31 [volume 5, page 67] is correct: "In these letters which I write, in the testimonies I bear, I am presenting to you that which the Lord has presented to me. I do not write one article in the paper expressing merely my own ideas. They are what God has opened before me in vision —the precious rays of light shining from the throne." It is true concerning the articles in our papers and in the many volumes of my books. I have been instructed in accordance with the Word in the precepts of the law of God. I have been instructed in selecting from the lessons of Christ. Are not the positions taken in my writings in harmony with the teachings of Jesus Christ?

Peril of Deceptive Representations

To some of the questions you have asked, I am not to answer Yes or No. I must not make statements that can be misconstrued. I see and feel the peril of those who, I have been instructed, are endangering their souls at times

by listening to deceptive representations regarding the
messages that God has given me. Through many twistings
and turnings and false reasonings on what I have written,
they try to vindicate their personal unbelief. I am sorry
for my brethren who have been walking in the mist of sus-
picion and skepticism and false reasoning. I know that
some of them would be blessed by messages of counsel if
the clouds obscuring their spiritual vision could be driven
back, and they could see aright. But they do not see clearly.
Therefore I dare not communicate with them. When the
Spirit of God clears away the mysticism, there will be
found just as complete comfort and faith and hope in the
messages that I have been instructed to give, as were found
in them in years past.

Truth will surely bear away the victory. The One who
gave His life to ransom man from the delusions of Satan,
is not asleep, but watching. When His sheep turn away
from following the voice of a stranger, whose sheep they
are not, they will rejoice in the voice they have loved to
follow.

We can learn precious lessons from the study of the
life of Christ. The envious Pharisees misinterpreted the
acts and words of Christ, which, if properly received,
would have been beneficial to their spiritual understanding.
Instead of admiring His goodness, they charged Him, in
the presence of His disciples, with impiety—"Why eateth
your Master with publicans and sinners?" (Matt. 9:11).
Instead of addressing our blessed Saviour Himself, whose
answer would at once have convicted them of their malice,
they talked with the disciples, and made their charges
where, as a leaven of evil, they would do great harm. If
Christ had been an impious man, He would have lost His
hold upon the hearts of His believing followers. But because of their confidence in Christ, the disciples would not
give ear to the insinuations of His wicked accusers.

Desiring to bring censure upon the disciples, these
wicked accusers went again and again to Christ with the
question, Why do Thy disciples that which is not lawful?
And when they judged our Lord to have transgressed, they

spoke, not to Himself, but to His disciples, to plant the seeds of unbelief in the hearts of His followers.

Thus they worked to bring in doubt and dissension. Every method was tried to bring doubt into the hearts of the little flock, that it might cause them to watch for something that would check the good and gracious work of the gospel of Jesus Christ.

Work of this same character will be brought to bear upon true believers today. The Lord Jesus reads the heart; He discerns the interests and purposes of the thoughts of all men concerning Himself and His believing disciples. He answers their thoughts concerning the faultfinding ones, "They that be whole need not a physician, but they that are sick" (Matt. 9:12). The insolent Pharisees had an exalted idea of their own piety and holiness, while they were ready to pass censure on the lives of others.— Letter 206, 1906.

THE LORD'S MESSENGER

Last night, in vision, I was standing before an assembly of our people, bearing a decided testimony regarding present truth and present duty. After the discourse, many gathered about me, asking questions. They desired so many explanations about this point, and that point, and another point, that I said, "One at a time, if you please, lest you confuse me."

And then I appealed to them, saying: "For years you have had many evidences that the Lord has given me a work to do. These evidences could scarcely have been greater than they are. Will you brush away all these evidences as a cobweb, at the suggestion of a man's unbelief? That which makes my heart ache is the fact that many who are now perplexed and tempted are those who have had abundance of evidence and opportunity to consider and pray and understand; and yet they do not discern the nature of the sophistries that are presented to influence them to reject the warnings God has given to save them from the delusions of these last days."

Some have stumbled over the fact that I said I did not

claim to be a prophet;* and they have asked, Why is this?

I have had no claims to make, only that *I am instructed that I am the Lord's messenger;* that He called me in my youth to be His messenger, to receive His word, and to give a clear and decided message in the name of the Lord Jesus.

Early in my youth I was asked several times, Are you a prophet? I have ever responded, I am the Lord's messenger. I know that many have called me a prophet, but I have made no claim to this title. My Saviour declared me to be His messenger. "Your work," He instructed me, "is to bear My word. Strange things will arise, and in your youth I set you apart to bear the message to the erring ones, to carry the word before unbelievers, and with pen and voice to reprove from the Word actions that are not right. Exhort from the Word. I will make My Word open to you. It shall not be as a strange language. In the true eloquence of simplicity, with voice and pen, the messages that I give shall be heard from one who has never learned in the schools. My Spirit and My power shall be with you.

"Be not afraid of man, for My shield shall protect you. It is not you that speaketh: it is the Lord that giveth the messages of warning and reproof. Never deviate from the truth *under any circumstances.* Give the light I shall give you. The messages for these last days shall be written in books, and shall stand immortalized, to testify against those who have once rejoiced in the light, but who have been led to give it up because of the seductive influences of evil."

Why have I not claimed to be a prophet?—Because in these days many who boldly claim that they are prophets are a reproach to the cause of Christ; and because my work includes much more than the word "prophet" signifies.

When this work was first given me, I begged the Lord to lay the burden on someone else. The work was so large and broad and deep that I feared I could not do it. But by

---

* Reference is here made to a discourse given at Battle Creek, October 2, 1904, in which she said, "I do not claim to be a prophetess."
—COMPILERS.

His Holy Spirit the Lord has enabled me to perform the work which He gave me to do.

A Work of Many Features

God has made plain to me the various ways in which He would use me to carry forward a special work. Visions have been given me, with the promise, "If you deliver the messages faithfully and endure to the end, you shall eat of the fruit of the tree of life, and drink of the water of the river of life."

The Lord gave me great light on health reform. In connection with my husband, I was to be a medical missionary worker. I was to set an example to the church by taking the sick to my home and caring for them. This I have done, giving the women and children vigorous treatment. I was also to speak on the subject of Christian temperance, as the Lord's appointed messenger. I engaged heartily in this work, and spoke to large assemblies on temperance in its broadest and truest sense.

I was instructed that I must ever urge upon those who profess to believe the truth, the necessity of practicing the truth. This means sanctification, and sanctification means the culture and training of every capability for the Lord's service.

I was charged not to neglect or pass by those who were being wronged. I was specially charged to protest against any arbitrary or overbearing action toward the ministers of the gospel by those having official authority. Disagreeable though the duty may be, I am to reprove the oppressor, and plead for justice. I am to present the necessity of maintaining justice and equity in all our institutions.

If I see those in positions of trust neglecting aged ministers, I am to present the matter to those whose duty it is to care for them. Ministers who have faithfully done their work are not to be forgotten or neglected when they have become feeble in health. Our conferences are not to disregard the needs of those who have borne the burdens of the work. It was after John had grown old in the service of the Lord that he was exiled to Patmos. And on that lonely isle he received more communications from heaven than he had received during the rest of his lifetime.

After my marriage I was instructed that I must show a special interest in motherless and fatherless children, taking some under my own charge for a time, and then finding homes for them. Thus I would be giving others an example of what they could do.

Although called to travel often, and having much writing to do, I have taken children of three and five years of age, and have cared for them, educated them, and trained them for responsible positions. I have taken into my home from time to time boys from ten to sixteen years of age, giving them motherly care, and a training for service. I have felt it my duty to bring before our people that work for which those in every church should feel a responsibility.

While in Australia I carried on this same line of work, taking into my home orphan children, who were in danger of being exposed to temptations that might cause the loss of their souls.

In Australia we* also worked as Christian medical missionaries. At times I made my home in Cooranbong an asylum for the sick and afflicted. My secretary, who had received a training in the Battle Creek Sanitarium, stood by my side, and did the work of a missionary nurse. No charge was made for her services, and we won the confidence of the people by the interest that we manifested in the sick and suffering. After a time the Health Retreat at Cooranbong was built, and then we were relieved of this burden.

No Boastful Claims

To claim to be a prophetess is something that I have never done. If others call me by that name, I have no controversy with them. But my work has covered so many lines that I cannot call myself other than a messenger, sent to bear a message from the Lord to His people, and to take up work in any line that He points out.

---

* Reference here is to her associate workers. James White died in 1881.

When I was last in Battle Creek, I said before a large congregation that I did not claim to be a prophetess. Twice I referred to this matter, intending each time to make the statement, "I do not claim to be a prophetess." If I spoke otherwise than this, let all now understand that what I had in mind to say was that I do not claim the title of prophet or prophetess.

I understood that some were anxious to know if Mrs. White still held the same views that she did years ago when they had heard her speak in the sanitarium grove, in the Tabernacle, and at the camp meetings held in the suburbs of Battle Creek. I assured them that the message she bears today is the same that she has borne during the sixty years of her public ministry. She has the same service to do for the Master that was laid upon her in her girl-hood. She receives lessons from the same Instructor. The directions given her are, "Make known to others what I have revealed to you. Write out the messages that I give you, that the people may have them." This is what she has endeavored to do.

I have written many books, and they have been given a wide circulation. Of myself I could not have brought out the truth in these books, but the Lord has given me the help of His Holy Spirit. These books, giving the instruction that the Lord has given me during the past sixty years, contain light from heaven, and will bear the test of investigation.

At the age of seventy-eight I am still toiling. We are all in the hands of the Lord. I trust in Him; for I know that He will never leave nor forsake those who put their trust in Him. I have committed myself to His keeping.

"And I thank Christ Jesus our Lord, who hath enabled me, for that he counted me faithful, putting me into the ministry" (1 Tim. 1:12).—*The Review and Herald,* July 26, 1906.

The Work of a Prophet and More

During the discourse, I said that I did not claim to be a prophetess. Some were surprised at this statement, and as much is being said in regard to it, I will make an explanation. Others have called me a prophetess, but I have never assumed that title. I have not felt that it was my duty thus to designate myself. Those who boldly assume that they are prophets in this our day are often a reproach to the cause of Christ.

My work includes much more than this name signifies. I regard myself as a messenger, entrusted by the Lord with messages for His people.—Letter 55, 1905.

I am now instructed that I am not to be hindered in my work by those who engage in suppositions regarding its nature, whose minds are struggling with so many intricate problems connected with the supposed work of a prophet. My commission embraces the work of a prophet, but it does not end there. It embraces much more than the minds of those who have been sowing the seeds of unbelief can comprehend.—Letter 244, 1906. (Addressed to elders of Battle Creek church.)

RECEIVING AND IMPARTING THE LIGHT

As inquiries are frequently made as to my state in vision, and after I come out, I would say that when the Lord sees fit to give a vision, I am taken into the presence of Jesus and angels, and am entirely lost to earthly things. I can see no farther than the angel directs me. My attention is often directed to scenes transpiring upon earth.

At times I am carried far ahead into the future and shown what is to take place. Then again I am shown things as they have occurred in the past. After I come out of vision I do not at once remember all that I have seen, and the matter is not so clear before me until I write, then the scene rises before me as was presented in vision, and I can write with freedom. Sometimes the things which I have seen are hid from me after I come out of vision, and I cannot call them to mind until I am brought before a company where that vision applies, then the things which I have seen come to my mind with force. I am just as dependent upon the Spirit of the Lord in relating or writing a vision, as in having the vision. It is impossible for me to call up things which have been shown me unless the Lord brings them before me at the time that He is pleased to have me relate or write them.—*Spiritual Gifts* (1860), vol. 2, pp. 292, 293.

Although I am as dependent upon the Spirit of the Lord in writing my views as I am in receiving them, yet the words I employ in describing what I have seen are my own, unless they be those spoken to me by an angel, which I always enclose in marks of quotation.—*The Review and Herald,* Oct. 8, 1867.

The question is asked, How does Sister White know in regard to the matters of which she speaks so decidedly, as if she had authority to say these things? I speak thus because they flash upon my mind when in perplexity like lightning out of a dark cloud in the fury of a storm. Some scenes presented before me years ago have not been retained in my memory, but when the instruction then given is needed, sometimes even when I am standing before the people, the remembrance comes sharp and clear, like a flash of lightning, bringing to mind distinctly that particular instruction. At such times I cannot refrain from saying the things that flash into my mind, not because I have had a new vision, but because that which was presented to me perhaps years in the past has been recalled to my mind forcibly.—*The Writing and Sending Out of the Testimonies,* p. 24.

No Claim to Infallibility

We have many lessons to learn, and many, many to unlearn. God and heaven alone are infallible. Those who think that they will never have to give up a cherished view, never have occasion to change an opinion, will be disappointed. As long as we hold to our own ideas and opinions with determined persistency, we cannot have the unity for which Christ prayed.—*The Review and Herald,* July 26, 1892.

In regard to infallibility, I never claimed it; God alone is infallible. His word is true, and in Him is no variableness, or shadow of turning.—Letter 10, 1895.

THE SACRED AND THE COMMON

Sanitarium, California
March 5, 1909

I am troubled in regard to Brother A, who for some years has been a worker in southern California. He has made some strange statements, and I am pained to see him denying the testimonies as a whole because of what seems to him an inconsistency—a statement made by me in regard to the number of rooms in the Paradise Valley Sanitarium. Brother A says that in a letter written to one of the brethren in southern California, the statement was made by me that the sanitarium contained forty rooms, when there were really only thirty-eight. This, Brother A gives to me as the reason why he has lost confidence in the testimonies. . . .

The information given concerning the number of rooms in the Paradise Valley Sanitarium was given, not as a revelation from the Lord, but simply as a human opinion. There has never been revealed to me the exact number of rooms in any of our sanitariums; and the knowledge I have obtained of such things I have gained by inquiring of those who were supposed to know. In my words, when speaking upon these common subjects, there is nothing to lead minds to believe that I receive my knowledge in a vision from the Lord and am stating it as such. . . .

When the Holy Spirit reveals anything regarding the institutions connected with the Lord's work, or concerning the work of God upon human hearts and minds, as He has revealed these things through me in the past, the message given is to be regarded as light given of God for those who need it. But for one to mix the sacred with the common is a great mistake. In a tendency to do this we may see the working of the enemy to destroy souls.

To every soul whom God has created He has given capabilities to serve Him, but Satan seeks to make this work of service hard by his constant temptation to mislead souls. He works to dim the spiritual perceptions that men may not distinguish between that which is common and that which is holy. I have been made to know this distinction through a life's service for my Lord and Master. . . .

The message came to me, Dedicate yourself to the highest work ever committed to mortals. I will give you high aspirations and powers and a true sense of the work of Christ. You are not your own, for you are bought with a price, by the life and death of the Son of God. God calls for your child's heart and service under the sanctification of the Holy Spirit.

I gave myself, my whole being, to God, to obey His call in everything, and since that time my life has been spent in giving the message, with my pen and in speaking before large congregations. It is not I who controls my words and actions at such times.

But there are times when common things must be stated, common thoughts must occupy the mind, common letters must be written and information given that has passed from one to another of the workers. Such words, such information, are not given under the special inspiration of the Spirit of God. Questions are asked at times that are not upon religious subjects at all, and these questions must be answered. We converse about houses and lands, trades to be made, and locations for our institutions, their advantages and disadvantages.

I receive letters asking for advice on many strange subjects, and I advise according to the light that has been given me. Men have again and again opposed the counsel that I have been instructed to give because they did not want to receive the light given, and such experiences have led me to seek the Lord most earnestly.—Manuscript 107, 1909.

3.

Attitudes Toward the

Testimonies

~~~~~~~~~~~~~~~~

AN EARLY STATEMENT

I saw the state of some who stood on present truth, but disregarded the visions—the way God had chosen to teach in some cases, those who erred from Bible truth. I saw that in striking against the visions they did not strike against the worm—the feeble instrument that God spake through—but against the Holy Ghost. I saw it was a small thing to speak against the instrument, but it was dangerous to slight the words of God. I saw if they were in error and God chose to show them their errors through visions, and they disregarded the teachings of God through visions, they would be left to take their own way, and run in the way of error, and think they were right, until they would find it out too late. Then in the time of trouble I heard them cry to God in agony, "Why didst Thou not show us our wrong, that we might have got right and been ready for this time?" Then an angel pointed to them and said, "My Father taught, but you would not be taught. He spoke through visions, but you disregarded His voice, and He gave you up to your own ways, to be filled with your own doings."—Broadside, *To Those Who Are Receiving the Seal of the Living God,* Jan. 31, 1849.

SAFE INSTRUCTION FOR CLOSING DAYS

A wealth of moral influence has been brought to us in the last half century. Through His Holy Spirit the voice of God has come to us continually in warning and instruction, to confirm the faith of the believers in the Spirit of prophecy. Repeatedly the word has come, Write the things that I have given you to confirm the faith of My people in the position they have taken. Time and trial have not made void the instruction given, but through years of suffering and self-sacrifice have established the truth of the testimony given. The instruction that was given in the early days of the message is to be held as safe instruction to follow in these its closing days. Those who are indifferent to this light and instruction must not expect to escape the snares which we have been plainly told will cause the rejecters of light to stumble, and fall, and be snared, and be taken. If we study carefully the second chapter of Hebrews, we shall learn how important it is that we hold steadfastly to every principle of truth that has been given.—*The Review and Herald,* July 18, 1907.

VARYING ATTITUDES ENUMERATED

Soon every possible effort will be made to discount and pervert the truth of the testimonies of God's Spirit. We must have in readiness the clear, straight messages that since 1846 have been coming to God's people.

There will be those once united with us in the faith who will search for new, strange doctrines, for something odd and sensational to present to the people. They will bring in all conceivable fallacies, and will present them as coming from Mrs. White, that they may beguile souls. . . .

Those who have treated the light that the Lord has given as a common thing will not be benefited by the instruction presented.

There are those who will misinterpret the messages that God has given, in accordance with their spiritual blindness.

Some will yield their faith, and will deny the truth of the messages, pointing to them as falsehoods.

Some will hold them up to ridicule, working against the light that God has been giving for years, and some who are weak in the faith will thus be led astray.

But others will be greatly helped by the messages. Though not personally addressed, they will be corrected, and will be led to shun the evils specified. . . . The Spirit of the Lord will be in the instruction, and doubts existing in many minds will be swept away. The testimonies themselves will be the key that will explain the messages given, as scripture is explained by scripture. Many will read with eagerness the messages reproving wrong, that they may learn what they may do to be saved. . . . Light will dawn upon the understanding, and the Spirit will make an impression on minds, as Bible truth is clearly and simply presented in the messages that since 1846 God has been sending His people. These messages are to find their place in hearts, and transformations will take place.—Letter 73, 1903.

PERILS OF DISSECTING INSPIRED MESSAGES

Some sit in judgment on the Scriptures, declaring that this or that passage is not inspired, because it does not strike their minds favorably. They cannot harmonize it with their ideas of philosophy and science, "falsely so called" (1 Tim. 6:20). Others for different reasons question portions of the Word of God. Thus many walk blindly where the enemy prepares the way. Now, it is not the province of any man to pronounce sentence upon the Scriptures, to judge or condemn any portion of God's Word. When one presumes to do this, Satan will create an atmosphere for him to breathe which will dwarf spiritual growth. When a man feels so very wise that he dares to dissect God's Word, his wisdom is, with God, counted foolishness. When he knows more, he will feel that he has everything to learn. And his very first lesson is to become teachable. "Learn of me," says the Great Teacher; "for I am meek and lowly in heart: and ye shall find rest unto your souls" (Matt. 11:29).

You who have been educating yourselves and others

in a spirit of criticism and accusing, remember that you are imitating the example of Satan. When it suits your purpose, you treat the Testimonies as if you believed them, quoting from them to strengthen any statement you wish to have prevail. But how is it when light is given to correct your errors? Do you then accept the light? When the Testimonies speak contrary to your ideas, you treat them very lightly.

It does not become anyone to drop a word of doubt here and there that shall work like poison in other minds, shaking their confidence in the messages which God has given, which have aided in laying the foundation of this work, and have attended it to the present day, in reproofs, warnings, corrections, and encouragements. To all who have stood in the way of the Testimonies, I would say, God has given a message to His people, and His voice will be heard, whether you hear or forbear. Your opposition has not injured me; but you must give an account to the God of heaven, who has sent these warnings and instructions to keep His people in the right way. You will have to answer to Him for your blindness, for being a stumbling block in the way of sinners.

"To the law and to the testimony: if they speak not according to this word, it is because there is no light in them" (Isa. 8:20). Even the work of the Holy Spirit upon the heart is to be tested by the Word of God. The Spirit which inspired the Scriptures, always leads to the Scriptures.—*General Conference Daily Bulletin, April 13, 1891.*

INSPIRED MESSAGES WRONGLY APPLIED

One man, B by name, came all the way from Michigan with a special message for Sister White. He said that Sister White had been appointed by God to occupy the position occupied by Moses, and that he, B, was to occupy the position of Joshua. Thus the work was to be carried forward. Sister White's work was to be united with his work, and we were to proclaim the truth with power.

This man took the liberty, as many others have done, to mingle a great deal of Scripture with his message,

quoting passages which he applied to Seventh-day Adventists. During my connection with the work many such men
have arisen. They have selected and arranged scriptures
which they made applicable to the people of God. Mr. B
read with a loud, strong voice the passages he had selected, declaring them to be applicable to us as a people.
He said that I must see that he was right; for was it not the
Bible he was reading.

"Yes," I said, "you have selected and put these scriptures together, but like many who have arisen as you have,
you are wresting the Scriptures, interpreting them to mean
thus and so, when I know they do not apply as you have
applied them.

"You, or any other deluded person, could arrange and
have arranged certain scriptures of great force, and applied
them according to your own ideas. Any man could misinterpret and misapply God's Word, denouncing people
and things, and then take the position that those who
refused to receive his message had rejected the message
of God, and decided their destiny for eternity.". . .

From the various letters which have come to me, I see
that when such men as B, claiming to be sent by God, go
to those who are more or less isolated from our people,
these souls are ready to grasp anything that purports to be
of heavenly origin. Letters come to me entreating an
answer; I know that many men take the testimonies the
Lord has given, and apply them as they suppose they
should be applied, picking out a sentence here and there,
taking it from its proper connection, and applying it according to their idea. Thus poor souls become bewildered,
when could they read in order all that has been given,
they would see the true application, and would not become
confused. Much that purports to be a message from Sister
White, serves the purpose of misrepresenting Sister White,
making her testify in favor of things that are not in
accordance with her mind or judgment. This makes her
work very trying. Reports fly from one to another regarding
what Sister White has said. Each time the report is repeated, it grows larger. If Sister White has anything to

say, leave her to say it. No one is called upon to be a mouthpiece for Sister White. . . . Please let Sister White bear her own message. It will come with a better grace from her than from the one who reports her.—Manuscript 21, 1901.

DOUBTING THE TESTIMONIES*

When you find men questioning the testimonies, finding fault with them, and seeking to draw away the people from their influence, be assured that God is not at work through them. It is another spirit. Doubt and unbelief are cherished by those who do not walk circumspectly. They have a painful consciousness that their life will not abide the test of the Spirit of God, whether speaking through His Word or through the testimonies of His Spirit that would bring them to His Word. Instead of beginning with their own hearts, and coming into harmony with the pure principles of the gospel, they find fault, and condemn the very means that God has chosen to fit up a people to stand in the day of the Lord.

Let some skeptical one come along, who is not willing to square his life by the Bible rule, who is seeking to gain the favor of all, and how soon the class that are not in harmony with the work of God are called out. Those who are converted, and grounded in the truth, will find nothing pleasing or profitable in the influence or teaching of such a one. But those who are defective in character, whose hands are not pure, whose hearts are not holy, whose habits of life are loose, who are unkind at home, or untrustworthy in deal—all these will be sure to enjoy the new sentiments presented. All may see, if they will, the true measure of the man, the nature of his teaching, from the character of his followers.

Those who have most to say against the testimonies are generally those who have not read them, just as those who boast of their disbelief of the Bible are those who have

* Extract from a sermon at the General Conference of 1883, appearing in *Notebook Leaflets*, The Church, No. 6.

little knowledge of its teachings. They know that it condemns them, and their rejection of it gives them a feeling of security in their sinful course.

Error's Bewitching Power

There is in error and unbelief that which bewilders and bewitches the mind. To question and doubt and cherish unbelief in order to excuse ourselves in stepping aside from the straight path is a far easier matter than to purify the soul through a belief of the truth, and obedience thereto. But when better influences lead one to desire to return, he finds himself entangled in such a network of Satan, like a fly in a spider's web, that it seems a hopeless task to him, and he seldom recovers himself from the snare laid for him by the wily foe.

When once men have admitted doubt and unbelief of the testimonies of the Spirit of God, they are strongly tempted to adhere to the opinions which they have avowed before others. Their theories and notions fix themselves like a gloomy cloud over the mind, shutting out every ray of evidence in favor of the truth. The doubts indulged through ignorance, pride, or love of sinful practices, rivet upon the soul fetters that are seldom broken. Christ, and He alone, can give the needed power to break them.

The testimonies of the Spirit of God are given to direct men to His Word, which has been neglected. Now if their messages are not heeded, the Holy Spirit is shut away from the soul. What further means has God in reserve to reach the erring ones, and show them their true condition?

The churches that have cherished influences which lessen faith in the testimonies, are weak and tottering. Some ministers are working to attract the people to themselves. When an effort is made to correct any wrong in these ministers, they stand back in independence and say, "My church accepts my labors."

Jesus said, "Every one that doeth evil, hateth the light, neither cometh to the light, lest his deeds should be reproved." There are many today pursuing a similar course.

In the testimonies are specified the very sins of which they are guilty; hence they have no desire to read them. There are those who from their youth up have received warning and reproofs through the testimonies; but have they walked in the light and reformed?—Not at all. They still indulge the same sins; they have the same defects of character. These evils mar the work of God, and make their impress upon the churches. The work the Lord would do to set the churches in order is not done, because the individual members—and especially the leaders of the flock—would not be corrected.

Many a man professes to accept the testimonies, while they have no influence upon his life or character. His faults become stronger by indulgence until, having been often reproved and not heeding the reproof, he loses the power of self-control, and becomes hardened in a course of wrongdoing. If he is overworked, if weakness comes upon him, he has not moral power to rise above the infirmities of character which he did not overcome; they become his strongest points, and he is overborne by them. Then bring him to the test and ask, "Did not God reprove this phase in your character by the testimonies years ago?" He will answer, "Yes, I received a written testimony saying that I was wrong in these things." "Why, then, did you not correct these wrong habits?" "I thought the reprover must have made a mistake; that which I could see, I accepted; that which I could not see, I said was the mind of the one who gave the message. I did not accept the reproof."

In some cases the very faults of character which God would have His servants see and correct, but which they refuse to see, have cost these men their life. They might have lived to be channels of light. God wanted them to live, and sent them instruction in righteousness, that they might preserve their physical and mental powers to do acceptable service for Him; and had they received the counsel of God, and become altogether such as He would have them, they would have been able workmen for the advancement of the truth, men who would have stood high in the affections and confidence of our people. But they are sleeping in the grave, because they did not see that God knew them better than they knew themselves. His thoughts were not their thoughts, nor His ways, their ways. These one-sided men have molded the work wherever they have labored. The churches under their management have been greatly weakened.

God reproves men because He loves them. He wants them to be strong in His strength, to have well-balanced minds and symmetrical characters; then they will be examples to the flock of God, leading them by precept and example nearer to heaven. Then they will build up a holy temple for God.—Manuscript 1, 1883.

Searching the Testimonies for an Excuse

Some who are not willing to receive the light, but who prefer to walk in ways of their own choosing, will search the testimonies to find something in them to encourage the spirit of unbelief and disobedience. Thus a spirit of disunion will be brought in; for the spirit which leads them to criticize the testimonies will also lead them to watch their brethren to find in them something to condemn.—Manuscript 73, 1908.

The Last Deception of Satan

Satan is . . . constantly pressing in the spurious—to lead away from the truth. The very last deception of Satan will be to make of none effect the testimony of the Spirit of God. "Where there is no vision, the people perish" (Prov. 29:18). Satan will work ingeniously, in different ways and through different agencies, to unsettle the confidence of God's remnant people in the true testimony.—Letter 12, 1890.

There will be a hatred kindled against the testimonies which is satanic. The workings of Satan will be to unsettle the faith of the churches in them, for this reason: Satan cannot have so clear a track to bring in his deceptions and bind up souls in his delusions if the warnings and reproofs and counsels of the Spirit of God are heeded.—Letter 40, 1890.

4.

The Writing and Sending Out of the Testimonies to the Church*

~~~~~~~~~~~~~~~~

A REVIEW OF THE WORK

Sanitarium, California
July 8, 1906

DEAR BROTHER:

There are some who think they are able to measure the character and to estimate the importance of the work the Lord has given me to do. Their own mind and judgment is the standard by which they would weigh the testimonies.

My Instructor said to me, Tell these men that God has not committed to them the work of measuring, classifying, and defining the character of the testimonies. Those who attempt this are sure to err in their conclusions. The Lord would have men adhere to their appointed work. If they will keep the way of the Lord, they will be able to discern clearly that the work which He has appointed me to do is not a work of human devising.

Those who carefully read the testimonies as they have appeared from the early days, need not be perplexed as to

---

* The material comprising this chapter appeared in a leaflet in 1913.

their origin. The many books, written by the help of the Spirit of God, bear a living witness to the character of the testimonies.

In the early days of our experience in the message, the Spirit of God often came upon a few of us as we were assembled, and I was taken away in vision. The Lord gave such light and evidence, such comfort and hope and joy, that His praises were upon our lips.

Assisted by Literary Helpers

While my husband lived, he acted as a helper and counselor in the sending out of the messages that were given to me. We traveled extensively. Sometimes light would be given to me in the night season, sometimes in the daytime before large congregations. The instruction I received in vision was faithfully written out by me, as I had time and strength for the work. Afterward we examined the matter together, my husband correcting grammatical errors and eliminating needless repetition. Then it was carefully copied for the persons addressed, or for the printer.

As the work grew, others assisted me in the preparation of matter for publication. After my husband's death, faithful helpers joined me, who labored untiringly in the work of copying the testimonies and preparing articles for publication.

But the reports that are circulated, that any of my helpers are permitted to add matter or change the meaning of the messages I write out, are not true.

While we were in Australia the Lord instructed me that W. C. White should be relieved from the many burdens his brethren would lay upon him, that he might be more free to assist me in the work the Lord has laid upon me. The promise had been given, "I will put My Spirit upon him, and give him wisdom."

Since my return to America I have several times received instruction that the Lord has given me W. C. White to be my helper, and that in this work the Lord will give him of His Spirit.

Proper Time and Manner of Presentation

It requires much wisdom and sound judgment, quickened by the Spirit of God, to know the proper time and manner to present the instruction that has been given. When the minds of persons reproved are under a strong deception, they naturally resist the testimony; and having taken an attitude of resistance, it is difficult for them afterward to acknowledge that they have been wrong.

In the early days of this cause, if some of the leading brethren were present when messages from the Lord were given, we would consult with them as to the best manner of bringing the instruction before the people. Sometimes it was decided that certain portions would better not be read before a congregation. Sometimes those whose course was reproved would request that the matters pointing out their wrongs and dangers should be read before others, that they, too, might be benefited.

Often after testimonies of reproof were read, hearty confessions were made. Then we would unite in a season of prayer, and the Lord would manifest His pardoning grace to those who had confessed their sins. The acceptance of the testimonies brought the rich blessing of God into our assemblies.

Faithfully I endeavor to write out that which is given me from time to time by the divine Counselor. Some portions of that which I write are sent out immediately to meet the present necessities of the work. Other portions are held until the development of circumstances makes it evident to me that the time has come for their use. Sometimes in ministers and physicians bearing responsibilities there has developed a disposition to discard the testimonies, and I have been instructed not to place testimonies in their hands; for having yielded to the spirit that tempted and overcame Adam and Eve, they have opened mind and heart to the control of the enemy. Being on a false track, and laboring under deceptive imaginings, they will read into the testimonies things that are not there, but which are in agreement with the false statements that they have listened to. By reading the testimonies in the light of their own kindling, they are deceived, and will deceive others.

Sometimes, after very clear-cut, decided reproofs have been written out, they are held for a time until by personal correspondence I have endeavored to change the spirit of those to whom they are addressed. If these efforts are unsuccessful, the messages, with all their strength of rebuke or reproof, are sent to them, whether they will hear, or whether they will deny the truthfulness of the message.

If those whose errors are pointed out make confession of their wrongdoing, the spell of the enemy may be broken. If they will repent and forsake their sins, God is faithful and just to forgive their sins, and to cleanse them from all unrighteousness. Christ, the sin-pardoning Redeemer, will remove the filthy garments from them, give them change of raiment, and set a fair miter upon their head. But so long as they refuse to turn from iniquity they cannot develop a character that will stand in the great day of judgment.

Often concealed wrongs in the life of individuals are opened before me, and I am bidden to bear a message of reproof and warning.

I have been told that many who give heed to the false science of the enemy would denounce my work as that of a false prophet, and would place upon the testimony such interpretations as tend to change the truth of God into a lie. Satan is on the alert; and some who in the past have been used by the Lord in doing His work, but who have permitted themselves to be deceived, will be stirred up to make an improper use of the messages given. Because they do not wish to listen to the words of reproof, because they will not hear counsel, and improve their course of action, and do their appointed work, they will misconstrue the messages to the church, and confuse many minds.

Nevertheless, I am to bear the message that is given me to bear, so long as the Lord shall choose. He has not given me the work of settling all the misunderstandings that are cherished in hearts of unbelief. Just as long as a door is open to receive the tempter's suggestions, difficulties will multiply. The hearts of those who will not come to the light are open to unbelief. If my time and strength are consumed upon such matters, this serves Satan's purposes. The Lord has said to me: "Bear the testimonies. Your work is not to settle difficulties; your work is to reprove, and to present the righteousness of Christ."

An Incident

At one time in the early days of the message, Father Butler and Elder Hart became confused in regard to the testimonies. In great distress they groaned and wept, but for some time they would not give the reasons for their perplexity. However, being pressed to give a reason for their faithless speech and manner, Elder Hart referred to a small pamphlet that had been published as the visions of Sister White, and said that to his certain knowledge, some visions were not included. Before a large audience, these brethren both talked strongly about their losing confidence in the work.

My husband handed the little pamphlet to Elder Hart, and requested him to read what was printed on the title page. *"A Sketch of the Christian Experience and Views of Mrs. E. G. White,"* he read.

For a moment there was silence, and then my husband explained that we had been very short of means, and were able to print at first only a small pamphlet, and he promised the brethren that when sufficient means was raised, the visions should be published more fully in book form.

Elder Butler was deeply moved, and after the explanation had been made, he said, "Let us bow before God." Prayers, weeping, and confessions followed, such as we have seldom heard.

Father Butler said: "Brother White, forgive me; I was afraid you were concealing from us some of the light we ought to have. Forgive me, Sister White." Then the power of God came into the meeting in a wonderful manner.—*The Writing and Sending Out of the Testimonies to the Church,* pp. 3-9.

The Work and the Helpers

Sanitarium, California
October 23, 1907

Dear Brother [F. M.] Wilcox:

I received and read your recent letter. Regarding the sister who thinks that she has been chosen to fill the position that Sister White has occupied, I have this to say: She may be honest, but she is certainly deceived.

About a year after the death of my husband, I was very feeble, and it was feared that I might live but a short time. At the Healdsburg camp meeting, I was taken into the tent where there was a large gathering of our people. I asked to be raised up from the lounge on which I was lying, and assisted to the speaker's platform, that I might say a few words of farewell to the people. As I tried to speak, the power of God came upon me, and thrilled me through and through. Many in the congregation observed that I was weak, and that my face and hands seemed bloodless; but as I began speaking they saw the color coming into my lips and face, and knew that a miracle was being wrought in my behalf. I stood before the people healed, and spoke with freedom.

After this experience, light was given me that the Lord had raised me up to bear testimony for Him in many countries, and that He would give me grace and strength for the work. It was also shown me that my son, W. C. White, should be my helper and counselor, and that the Lord would place on him the spirit of wisdom and of a sound mind. I was shown that the Lord would guide him, and that he would not be led away, because he would recognize the leadings and guidance of the Holy Spirit.

The assurance was given me: "You are not alone in the work the Lord has chosen you to do. You will be taught of God how to bring the truth in its simplicity before the people. The God of truth will sustain you, and convincing proof will be given that He is leading you. God will give you of His Holy Spirit, and His grace and wisdom and keeping power will be with you. . . .

"The Lord will be your instructor. You will meet with deceptive influences; they will come in many forms, in pantheism and other forms of infidelity; but follow where I shall guide you, and you will be safe. I will put My Spirit upon your son, and you will strengthen him to do his work. He has the grace of humility. The Lord has selected him to act an important part in His work. For this purpose was he born."

This word was given me in 1882, and since that time I have been assured that the grace of wisdom was given to him. More recently, in a time of perplexity, the Lord said: "I have given you My servant, W. C. White, and I will give him judgment to be your helper. I will give him skill and understanding to manage wisely."

The Lord has given me other faithful helpers in my work. Many of my discourses have been reported, and have been put before the people in printed form. Through nearly the whole of my long experience I have endeavored, day by day, to write out that which was revealed to me in visions of the night. Many messages of counsel and reproof and encouragement have been sent out to individuals, and much of the instruction that I have received for the church has been published in periodicals and books, and circulated in many lands. . . .

The work is constantly moving forward. We are making earnest efforts to place my writings before the people. We hope that several new books will go to press shortly. If I am incapacitated for labor, my faithful workers are prepared to carry forward the work.

My Writings Will Constantly Speak

Abundant light has been given to our people in these last days. Whether or not my life is spared, my writings will constantly speak, and their work will go forward as long as time shall last. My writings are kept on file in the office, and even though I should not live, these words that have been given to me by the Lord will still have life and will speak to the people. But my strength is yet spared, and I hope to continue to do much useful work. I may live until the coming of the Lord; but if I should not, I trust it may be said of me, "Blessed are the dead which die in the Lord from henceforth: Yea, saith the Spirit, that they may rest from their labours; and their works do follow them" (Rev. 14:13). . . .

I thank God for the assurance of His love, and that I have daily His leading and guidance. I am very busy with my writing. Early and late, I am writing out the matters that the Lord opens before me. The burden of my work is to prepare a people to stand in the day of the Lord. The promise of Christ is sure. The time is not long. We must work and watch and wait for the Lord Jesus. We are called upon to be steadfast, unmovable, always abounding in the work of the Lord. All our hopes have their foundation in Christ.

Are our people reviewing the past and the present and the future, as it is unfolding before the world? Are they heeding the messages of warning given them? Is it our greatest concern today that our lives shall be refined and purified, and that we shall reflect the similitude of the divine? This must be the experience of all who join that company who are washed and made white in the blood of the Lamb. They must be arrayed in the righteousness of Christ. His name must be written in their foreheads. They must rejoice in the hope of the glory of God. Christ has engraved the names of His people on the palms of His hands. He will never lose His interest in any dependent soul.

Say to the church members that there is need of thorough consecration to God. Let all understand that they must make a covenant with God by sacrifice. We need the blessings of the gospel every day and every hour. Every proof of the Lord's power, His presence, and His love, is to be recognized with grateful thanks. Happiness is to be achieved by the right action of the soul toward God. I thank the Lord for this precious thought. Let Him be glorified by the sentiments expressed and by the actions performed. . . . Never have testimonies been more clearly brought before the people than those that have recently been traced by my pen. God bids me urge upon the attention of our people the importance of their study. Let this work begin now. Then, whether I am permitted to labor or am laid away to rest until Jesus comes, these messages are immortalized.

To my brethren I now say: Speak words that will draw souls to Christ. Bring forth fruit in good works. "He that believeth on the Son hath everlasting life" (John 3: 36). Every conceivable thing will be brought in to deceive, if possible, the very elect; but the Lord will certainly take care of His work.—*The Writing and Sending Out of the Testimonies to the Church,* pp. 10-16.

THE USE OF THE TESTIMONIES

Time and Place to be Considered

Regarding the testimonies, nothing is ignored; nothing is cast aside; but time and place must be considered. Nothing must be done untimely. Some matters must be withheld because some persons would make an improper use of the light given. Every jot and tittle is essential and must appear at an opportune time. In the past, the testimonies were carefully prepared before they were sent out for publication. And all matter is still carefully studied after the first writing.

Tell them to eat the flesh and drink the blood of the Son of God. Place His Word before them. There will be those who will misinterpret and misrepresent. Their eyes have been blinded, and they set forth the figures and interpretations that Satan has worked out for them, and an entirely wrong meaning will be placed upon the words that Sister White has spoken. Satan is just as verily claiming to be Christ's child as did Judas, who was on the accusing side. They have educated themselves in Satan's school of misstating. A description of them is given in the third chapter of Zechariah. Nothing in the world is so dear to God as His church. Satan has worked upon human minds, and will continue to betray sacred trust in a spurious way.

The Publishing of Compilations

I can see plainly that should every one who thinks he is qualified to write books, follow his imagination and have his productions published, insisting that they be recommended by our publishing houses, there would be plenty of tares sown broadcast in our world. Many from among our own people are writing to me, asking with earnest determination the privilege of using my writings to give force to certain subjects which they wish to present to the people in such a way as to leave a deep impression upon them.

It is true that there is a reason why some of these matters should be presented: but I would not venture to give my approval in using the testimonies in this way, or to sanction the placing of matter which is good in itself in the way which they propose.

The persons who make these propositions, for ought I know, may be able to conduct the enterprise of which they write in a wise manner; but nevertheless I dare not give the least license for using my writings in the manner which they propose. In taking account of such an enterprise, there are many things that must come into consideration; for in using the testimonies to bolster up some subject which may impress the mind of the author, the extracts may give a different impression than that which they would were they read in their original connection.— *The Writing and Sending Out of the Testimonies to the Church,* pp. 25, 26.

5.

An Explanation of

Early Statements

~~~~~~~~~~~~~~~~

An Answer to a Challenge

[Soon after the republication in 1882 of the three earliest E. G. White books, *A Sketch of the Christian Experience and Views of Ellen G. White, A Supplement to Experience and Views,* and *Spiritual Gifts,* vol. 1, all three of which today comprise *Early Writings,* certain questions were raised concerning the completeness of some of the articles and the significance of certain statements appearing here or in still earlier published articles. Mrs. White answered these questions in 1883 in the following statement. Reference is made to the teachings on the "shut door." For another reference to the significance of the "shut door" see *The Great Controversy,* pages 429-432.—COMPILERS.]

My attention has recently been called to a sixteen-page pamphlet published by C, of Marion, Iowa, entitled *Comparison of the Early Writings of Mrs. White With Later Publications.* The writer states that portions of my earlier visions, as first printed, have been suppressed in the work recently published under the title *Early Writings of Mrs. E. G. White,* and he conjectures as a reason for such suppression that these passages teach doctrines now repudiated by us as a people.

He also charges us with willful deception in representing *Early Writings* as a complete republication of my earliest views, with only verbal changes from the original work.

Before I notice separately the passages which are said

to have been omitted, it is proper that several facts be stated. When my earliest views were first published in pamphlet form,* the edition was small, and was soon sold. This was in a few years followed by a larger book, *The Christian Experience and Views of Mrs. E. G. White,* printed in 1851, and containing much additional matter.

In our frequent change of location in the earlier history of the publishing work, and then in almost incessant travel as I have labored from Maine to Texas, from Michigan to California—and I have crossed the plains no less than seventeen times—I lost all trace of the first published works. When it was decided to publish *Early Writings* at Oakland last fall, we were obliged to send to Michigan to borrow a copy of *Experience and Views.* And in doing this we supposed that we had obtained an exact copy of the earliest visions as first published. This we reprinted, as stated in the preface to *Early Writings,* with only verbal changes from the original work.

And here I will pause to state that any of our people having in their possession a copy of any or all of my first views, as published prior to 1851, will do me a great favor if they will send them to me without delay. I promise to return the same as soon as a copy can be produced.

So far from desiring to withhold anything that I have ever published, I would feel great satisfaction in giving to the public every line of my writings that has ever been printed.

Testimonies Garbled by Eli Curtis

There is another fact that should be stated here. I am not responsible for all that has been printed as coming from me. About the time that my earliest visions were first published, several articles did appear purporting to have been written by me, and to relate what the Lord had shown me, but sanctioning doctrines which I did not believe. These were published in a paper edited by a Mr.

---

* Reference is here made to the 24-page pamphlet "A Word to the Little Flock," published by James White in 1847, containing three Ellen G. White communications.—COMPILERS.

Curtis. Of the name of the paper I am not certain. In the years of care and labor that have passed since then, some of these less important particulars have been forgotten, but the main points are still distinct in my mind.

This man took articles that came from my pen, and wholly transformed and distorted them, picking out a sentence here and there, without giving the connection, and then, after inserting his own ideas, he attached my name to them as if they came direct from me.

On seeing these articles, we wrote to him, expressing our surprise and disapprobation, and forbidding him thus to misconstrue my testimonies. He answered that he should publish what he pleased, that he knew the visions ought to say what he had published, and that if I had written them as the Lord gave them to me, they would have said these things. He asserted that if the visions had been given for the benefit of the church, he had a right to use them as he pleased.

Some of these sheets may still be in existence, and may be brought forward as coming from me, but I am not responsible for them. The articles given in *Early Writings* did pass under my eye; and as the edition of *Experience and Views* published in 1851 was the earliest which we possessed, and as we had no knowledge of anything additional in papers or pamphlets of earlier date, I am not responsible for the omissions which are said to exist.

The First Omission

The first quotation mentioned by C is from a pamphlet of twenty-four pages published in 1847, entitled *A Word to the Little Flock*. Here are the lines omitted in *Experience and Views*:

"It was just as impossible for them [those that gave up their faith in the '44 movement] to get on the path again and go to the city, as all the wicked world which God had rejected. They fell all the way along the path one after another."

I will give the context, that the full force of the expressions may be clearly seen:

"While praying at the family altar, the Holy Ghost fell on me, and I seemed to be rising higher and higher, far above the dark world. I turned to look for the advent people in the world, but could not find them—when a voice said to me, 'Look again, and look a little higher.' At this I raised my eyes and saw a straight and narrow path, cast up high above the world. On this path the advent people were traveling to the city, which was at the farther end of the path. They had a bright light set up behind them at the first end of the path, which an angel told me was the midnight cry. This light shone all along the path, and gave light for their feet so they might not stumble. And if they kept their eyes fixed on Jesus, who was just before them, leading them to the city, they were safe. But soon some grew weary, and they said the city was a great way off, and they expected to have entered it before. Then Jesus would encourage them by raising His glorious right arm, and from His arm came a glorious light which waved over the advent band, and they shouted, Hallelujah! Others rashly denied the light behind them, and said that it was not God that had led them out so far. The light behind them went out, leaving their feet in perfect darkness, and they stumbled and got their eyes off the mark and lost sight of Jesus, and fell off the path down into the dark and wicked world below."

Now follows the passage said to be in the original work, but not found in *Experience and Views* nor in *Early Writings:*

"It was just as impossible for them [those that gave up their faith in the '44 movement] to get on the path again and go to the city, as all the wicked world which God had rejected. They fell all the way along the path one after another."

The "Shut Door" Defined

It is claimed that these expressions prove the shut-door doctrine, and that this is the reason of their omission in later editions. But in fact they teach only that which has been and is still held by us as a people, as I shall show.

For a time after the disappointment in 1844, I did hold, in common with the advent body, that the door of mercy was then forever closed to the world. This position was taken before my first vision was given me. It was the light given me of God that corrected our error, and enabled us to see the true position.

I am still a believer in the shut-door theory, but not in the sense in which we at first employed the term or in which it is employed by my opponents.

There was a shut door in Noah's day. There was at that time a withdrawal of the Spirit of God from the sinful race that perished in the waters of the Flood. God Himself gave the shut-door message to Noah:

"My spirit shall not always strive with man, for that he also is flesh: yet his days shall be an hundred and twenty years" (Gen. 6:3).

There was a shut door in the days of Abraham. Mercy ceased to plead with the inhabitants of Sodom, and all but Lot, with his wife and two daughters, were consumed by the fire sent down from heaven.

There was a shut door in Christ's day. The Son of God declared to the unbelieving Jews of that generation, "Your house is left unto you desolate" (Matt. 23:38).

Looking down the stream of time to the last days, the same infinite power proclaimed through John:

"These things saith he that is holy, he that is true, he that hath the key of David, he that openeth, and no man shutteth; and shutteth, and no man openeth" (Rev. 3:7).

I was shown in vision, and I still believe, that there was a shut door in 1844. All who saw the light of the first and second angels' messages and rejected that light, were left in darkness. And those who accepted it and received the Holy Spirit which attended the proclamation of the message from heaven, and who afterward renounced their faith and pronounced their experience a delusion, thereby rejected the Spirit of God, and it no longer pleaded with them.

Those who did not see the light, had not the guilt of its rejection. It was only the class who had despised the light from heaven that the Spirit of God could not reach. And this class included, as I have stated, both those who refused to accept the message when it was presented to them, and also those who, having received it, afterward renounced their faith. These might have a form of godliness, and profess to be followers of Christ; but having no living connection with God, they would be taken captive by the delusions of Satan. These two classes are brought to view in the vision—those who declared the light which they had followed a delusion, and the wicked of the world who, having rejected the light, had been rejected of God. No reference is made to those who had not seen the light, and therefore were not guilty of its rejection.

In order to prove that I believed and taught the shut-door doctrine, Mr. C gives a quotation from the *Review* of June 11, 1861, signed by nine of our prominent members. The quotation reads as follows:

"Our views of the work before us were then mostly vague and indefinite, some still retaining the idea adopted by the body of advent believers in 1844, with William Miller at their head, that our work for 'the world' was finished, and that the message was confined to those of the original advent faith. So firmly was this believed that one of our number was nearly refused the message, the individual presenting it having doubts of the possibility of his salvation because he was not in 'the '44 move.' "

To this I need only to add, that in the same meeting in which it was urged that the message could not be given to this brother, a testimony was given me through vision to encourage him to hope in God and to give his heart fully to Jesus, which he did then and there.

An Unreasonable Conjecture

In another passage from the book *A Word to the Little Flock,* I speak of scenes upon the new earth, and state that I there saw holy men of old, "Abraham, Isaac, Jacob, Noah, Daniel and many like them." Because I speak of having seen these men, our opponents *conjecture* that I then believed in the immortality of the soul and that having since changed my views upon this point, I found it necessary to suppress that passage. They are as near the truth here as in other conjectures.

In the year 1844 I accepted the doctrine we now hold, concerning the nonimmortality of the soul, as may be seen by reference to *Life Sketches,* pages 170, 171 [1880 edition. See also 1915 edition, page 49; *Testimonies,* volume 1, pages 39, 40], and I have never, by voice or pen, advocated any other. Had we suppressed this passage on account of its teaching the immortality of the soul, we would have found it necessary to suppress other passages.

In relating my first vision, page 13 of *Early Writings* [1882 edition, present edition, page 17], I speak of having seen brethren who had but a short time previous fallen asleep in Jesus, and on page 14 [present edition, pages 18, 19] I state that I was shown a great company who had suffered martyrdom for their faith.

The immortality of the soul is no more taught in the "suppressed" passage than in the two last cited.

The fact in the case is, that in these visions I was carried forward to the time when the resurrected saints shall be gathered into the kingdom of God. In the same manner the judgment, the second coming of Christ, the establishment of the saints upon the new earth have been presented before me. Does anyone suppose that these scenes have yet transpired? My adversaries show the spirit by which they are actuated in thus accusing me of deception on the strength of a mere "conjecture."

A Misquotation

In this quotation are also found the words, "I saw two long golden rods on which hung silver wires, and on the wires were glorious grapes."

My opponents ridicule "that weak and childish expression of glorious grapes growing on silver wires, and these wires attached to golden rods."

What motive impelled the writer of the above to misstate my words? I do not state that grapes were *growing* on silver wires. That which I beheld is described as it

1-3

appeared to me. It is not to be supposed that grapes were attached to silver wires or golden rods, but that such was the appearance presented. Similar expressions are daily employed by every person in ordinary conversation. When we speak of golden fruit, we are not understood as declaring that the fruit is composed of that precious metal, but simply that it has the appearance of gold. The same rule applied to my words removes all excuse for misapprehension.

The Seal of God

Another "suppression" reads as follows: "Well, bless the Lord, brethren and sisters, it is an extra meeting for those that have the seal of the living God."

There is nothing in this that we do not still hold. Reference to our published works will show our belief that the living righteous will receive the seal of God prior to the close of probation; also that these will enjoy special honors in the kingdom of God.

Renouncing the Sabbath

The following passage is said to be omitted from the vision related on pages 25-28 [pages 32-35, present edition] of *Early Writings:*

"And if one believed, and kept the Sabbath, and received the blessing attending it, and then gave it up, and broke the holy commandment, they would shut the gates of the Holy City against themselves, as sure as there was a God that rules in heaven above."

Those who have clearly seen and fully accepted the truth upon the fourth commandment, and have received the blessing attending obedience, but have since renounced their faith, and dared to violate the law of God, will find, if they persist in this path of disobedience, the gates of the city of God closed against them.

"Time Nearly Finished"

A statement published in 1851 in *Experience and Views,* and found on page 49 [page 58, present edition] of *Early Writings* is quoted as proving my testimonies false:

"I saw that the time for Jesus to be in the most holy place was nearly finished, and that time can last but a very little longer."

As the subject was presented before me, the period of Christ's ministration seemed almost accomplished. Am I accused of falsehood because time has continued longer than my testimony seemed to indicate? How is it with the testimonies of Christ and His disciples? Were they deceived?

Paul writes to the Corinthians:

"But this I say, brethren, *the time is short:* it remaineth, that both they that have wives be as though they had none; and they that weep, as though they wept not; and they that rejoice, as though they rejoiced not" (1 Cor. 7:29, 30).

Again, in his epistle to the Romans, he says:

"The night is far spent, the day is *at hand:* let us therefore cast off the works of darkness, and let us put on the armour of light" (Rom. 13:12).

And from Patmos, Christ speaks to us by the beloved John:

"Blessed is he that readeth, and they that hear the words of this prophecy, and keep those things which are written therein: for the *time is at hand*" (Rev. 1:3). "The Lord God of the holy prophets sent his angel to shew unto his servants the things which must *shortly* be done. Behold, I come *quickly;* blessed is he that keepeth the sayings of the prophecy of this book" (Rev. 22:6, 7).

The angels of God in their messages to men represent time as very short. Thus it has always been presented to me. It is true that time has continued longer than we expected in the early days of this message. Our Saviour did not appear as soon as we hoped. But has the word of the Lord failed? Never! It should be remembered that the promises and threatenings of God are alike conditional.

God had committed to His people a work to be accomplished on earth. The third angel's message was to be given, the minds of believers were to be directed to the heavenly sanctuary, where Christ had entered to make atonement for His people. The Sabbath reform was to be carried forward. The breach in the law of God must be made up. The message must be proclaimed with a loud voice, that all the inhabitants of earth might receive the warning. The people of God must purify their souls through obedience to the truth, and be prepared to stand without fault before Him at His coming.

Had Adventists, after the great disappointment in 1844, held fast their faith, and followed on unitedly in the opening providence of God, receiving the message of the third angel and in the power of the Holy Spirit proclaiming it to the world, they would have seen the salvation of God, the Lord would have wrought mightily with their efforts, the work would have been completed, and Christ would have come ere this to receive His people to their reward.

But in the period of doubt and uncertainty that followed the disappointment, many of the advent believers yielded their faith. Dissensions and divisions came in. The majority opposed with voice and pen the few who, following in the providence of God, received the Sabbath reform and began to proclaim the third angel's message. Many who should have devoted their time and talents to the one purpose of sounding warning to the world, were absorbed in opposing the Sabbath truth, and in turn, the labor of its advocates was necessarily spent in answering these opponents and defending the truth. Thus the work was hindered, and the world was left in darkness. Had the whole Adventist body united upon the commandments of God and the faith of Jesus, how widely different would have been our history!

It was not the will of God that the coming of Christ should be thus delayed. God did not design that His people, Israel, should wander forty years in the wilderness. He promised to lead them directly to the land of Canaan, and establish them there a holy, healthy, happy people. But those to whom it was first preached, went not in "because of unbelief" (Heb. 3:19). Their hearts were filled with murmuring, rebellion, and hatred, and He could not fulfill His covenant with them.

For forty years did unbelief, murmuring, and rebellion shut out ancient Israel from the land of Canaan. The same sins have delayed the entrance of modern Israel into the heavenly Canaan. In neither case were the promises of God at fault. It is the unbelief, the worldliness, unconsecration, and strife among the Lord's professed people that have kept us in this world of sin and sorrow so many years.

There are two other passages said to be found in my first book, but not given in my later writings. Concerning these I shall only say, when I can obtain a book containing them, so that I can be assured of the correctness of the quotations and can see for myself their connection, I shall be prepared to speak understandingly in regard to them.

Last-Day Scoffers

From the beginning of my work, I have been pursued by hatred, reproach, and falsehood. Base imputations and slanderous reports have been greedily gathered up and widely circulated by the rebellious, the formalist, and the fanatic. There are ministers of the so-called orthodox churches traveling from place to place to war against Seventh-day Adventists, and they make Mrs. White their textbook. The scoffers of the last days are led on by these ministers professing to be God's watchmen.

The unbelieving world, the ministers of the fallen churches, and the first-day Adventists are united in the work of assailing Mrs. White. This warfare has been kept up for nearly forty years, but I have not felt at liberty even to notice their vile speeches, reproaches, and insinuations. And I would not now depart from this custom, were it not that some honest souls may be misled by the enemies of the truth who are so exultantly declaring me a deceiver. In the hope of helping the minds of the honest, I make the statements that I do.

I do not expect to reach those who, having seen the light of truth, refuse to heed it, those who have given themselves up to prejudice, and entrenched their souls in unbelief.

Jesus, the Majesty of heaven, He who was equal with

God, was in the world thirty-three years, and yet there were but few who acknowledged His divine character. And can I, who am so weak, so unworthy, a frail creature of humanity, expect greater success than was enjoyed by the Saviour of the world?

When I first gave myself to this work, to go when God should bid me, to speak the words which He should give me for the people, I knew that I should receive opposition, reproach, persecution. I have not been disappointed. Had I depended on human applause, I would long ago have become discouraged. But I looked to Jesus, and saw that He who was without a fault was assailed by slanderous tongues. Those who made high pretensions to godliness followed as spies upon the Saviour's course, and made every exertion in their power to hedge up His way. But although He was all-powerful, He did not visit His adversaries as their sins deserved. He might have launched forth against them the bolts of His vengeance, but He did not. He administered scathing rebukes for their hypocrisy and corruption, and when His message was rejected and His life threatened, He quietly passed to another place to speak the words of life. I have tried, in my weakness, to follow the example of my Saviour.

Enmity Against Advocates of Truth

How eagerly the Pharisees sought to prove Christ a deceiver! How they watched His every word, seeking to misrepresent and misinterpret all His sayings! Pride and prejudice and passion closed every avenue of the soul against the testimony of the Son of God. When He plainly rebuked their iniquity and declared that their works proved them to be the children of Satan, they angrily flung back the accusation, saying, "Say we not well that thou art a Samaritan, and hast a devil?"

All the arguments urged against Christ were founded in falsehood. So was it in the case of Stephen, and of Paul. But the weakest and most unreliable statements made on the wrong side had an influence, because there were so many whose hearts were unsanctified, who desired those statements to be true. Such are ever eager to fasten upon any supposed error or mistake in those who speak to them the unpalatable truth.

It should not surprise us when evil conjectures are greedily seized upon as undoubted facts by those who have an appetite for falsehood. The opposers of Christ were again and again confounded and put to silence by the wisdom of His words; yet they still eagerly listened to every rumor, and found some pretext to ply Him again with opposing questions. They were determined not to abandon their purpose. They well knew that if Jesus should continue His work, many would believe on Him, and the scribes and Pharisees would lose their power with the people. Hence they were ready to stoop to any base or contemptible measure to accomplish their malicious intentions against Him. They hated the Herodians, yet they joined these inveterate enemies in order to invent some plan to rid the earth of Christ.

Such was the spirit with which the Son of God was met by those whom He came to save. Can any who are seeking to obey God, and to bear to the world the message of His truth, expect a more favorable reception than was granted Christ?

I have no ill will toward those who are seeking to make of none effect the message which God has given to reprove, warn, and encourage His people. But as the ambassador of Christ, I must stand in defense of the truth. Who are those that so zealously array themselves against me? Are they the pure and holy children of faith? Have they been born again? Are they partakers of the divine nature? Do they love Jesus, and manifest His spirit of meekness and humility? "By their fruits ye shall know them" (Matt. 7:20). Do they resemble the early disciples, or those cunning scribes and Pharisees who were constantly watching to entrap Christ in His words? Notice the sharp practice of those ancient opposers of the faith—how lawyers, priests, scribes, and rulers combined to find something against Him who was the light of the world.

And why were they so intent upon condemning

Christ? They did not love His doctrines and precepts, and they were displeased as they saw the attention of the people turned to Him and away from their former leaders.

Human nature is human nature still. Let not those who seek to hedge up my way and destroy the influence of my words, deceive themselves with the belief that they are doing God service. They are serving another master, and they will be rewarded according to their work.

Rebellion will exist as long as Satan exists. Those who are actuated by his spirit will not discern the Spirit of God or listen to its voice until the mandate shall go forth, "He that is unjust, let him be unjust still: and he which is filthy, let him be filthy still: and he that is righteous, let him be righteous still: and he that is holy, let him be holy still" (Rev. 22:11). I expect to encounter the malice of those who despise the light which God has been pleased to give me.

Sufficient Evidence for the Honest in Heart

It is God's plan to give sufficient evidence of the divine character of His work to convince all who honestly desire to know the truth. But He never removes all opportunity for doubt. All who desire to question and cavil will find occasion.

I pity those who have set their feet in the path of doubt and unbelief. I would gladly help them if I could, but the experience of the past gives me little hope that they will ever come to the light. No amount of evidence will convince men of the truth so long as they are unwilling to yield their pride, subdue their carnal nature, and become learners in the school of Christ.

Self-will and pride of opinion lead many to reject the light from heaven. They cling to pet ideas, fanciful interpretations of Scripture, and dangerous heresies; and if a testimony is borne to correct these errors, they will, like many in Christ's day, go away displeased.

It matters not how blameless the character and life of those who speak to the people the words of God; this procures for them no credit. And why? Because they tell the people the truth. This, brethren, is my offense. But if a false report is circulated, if by some inference or conjecture an imputation is cast upon the character of Christ's ambassador, with what absurd credulity is it received! How many are ready to magnify and spread the slander! Such are revealing their real character. "He that is of God heareth God's words: ye therefore hear them not, because ye are not of God" (John 8:47).

Calumny and reproach will be the recompense of those who stand for the truth as it is in Jesus. "All that will live godly in Christ Jesus shall suffer persecution" (2 Tim. 3:12). Those who bear a plain testimony against sin will as surely be hated as was the Master who gave them this work to do in His name. Like Christ, they will be called the enemies of the church and of religion, and the more earnest and true their efforts to honor God, the more bitter will be the enmity of the ungodly and hypocritical. But we should not be discouraged when thus treated.

I Shall Go Forward With My Work

We may be called "weak and foolish," enthusiastic, even insane. It may be said of us as it was of Christ, "He hath a devil" (John 10:20). But the work which the Master has given us to do is our work still. We must direct minds to Jesus, not seeking praise or honor of men, but committing ourselves to Him who judgeth righteously. He knows how to help those who while following in His steps suffer in a limited degree the reproach He bore. He was tempted in all points like as we are, that He might know how to succor those who should be tempted.

Whatever wrong construction may be placed upon my testimony by those who profess righteousness, yet know not God, I shall in humility go forward with my work. I will speak the words which God gives me to speak in encouragement, reproof, and warning. There remains but a little remnant of my life on earth. The work that my Father hath given me, I will, by His grace, perform with fidelity, knowing that all my deeds must pass the scrutiny of Jehovah.—Manuscript 4, 1883.

Ellen G. White Experience on Shut-Door Question Recounted*

Battle Creek, Michigan
August 24, 1874

Dear Brother Loughborough:

I hereby testify in the fear of God that the charges of Miles Grant, of Mrs. Burdick, and others published in the *Crisis* are not true. The statements in reference to my course in forty-four are false.

With my brethren and sisters, after the time passed in forty-four I did believe no more sinners would be converted. But I never had a vision that no more sinners would be converted. And am clear and free to state no one has ever heard me say or has read from my pen statements which will justify them in the charges they have made against me upon this point.

It was on my first journey east to relate my visions that the precious light in regard to the heavenly sanctuary was opened before me and I was shown the open and shut door. We believed that the Lord was soon to come in the clouds of heaven. I was shown that there was a great work to be done in the world for those who had not had the light and rejected it. Our brethren could not understand this with our faith in the immediate appearing of Christ. Some accused me of saying that my Lord delayeth His coming, especially the fanatical ones. I saw that in '44 God had opened a door and no man could shut it, and shut a door and no man could open it. Those who rejected the light which was brought to the world by the message of the second angel went into darkness, and how great was that darkness.

I never have stated or written that the world was doomed or damned. I never have under any circumstances used this language to any one, however sinful. I have ever had messages of reproof for those who used these harsh expressions.—Letter 2, 1874.

---

* See *The Great Controversy*, pages 426-432, for a fuller presentation of the "shut door."

STATEMENT ON THE DAY AND HOUR OF CHRIST'S COMING

DEAR SISTER:

You state that "some claim among other things that there is dishonesty in suppressing your former writings." Will those who say these things please give proof of their statements? I know that this has been often repeated but not proved. "Claiming that in your original testimonies, volume 1, which they have preserved, you distinctly declare that you were shown the day and hour of Christ's second coming. Their argument is that this statement of yours will not stand the Bible test; as Christ Himself declares that no man knoweth the day or the hour, no not even the angels of God." . . .

In my first book you will find the only statement in regard to the day and hour of Christ's coming that I have made since the passing of the time in 1844. It is found in *Early Writings,* pages 11, 27, and 145, 146 [pages 15, 34, and 285, present edition]. All refer to the announcement that will be made just before the second coming of Christ.

By turning to page 145 [page 285, present edition] and reading from the commencement of the chapter you will see that the statements made refer to the deliverance of the saints from the time of trouble by the voice of God. Please obtain this book if you do not have it, and read the statements therein. They are just as printed from the first article published. "The sky opened and shut, and was in commotion." "The mountains shook like a reed in the wind, and cast out ragged rocks all around. The sea boiled like a pot, and cast out stones upon the ground. And as God spoke the day and hour of Jesus' coming, and delivered the everlasting covenant to His people, He spoke one sentence and then paused while the words were rolling through the earth."

This is a portion of the paragraph. The statements in pages 11 and 27 [pages 15 and 34, present edition] refer to the same time. They contain all that I have ever been shown in regard to the definite time of the Lord's coming.

I have not the slightest knowledge as to the time spoken by the voice of God. I heard the hour proclaimed, but had no remembrance of that hour after I came out of vision. Scenes of such thrilling, solemn interest passed before me as no language is adequate to describe. It was all a living reality to me, for close upon this scene appeared the great white cloud, upon which was seated the Son of man.— Letter 38, 1888.

An Early View of Jets of Light

In my very girlhood the Lord saw fit to open before me the glories of heaven. I was in vision taken to heaven, and the angel said to me, "Look!" I looked to the world as it was in dense darkness. The agony that came over me was indescribable as I saw this darkness.

Again the word came, "Look ye." And again I looked intensely over the world, and I began to see jets of light like stars dotted all through this darkness; and then I saw another and another added light, and so all through this moral darkness the star-like lights were increasing. And the angel said, "These are they that believe on the Lord Jesus Christ, and are obeying the words of Christ. These are the light of the world; and if it were not for these lights, the judgments of God would immediately fall upon the transgressors of God's law." I saw then these little jets of light growing brighter, shining forth from the east and the west, from the north and the south, and lighting the whole world.

Occasionally one of these lights would begin to grow dim, and others would go out, and every time this occurred there was sadness and weeping in heaven. And some of the lights would grow brighter and brighter, and their brightness was far-reaching, and many more lights were added to it. Then there was rejoicing in heaven. I saw that the rays of light came directly from Jesus, to form these precious jets of light in the world.—*Gospel Workers,* pp. 378-379 (1892 edition).

SECTION II

Christian Experience

INTRODUCTION

~~~~~~~~~~~~~~~~~~~~~~~~~~~~~~~~~~~

Some fifteen years after Mrs. White's death the files of her unpublished writings—then at the Elmshaven office in California—were reindexed, and certain choice materials drawn from her letters and manuscripts were at that time published in leaflet form. These covered various topics of interest especially to Seventh-day Adventist workers, such as "Christian Experience," "Methods of Labor," "Education," "The Church," et cetera. These were first published as the "Elmshaven Leaflets," but were later issued under the title *Notebook Leaflets*. The series grew to a total of forty-two separate items, tied together as a unit.

In the years succeeding the publication of *Notebook Leaflets,* such Ellen G. White works as *Medical Ministry, Evangelism, Child Guidance, Welfare Ministry, The Adventist Home,* drew heavily on the manuscript sources from which the leaflets were originally selected, and provided much of the material, or closely paralleling material, in permanent book form. This has greatly lessened the mission of and the demand for the *Notebook Leaflets.*

Certain of the leaflets, however, miscellaneous in nature and character, relating to Christian experience and some other important topics, have not been paralleled or duplicated in the Ellen G. White books issued since her death. These are now found, here and there, in *Selected Messages.* The largest grouping of such *Notebook Leaflets* materials appears in this section dealing with Christian experience.—WHITE TRUSTEES.

6.

*The Loving Watchcare of Jesus**

~~~~~~~~~~~~~~~~~~~~~~~~~~

As I write I have a deep sense of gratitude for the loving watchcare of our Saviour over us all. As I read the Word of God and kneel in prayer, I am so impressed with the goodness and mercy of God that I cannot offer my petition without weeping. My heart is subdued and broken as I think of my heavenly Father's goodness and love. I hunger and thirst for more and still more of Jesus in *this* life. Christ was crucified for me, and shall I complain if I am crucified with Christ? . . .

We know not what is before us, and our only safety is in walking with Christ, our hand in His, our hearts filled with perfect trust. Has He not said, "Let him take hold of my strength, that he may make peace with me; and he shall make peace with me"? Let us keep close to the Saviour. Let us walk humbly with Him, filled with His meekness. Let self be hid with Him in God. . . .

The Outward Adorning

Those who cherish and flatter self, fostering pride and vanity, giving to dress and appearance the time and atten-

---

* Portion of a letter written February 18, 1904, published in *Notebook Leaflets,* Christian Experience, No. 1.

tion that ought to be given to the Master's work, are incur-
ring a fearful loss. Many who are clothed in beautiful outward garments know nothing of the inward adorning that
is in the sight of God of great price. Their fine clothing
covers a heart that is sinful and diseased, full of vanity and
pride. They know not what it means to "seek those things
which are above, where Christ sitteth on the right hand of
God" (Col. 3:1).

I long to be filled day by day with the Spirit of Christ.
The treasure of His grace is of more value to me than gold
or silver or costly array. I never felt a more earnest longing
for righteousness than at the present time.

When my sisters catch a glimpse of what Christ has
suffered in their behalf, that they might become children of
God by adoption, they will no longer be satisfied with
worldly pride and self-love. No longer will they worship
self. God will be the object of their supreme regard.

My heart aches as I am shown how many there are who
make self their idol. Christ has paid the redemption price
for them. To Him belongs the service of all their powers.
But their hearts are filled with self-love, and the desire for
self-adorning. They give no thought to the words, "Whosoever will come after me, let him deny himself, and take
up his cross, and follow me" (Mark 8:34). Self-gratification is hiding Christ from their view. They have no desire
to walk before God in meekness and lowliness. They are
not looking to Jesus. They are not praying that they may be
changed into His likeness. Their cases are represented by
the man who came to the king's banquet clothed in his
common citizen dress. He had refused to make the preparation required by the king. The garment provided for him
at great cost he disdained to wear. To the king's demand,
"How camest thou in hither not having a wedding garment?" (Matt. 22:12) he could answer nothing. He was
speechless; for he was self-condemned.

Many who profess to be Christians are such only in
name. They are not converted. They keep self prominent.
They do not sit at the feet of Jesus, as Mary did, to learn of
Him. They are not ready for Christ's coming.

A Great Surprise

In the night season I was in a company of people whose hearts were filled with vanity and conceit. Christ was hid from their eyes. Suddenly in loud, clear accents, the words were heard, "Jesus is coming to take to Himself those who on this earth have loved and served Him, to be with Him in His kingdom forever." Many of those in the company went forth in their costly apparel to meet Him. They kept looking at their dress. But when they saw His glory, and realized that their estimation of one another had been so largely measured by outward appearance, they knew that they were without the robe of Christ's righteousness, and that the blood of souls was on their garments.

When Christ took His chosen ones, they were left; for they were not ready. In their lives self had been given the first place, and when the Saviour came, they were not prepared to meet Him.

I awoke with the picture of their agonized countenances stamped on my mind. I cannot efface the impression. I wish I could describe the scene as it was presented to me. Oh, how sad was the disappointment of those who had not learned by experience the meaning of the words, "Ye are dead, and your life is hid with Christ in God" (Col. 3:3).

There are many professing Christians who know not Christ by an experimental knowledge. Oh, how my heart aches for these poor, deceived, unprepared souls! As I stand before congregations, and see the self-sufficient, self-righteous ones, and know that they are not preparing themselves to do acceptable work for Christ, and to meet Him in peace, I am so burdened that I cannot sleep. I ask myself, What can I say to these souls that will arouse them to a sense of their true condition? Self is the all-absorbing theme of their life. I long to reveal Christ so plainly that they will behold *Him,* and cease to center their attention on self. . . .

Among those to whom bitter disappointment will come at the day of final reckoning will be some who have been outwardly religious, and who apparently have lived Christian lives. But self is woven into all they do. They pride themselves on their morality, their influence, their ability to stand in a higher position than others, [and] their knowledge of the truth, for they think that these will win for them the commendation of Christ. "Lord," they plead, "we have eaten and drunk in thy presence, and thou hast taught in our streets" (Luke 13:26). "Have we not prophesied in thy name? and in thy name have cast out devils? and in thy name done many wonderful works?" (Matt. 7: 22).

But Christ says, "I tell you, I know you not whence ye are; depart from me." "Not every one that saith unto me, Lord, Lord, shall enter into the kingdom of heaven; but he that doeth the will of my Father which is in heaven" (Matt. 7:21).

There is no discussion; the time for that is past. The irrevocable sentence has been pronounced. They are shut out from heaven by their own unfitness for its companionship. (Read Matt. 7:24-27.)—Letter 91, 1904.

Through the plan of redemption, God has provided means for subduing every sinful trait, and resisting every temptation, however strong.—*The Review and Herald,* Dec. 22, 1885.

If God's people had the love of Christ in the heart; if every church member were thoroughly imbued with the spirit of self-denial; if all manifested thorough earnestness, there would be no lack of funds for home and foreign missions; our resources would be multiplied; a thousand doors of usefulness would be opened, and we would be invited to enter. Had the purpose of God been carried out by His people in giving the message of mercy to the world, Christ would have come to the earth, and the saints would ere this have received their welcome into the city of God. —*Union Conference Record* (Australasian), Oct. 15, 1898.

7.

*Christus Holds Control**

~~~~~~~~~~~~~~~~~~~~~~~~

The Gergesenes desired Christ to depart. They of Capernaum received Him, and among them He wrought wonderful miracles.

Christ has all power in heaven and in earth. He is the Great Physician, upon whom we are to call when suffering from physical or spiritual disease. Over the winds and the waves and over men possessed with demons, He showed that He possessed absolute control. To Him have been given the keys of death and of hell. Principalities and powers were made subject to Him, even while in His humiliation. . . .

Why do we not exercise greater faith in the Divine Physician? As He worked for the man with the palsy, so He will work today for those who come to Him for healing. We have great need of more faith. I am alarmed as I see the lack of faith among our people. We need to come right into the presence of Christ, believing that He will heal our physical and spiritual infirmities.

We are too faithless. Oh, how I wish that I could lead our people to have faith in God! They need not feel that in order to exercise faith they must be wrought up into a high

---

* Appeared in *Notebook Leaflets,* Christian Experience, No. 2.

state of excitement. All they have to do is to believe God's Word, just as they believe one another's word. He hath said it, and He will perform His Word. Calmly rely on His promise, because He means all that He says. Say, He has spoken to me in His Word, and He will fulfill every promise that He has made. Do not become restless. Be trustful. God's Word is true. Act as if your heavenly Father could be trusted. . . .

Men are appointed to proclaim the truth in new places. These men must have funds for their support. And they must have a fund to draw upon for the help of the poor and needy whom they meet in their work. The benevolence that they show toward the poor gives influence to their efforts to proclaim the truth. Their willingness to help those in need gains for them the gratitude of those they help, and the approval of Heaven.

These faithful workers should have the sympathies of the church. The Lord will hear prayer in their behalf. And the church should not fail to show a practical interest in their work.

No one lives to himself. In God's work each one is assigned a post of duty. The union of all strengthens the work of each. As the faith and love and unity of the church grow stronger their circle of influence enlarges, and ever they are to reach to the farthest limit of this influence, constantly extending the triumphs of the cross.

Arise, Shine

God calls upon us to burst the bands of our precise, indoor service. The message of the gospel is to be borne in the cities and outside of the cities. We are to call upon all to rally around the banner of the cross. When this work is done as it should be, when we labor with divine zeal to add converts to the truth, the world will see that a power attends the message of truth. The unity of the believers bears testimony to the power of the truth that can bring into perfect harmony men of different dispositions, making their interests one.

The prayers and offerings of the believers are combined

with earnest, self-sacrificing efforts, and they are indeed a spectacle to the world, to angels, and to men. Men are converted anew. The hand that once grasped for recompense in higher wages has become the helping hand of God. The believers are united by one interest—the desire to make centers of truth where God shall be exalted. Christ joins them together in holy bonds of union and love, bonds which have irresistible power.

It was for this unity that Jesus prayed just before His trial, standing but a step from the cross. "That they all may be one;" He said, "as thou, Father, art in me, and I in thee, that they also may be one in us: that the world may believe that thou hast sent me" (John 17:21).

God calls upon those who are half awake to arouse, and engage in earnest labor, praying to Him for strength for service. Workers are needed. It is not necessary to follow rules of exact precision. Receive the Holy Spirit, and your efforts will be successful. Christ's presence is that which gives power. Let all dissension and strife cease. Let love and unity prevail. Let all move under the guidance of the Holy Spirit. If God's people will give themselves wholly to Him, He will restore to them the power they have lost by division. May God help us all to realize that disunion is weakness and that union is strength.—Letter 32, 1903.

Talk Faith

Whatever may arise, never be discouraged. The Lord loves us, and He will perform His word. Try to encourage in the patients a trust in God. Bid them be of good courage. Talk hope, even to the last. If they are to die, let them die praising the Lord. He ever lives; and though some of His faithful followers may fall in death, their works will follow them, and theirs will be a joyous awakening in the resurrection morning.

Let us not be discouraged. Let us not talk doubt, but faith; for faith brings infinite power. If we lay hold upon this power, and do not trust in our own human strength, we shall see the salvation of God.—*The Review and Herald,* Dec. 30, 1909.

8.

Willing to Spend and Be Spent *

~~~~~~~~~~~~~~~~~~~

He who loves God supremely and his neighbor as himself will work with the constant realization that he is a spectacle to the world, to angels, and to men. Making God's will his will, he will reveal in his life the transforming power of the grace of Christ. In all the circumstances of life, he will take Christ's example as his guide.

Every true, self-sacrificing worker for God is willing to spend and be spent for the sake of others. Christ says, "He that loveth his life shall lose it; and he that hateth his life in this world shall keep it unto life eternal" (John 12:25). By earnest, thoughtful efforts to help where help is needed, the true Christian shows his love for God and for his fellow beings. He may lose his life in service. But when Christ comes to gather His jewels to Himself, he will find it again.

My brethren and sisters, do not spend a large amount of time and money on self, for the sake of appearance. Those who do this are obliged to leave undone many things that would have comforted others, sending a warm glow to their weary spirits. We all need to learn how to improve more faithfully the opportunities that so often come to us to bring light and hope into the lives of others. How can

* Appeared in *Notebook Leaflets,* Christian Experience, No. 3.

we improve these opportunities if our thoughts are centered upon self? He who is self-centered loses countless opportunities for doing that which would have brought blessing to others and to himself. It is the duty of the servant of Christ, under every circumstance, to ask himself, "What can I do to help others?" Having done his best, he is to leave the consequences with God.

I desire so to live that in the future life I can feel that during this life I did what I could. God has provided for every one pleasure that may be enjoyed by rich and poor alike—the pleasure found in cultivating pureness of thought and unselfishness of action, the pleasure that comes from speaking sympathizing words and doing kindly deeds. From those who perform such service the light of Christ shines to brighten lives darkened by many shadows.

God is dishonored when we fail to speak the truth plainly to one another. But we are to speak the truth in love, bringing tenderness and sympathy into our voices.

The perils of the last days are upon us. Those who live to please and gratify self are dishonoring the Lord. He cannot work through them, for they would misrepresent Him before those who are ignorant of the truth. Be very careful not to hinder, by an unwise expenditure of means, the work that the Lord would have done in proclaiming the warning message to a world lying in wickedness. Study economy, cutting down your personal expense to the lowest possible figure. On every hand the necessities of the cause of God are calling for help. God may see that you are fostering pride. He may see that it is necessary to remove from you blessings which, instead of improving, you have used for the gratification of selfish pride. . . .

Help in Every Time of Need

Those who are laboring in places where the work has not long been started, will often find themselves in great need of better facilities. Their work will seem to be hindered for lack of these facilities; but let them not worry. Let them take the whole matter to the Lord in prayer. When trying to build up the work in new territory, we have often gone to the limit of our resources. At times it seemed as if we could not advance farther. But we kept our petitions ascending to the heavenly courts, all the time denying self; and God heard and answered our prayers, sending us means for the advancement of the work.

Lay every care at the feet of the Redeemer. "Ask, and ye shall receive" (John 16:24). Work, and pray, and believe with the whole heart. Do not wait until the money is in your hands before doing anything. Walk out by faith. God has declared that the standard of truth is to be planted in many places. Learn to believe, as you pray to God for help. Practice self-denial; for Christ's whole life on this earth was one of self-denial. He came to show us what we must be and do in order to gain eternal life.

Do your best, and then wait, patiently, hopefully, rejoicingly, because the promise of God cannot fail. Failure comes because many who could put their means into circulation for the advancement of God's work are lacking in faith. The longer they withhold their means, the less faith they will have. They are barrier builders, who fearfully retard the work of God.

My dear fellow workers, be true, hopeful, heroic. Let every blow be made in faith. As you do your best, the Lord will reward your faithfulness. From the life-giving fountain draw physical, mental, and spiritual energy. Manliness, womanliness—sanctified, purified, refined, ennobled—we have the promise of receiving. We need that faith which will enable us to endure the seeing of Him who is invisible. As you fix your eyes upon Him, you will be filled with a deep love for the souls for whom He died, and will receive strength for renewed effort.

Christ is our only hope. Come to God in the name of Him who gave His life for the world. Rely upon the efficacy of His sacrifice. Show that His love, His joy, is in your soul, and that because of this your joy is full. Cease to talk unbelief. In God is our strength. Pray much. Prayer is the life of the soul. The prayer of faith is the weapon by which we may successfully resist every assault of the enemy.— Manuscript 24, 1904.

9.

Examine Yourselves *

~~~~~~~~~~~~~~~~~~~~~

"Examine yourselves, whether ye be in the faith; prove your own selves" (2 Cor. 13:5). Closely criticize the temper, the disposition, the thoughts, words, inclinations, purposes, and deeds. How can we ask intelligently for the things we need unless we prove by the Scriptures the condition of our spiritual health?

Many in their religious life are making crooked paths for their feet. Their prayers are offered in a loose, haphazard manner. He who is placed in a position of responsibility should remember that of himself he is not able to do that which is required of him. Every day he should remember that he is a spectacle unto the world, to angels, and to men.

No one is to wait to be borne to fields of labor and provided with costly facilities for doing good. He who serves must cheerfully take up his work, however humble it is, and wherever he may be placed. Christ, our example in all things, was poor, that through His poverty He might make many rich.

He whose heart is filled with the grace of God and love for his perishing fellow men will find opportunity,

---

* Appeared in *Notebook Leaflets,* Christian Experience, No. 12.

wherever he may be placed, to speak a word in season to
those who are weary. Christians are to work for their
Master in meekness and lowliness, holding fast to their
integrity amid the noise and bustle of life.

God calls upon men to serve Him in every transaction
of life. Business is a snare when the law of God is not
made the law of the daily life. He who has anything to do
with the Master's work is to maintain unswerving integrity.
In all business transactions, as verily as when on bended
knees he seeks help from on high, God's will is to be his
will. He is to keep the Lord ever before him, constantly
studying the subjects about which the Holy Word speaks.
Thus, though living amid that which would debase a man
of lax principles, the man of piety and stern integrity pre-
serves his Christianity.

The world is no more favorable today for the development of Christian character than in Noah's day. Then
wickedness was so widespread that God said, "I will destroy
man whom I have created from the face of the earth; both
man, and beast, and the creeping thing, and the fowls of
the air; for it repenteth me that I have made them. But
Noah found grace in the eyes of the Lord. . . . Noah was a
just man and perfect in his generations, and Noah walked
with God" (Gen. 6:7-9). Yes, amid the corruption of
that degenerate age, Noah was a pleasure to his Creator.

We are living in the last days of this earth's history, in
an age of sin and corruption, and like Noah we are to so
live that we shall be a pleasure to God, showing forth
the praises of Him "who hath called you out of darkness
into his marvelous light" (1 Peter 2:9). In the prayer
which Christ offered to His Father just before His crucifixion, He said, "I pray not that thou shouldest take them
out of the world, but that thou shouldest keep them from
the evil" (John 17:15).

The Highest Service

When men and women have formed characters which
God can endorse, when their self-denial and self-sacrifice
have been fully made, when they are ready for the final

test, ready to be introduced into God's family, what service will stand highest in the estimation of Him who gave Himself a willing offering to save a guilty race? What enterprise will be most dear to the heart of infinite love? What work will bring the greatest satisfaction and joy to the Father and the Son?—The salvation of perishing souls. Christ died to bring to men the saving power of the gospel. Those who cooperate with Him in carrying forward His great enterprise of mercy, laboring with all the strength God has given them to save those nigh and afar off, will share in the joy of the Redeemer when the redeemed host stand around the throne of God.

God has entrusted means and capabilities to His servants for the doing of a work far higher than that which to-day He looks upon.

"O," said the heavenly messenger, "the Lord's institutions are terribly behind the greatness of the truths which are being fulfilled at the present time. There is a fearful misconception of the claims of duty. The frosty atmosphere in which believers are content to live retards the self-sacrificing movements which should be made to warn the world and save souls.

"The powers of darkness are working with an intensity of effort, and year by year thousands of people, from all kindreds, nations, and tongues, pass into eternity, unwarned and unready. Our faith must mean something more definite, more decided, more important.

"Ask my institutions and churches, 'Do you believe the Word of God? What then are you doing in missionary lines? Are you working with self-denial and self-sacrifice? Do you believe that the Word of God means what it says? Your actions show that you do not. How will you meet at the bar of God the countless millions who, unwarned, are passing into eternity?

" 'Will there be a second probation? No, no. This fallacy might just as well be given up at once. The present probation is all that we shall have. Do you realize that the salvation of fallen human beings must be secured in this present life, or they will be forever lost?' "

Our Responsibilities

The Laodicean message is applicable to the church at this time. Do you believe this message? Have you hearts that feel? Or are you constantly saying, We are rich and increased in goods, and have need of nothing? Is it in vain that the declaration of eternal truth has been given to this nation to be carried to all the nations of the world? God has chosen a people and made them the repositories of truth weighty with eternal results. To them has been given the light that must illuminate the world. Has God made a mistake? Are we indeed His chosen instrumentalities? Are we the men and women who are to bear to the world the messages of Revelation fourteen, to proclaim the message of salvation to those who are standing on the brink of ruin? Do we act as if we were?

In a clear, determined voice the messenger said, "I ask you what you are doing? O that you could comprehend! O that you could understand the importance of the warning and what it means to you and to the world! If you did understand, if you were filled with the spirit of the One who gave His life for the life of the world, you would cooperate with Him, making earnest, self-sacrificing efforts to save sinners."

"He that saith, I know him, and keepeth not his commandments, is a liar, and the truth is not in him" (1 John 2:4). A great awakening must come to the church. If we only knew, if we only understood, how quickly the spirit of the message would go from church to church. How willingly would the possessions of believers be given to support the work of God. God calls upon us to pray and watch unto prayer. Cleanse your homes of the picture-idols* which have consumed the money that ought to have flowed into the Lord's treasury. The light must go forth as a lamp that burneth. Those who bear the message to the world should seek the Lord earnestly, that His Holy Spirit may be abundantly showered upon them. You have no time to lose. Pray

---

* See *Selected Messages,* Book II, pages 317-320 for a fuller discussion of the taking of pictures.—COMPILERS.

for the power of God, that you may work with successs for those nigh and afar off.

Warnings to Be Given

We must have genuine faith. As yet we scarcely grasp the reality of the truth. We only half believe the Word of God. A man will act out all the faith he has. Notwithstanding that the signs of the times are fulfilling all over the world, faith in the Lord's coming has been growing feeble. Clear, distinct, certain, the warnings are to be given. At the peril of our souls we are to learn the prescribed conditions under which we are to work out our own salvation, remembering that it is God which worketh in us, both to will and to do of His good pleasure.

It will not do for us to float along with the current, guided by tradition and presumptuous fallacies. We are called laborers together with God. Then let us arise and shine. There is no time to spend in controversy. Those who have a knowledge of the truth as it is in Jesus must now become one in heart and purpose. All differences must be swept away. The members of the church must work unitedly under the great Head of the church.

Let those who have a knowledge of the truth arise and shine. "Cry aloud, spare not, lift up thy voice like a trumpet" (Isa. 58:1). No longer mutilate the truth. Let the soul cry out for the living God. Cease ye from man, whose breath is in his nostrils. The Comforter will come to you, if you will open the door to Him. "Seeing then that we have a great high priest, that is passed into the heavens, Jesus the Son of God, let us hold fast our profession. For we have not an high priest which cannot be touched with the feeling of our infirmities; but was in all points tempted like as we are, yet without sin. Let us therefore come boldly unto the throne of grace, that we may obtain mercy, and find grace to help in time of need" (Heb. 4:14-16).—Manuscript 51, 1901.

10.

Good Angels More Powerful Than Evil Angels *

~~~~~~~~~~~~~~~~

It is expressly stated that Satan works in the children of disobedience, not merely having access to their minds, but working through their influence, conscious and unconscious, to draw others into the same disobedience. If evil angels have such power over the children of men in their disobedience, how much greater power the good angels have over those who are striving to be obedient. When we put our trust in Jesus Christ, working obedience unto righteousness, angels of God work in our hearts unto righteousness. . . .

Angels came and ministered to our Lord in the wilderness of temptation. Heavenly angels were with Him during all the period in which He was exposed to the assaults of satanic agencies. These assaults were more severe than man has ever passed through. Everything was at stake in behalf of the human family. In this conflict Christ did not frame His words even. He depended upon "It is written" (Matt. 4:4). In this conflict the humanity of Christ was taxed as none of us will ever know. The Prince of life and the prince of darkness met in terrible conflict, but Satan was unable to gain the least advantage in word or in action.

* Appeared in *Notebook Leaflets,* Christian Experience, No. 15.

These were real temptations, no pretense. Christ "suffered being tempted" (Heb. 2:18). Angels of heaven were on the scene on that occasion, and kept the standard uplifted, that Satan should not exceed his bounds and overpower the human nature of Christ.

In the last temptation Satan presented to Christ the prospect of gaining the whole world with all its glory if He would only worship him who claimed to be sent of God. Christ must then issue His command. He must then exercise authority above all satanic agencies. Divinity flashed through humanity, and Satan was peremptorily repulsed. "Get thee hence, Satan," Christ said, "for it is written, Thou shalt worship the Lord thy God, and him only shalt thou serve" (Matt. 4:10).

It was enough. Satan could go no further. Angels ministered to the Saviour. Angels brought Him food. The severity of this conflict no human mind can compass. The welfare of the whole human family and of Christ Himself was at stake. One admission from Christ, one word of concession, and the world would be claimed by Satan as his; and he, the prince of the power of darkness, would, he supposed, commence his rule. There appeared unto Christ an angel from heaven; for the conflict ended. Human power was ready to fail. But all heaven sang the song of eternal victory.

The human family have all the help that Christ had in their conflicts with Satan. They need not be overcome. They may be more than conquerors through Him who has loved them and given His life for them. "Ye are bought with a price" (1 Cor. 6:20). And what a price! The Son of God in His humanity wrestled with the very same fierce, apparently overwhelming temptations that assail men— temptations to indulgence of appetite, to presumptuous venturing where God has not led them, and to the worship of the god of this world, to sacrifice an eternity of bliss for the fascinating pleasures of this life. Everyone will be tempted, but the Word declares that we shall not be tempted above our ability to bear. We may resist and defeat the wily foe.

A Heaven to Win

Every soul has a heaven to win, and a hell to shun. And the angelic agencies are all ready to come to the help of the tried and tempted soul. He, the Son of the infinite God, endured the test and trial in our behalf. The cross of Calvary stands vividly before every soul. When the cases of all are judged, and they [the lost] are delivered to suffer for their contempt for God and their disregard of His honor in their disobedience, not one will have an excuse, not one will need to have perished. It was left to their own choice who should be their prince, Christ or Satan. All the help Christ received, every man may receive in the great trial. The cross stands as a pledge that not one need be lost, that abundant help is provided for every soul. We can conquer the satanic agencies, or we can join ourselves with the powers that seek to counterwork the work of God in our world. . . .

We have an Advocate pleading in our behalf. The Holy Ghost is continually engaged in beholding our course of action. We need now keen perception, that by our own practical godliness the truth may be made to appear truth as it is in Jesus. The angelic agencies are messengers from heaven, actually ascending and descending, keeping earth in constant connection with the heaven above. These angel messengers are observing all our course of action. They are ready to help all in their weakness, guarding all from moral and physical danger according to the providence of God. And whenever souls yield to the softening, subduing influence of the Spirit of God under these angel ministrations, there is joy in heaven; the Lord Himself rejoices with singing.

Men take altogether too much glory to themselves. It is the work of heavenly agencies cooperating with human agencies according to God's plan that brings the result in the conversion and sanctification of the human character. We cannot see and could not endure the glory of angelic ministrations if their glory was not veiled in condescension to the weakness of our human nature. The blaze of the heavenly glory, as seen in the angels of light, would extinguish earthly mortals. Angels are working upon human minds just as these minds are given to their charge; they bring precious remembrances fresh before the mind as they did to the women about the sepulcher.

A created instrumentality is used in heaven's organized plan for the renewing of our nature, working in the children of disobedience obedience unto God. The guardianship of the heavenly host is granted to all who will work in God's ways and follow His plans. We may in earnest, contrite prayer call the heavenly helpers to our side. Invisible armies of light and power will work with the humble, meek, and lowly one.—Letter 116, 1899.

Angels Looking for Cooperation

Satan uses human agents to bring the soul under the power of temptation, but the angels of God are searching for human agents through whom they may cooperate to save the tempted ones. Angels are looking for those who will work in Christ's lines, who will be moved by the realization that they belong to Christ. They are looking for those who will feel that those who fall under temptation, whether high or low, are the ones who need their special labors, and that Christ looks on those who are passed by, neglected, wounded, and bruised by the enemy, and ready to die, and is grieved at the hardness of men, who refuse to exercise the faith that works by love, which will purify the soul.

Angels of God will work with, and through, and by those who will cooperate with the heavenly agencies for the saving of a soul from death, and the hiding of a multitude of sins, that will lead them to consider themselves, lest they also be tempted.

It is the sick that need a physician, not those who are whole. When you expend labor on those who do not need it, and take no notice of the very ones whom your words and actions could bless, you are forming a character that is not after the likeness of Christ.—Letter 70, 1894.

11.

*What Are We Worth?**

~~~~~~~~~~~~~~

The Lord desires every one of us to be decidedly in earnest. We cannot afford to make a mistake in spiritual matters. The life-and-death question with us is, "What shall I do that I may be saved, eternally saved?" "What shall I do that I may inherit eternal life—a life that measures with the life of God?" This is a question that it becomes every one of us to consider carefully. . . .

While living in this world we are to be God's helping hand. Paul declared, "Ye are God's husbandry, ye are God's building" (1 Cor. 3:9). We are to cooperate with God in every measure that He desires to carry out. Are we fulfilling the purpose of the eternal God? Are we daily seeking to have the mind of Christ and to do His will in word and work?

What a condition the human family is in today! Have you ever seen before such a time of confusion—of violence, of murder, theft, and every other kind of crime? In this time, where are we individually standing?

In the fifty-eighth of Isaiah we have read of those who

_____

* Portion of a sermon delivered in the St. Helena Sanitarium chapel, January 23, 1904, and appearing in *Notebook Leaflets*, The Church, No. 7.

"fast for strife and debate, and to smite with the fist of wickedness" and we have learned that God will not accept such a fast. "Ye shall not fast as ye do this day," He declares, "to make your voice to be heard on high" (Isa. 58:4).

"Is it such a fast that I have chosen? a day for a man to afflict his soul? is it to bow down his head as a bulrush, and to spread sackcloth and ashes under him? wilt thou call this a fast, and an acceptable day to the Lord?

"Is not this the fast that I have chosen? to loose the bands of wickedness, to undo the heavy burdens [instead of binding them on], and to let the oppressed go free, and that ye break every yoke? Is it not to deal thy bread to the hungry, and that thou bring the poor that are cast out to thy house? when thou seest the naked, that thou cover him; and that thou hide not thyself from thine own flesh?" (Isa. 58:5-7).

The Reward

"Then [after they do these works of mercy and necessity] shall thy light break forth as the morning, and thine health shall spring forth speedily: and thy righteousness shall go before thee; the glory of the Lord shall be thy rereward" (Isa. 58:8).

We are to put into practice the precepts of the law, and thus have righteousness before us; the rearward will be God's glory. The light of the righteousness of Christ will be our front guard, and the glory of the Lord will be our rearward. Let us thank the Lord for this assurance. Let us constantly stand in a position where the Lord God of heaven can favor us. Let us consider that it is our high privilege to be in connection with God—to be His helping hand.

In God's great plan for the redemption of a lost race, He has placed Himself under the necessity of using human agencies as His helping hand. He must have a helping hand, in order to reach humanity. He must have the cooperation of those who will be active, quick to see opportunities, quick to discern what must be done for their fellow men.

Christ gave His life for sinful men and women. He desired to rescue the race from a life of transgression to a life of obedience and righteousness; and to those who accept Him as their Redeemer. He offers the richest reward that Heaven can bestow—even the inheritance of life eternal. . . .

O that we might comprehend more fully the infinite price that has been paid for our redemption! Paul declares, "Ye are bought with a price" (1 Cor. 6:20); and it is true; for the price paid is nothing less than the life of the only-begotten Son of God. Let us all consider this. We may refuse the invitations that Christ sends to us; we may neglect His offer of pardon and peace; but still it remains a fact that every one of us has been bought with a price, even with the precious blood of the Son of God. Therefore, "Consider him" (Heb. 12:3).

You have cost much. "Glorify God in your body, and in your spirit, which are God's" (1 Cor. 6:20). That which you may regard as your own is God's. Take care of His property. He has bought you with an infinite price. Your mind is His. What right has any person to abuse a body that belongs not to himself, but to the Lord Jesus Christ? What satisfaction can anyone take in gradually lessening the powers of body and mind by selfish indulgence of any form?

God has given to every human being a brain. He desires that it shall be used to His glory. By it, man is enabled to cooperate with God in efforts to save perishing fellow mortals. We have none too much brain power or reasoning faculties. We are to educate and train every power of mind and body—the human mechanism that Christ has bought—in order that we may put it to the best possible use. We are to do all we can to strengthen these powers; for God is pleased to have us become more and still more efficient colaborers with Him.

Of those who do their part faithfully, it is said, "We are labourers *together* with God" (1 Cor. 3:9). Apart from divine aid, man can do very little; but the heavenly Father and His Son are ready to work through everyone who consecrates himself wholly on the altar of service. Every soul before me may cooperate with God, and labor for Him acceptably. The Lord desires us all to come into line. To every man He has given an appointed work, according to their several ability. . . .

Personal Experience

At the age of seventeen, when all my friends thought I was an invalid for life on account of a severe accident I had sustained in my girlhood, a heavenly visitant came and spoke to me, saying, "I have a message for you to bear." "Why," I thought, "there certainly must be a great mistake somewhere." Again were spoken the words: "I have a message for you to bear. Write out for the people what I give you." Up to that time, my trembling hand had not been able to write a line. I replied, "I cannot do it; I cannot do it." "Write! write!" were the words spoken once again. I took the pen and paper, and I began to write; and how much I have written since, it is impossible to estimate. The strength, the power, was of God.

Since that time, the books that I have written have been published in many, many languages, and have gone to all parts of the earth. Just a short time ago I received word that a copy of one of my books had been graciously received by the queen of Germany, and that she had written a kind letter expressing her appreciation of the volume. To the Lord be all the praise.

Of ourselves we can do nothing good. But it is our privilege to place ourselves in right relation to God, and to determine that by His help we will do our part in this work, to make it better. In the lives of those who humbly yet unfalteringly carry out this resolution, will be revealed the glory of God. I know this by experience. I have had no power of my own. I have realized that I must hang my helpless soul on Jesus Christ; and as the result of doing this, of praying, and of believing, the salvation of God has gone before me, and the glory of the Lord has followed.

I tell you that which I know, for your encouragement and comfort. Let us all place ourselves in right relation to

God. What satisfaction is to be found in keeping pace with the fashions of this world? You have a better work to do. Fashion character. Use every ability, every nerve, every muscle, every thought, every action, to the glory of God. Then you will see, as you have never seen before, the salvation of God going before you.

Oh, I have nought to complain of. The Lord has never failed me. I laid my husband in the grave twenty-two years ago; and several years afterward, when the decision was made that more missionaries must go to Australia to unite with the few who had been sent, we went there ourselves to strengthen the hands of our brethren, and to establish the work on right lines in this new center. There we did much pioneer work.

Helping Establish a School

We saw the great need for a school in which promising young men and young women could be trained for the Master's service; and we went right into the woods in New South Wales, purchased fifteen hundred acres of land, and there established a training school away from the cities. . . .

Three years ago we returned to America. Others were sent to Australia to take our places. The work has continued to grow; prosperity has attended every effort. I wish you could read the letters that come to us. Doubtless you have heard of the dreadful drought that has caused famine in so many places in Australia during the past two years. Hundreds of thousands of sheep and cattle and horses have perished. In all the colonies, and especially in Queensland, the suffering and the financial loss have been great.

But the spot that was chosen for our training school, has had sufficient rainfall for good pasture land and bountiful crops; in fact, in legislative assemblies and in the newspapers of the great cities it has been specified as "the only green spot in all New South Wales."

Is not this remarkable? Has not the Lord blessed? From one of the reports received, we learn that last year seven thousand pounds of honey of the best quality has been made on the school estate. Large quantities of vegetables have been raised, and the sale of the surplus has been a source of considerable revenue to the school. All this is very encouraging to us; for we took the wild land, and helped to bring it to its present fruitful state. To the Lord we ascribe all the praise.

In every land and in every community there are many opportunities for helpful service. Even in these valleys in which we are now living, there are families that need help along spiritual lines. Look these ones up. Use your talent, your ability, by helping them. First give yourself to the Master; then He will work with you. To every man He gives his work.

Is Sister White Getting Rich?

Sometimes it has been reported that I am trying to get rich. Some have written to us, inquiring, "Is not Mrs. White worth millions of dollars?" I am glad that I can say, "No." I do not own in this world any place that is free from debt. Why?—Because I see so much missionary work to be done. Under such circumstances, could I hoard money?—No, indeed. I receive royalties from the sale of my books; but nearly all is spent in missionary work.

The head of one of our publishing houses in a distant foreign land, upon hearing from others recently that I was in need of means, sent me a bill of exchange for five hundred dollars; and in the letter accompanying the money, he said that in return for the thousands upon thousands of dollars royalty that I had turned over to their mission field for the translation and distribution of new books and for the support of new missionary enterprises, they regarded the enclosed five hundred dollars as a very small token of their appreciation. They sent this because of their desire to help me in my time of special need; but heretofore I have given, for the support of the Lord's cause in foreign lands, all the royalties that come from the sale of my foreign books in Europe; and I intend to return this five hundred dollars as soon as I can free myself from debt.

For the glory of God, I will tell you that about four years ago He enabled me to finish writing a book on the parables of Jesus, and then He put it into my heart to give this book for the advancement of our denominational educational work.

At that time some of our larger training schools and colleges were heavily in debt; but through the efforts of our people to sell this book and to devote the entire proceeds to the liquidation of these debts, over two hundred thousand dollars has already been raised and applied on the debts; and the good work is still going on. The success of this plan has been a source of great satisfaction to me. I am now completing another book, to be used in a similar way for other enterprises.

But the financial gain is not the most encouraging feature to me. I love to dwell on the thought that the circulation of these books is bringing many souls into the truth. This thought makes my heart glad indeed. I have no time to sit down and mourn. I go right on with my work, and constantly keep writing, writing, writing. Early in the morning, when the rest of you are asleep, I am generally up, writing.

Even affliction has not caused me to cease writing. Not long after going to Australia, I was stricken with disease. Because of the dampness of the houses, I suffered an attack of inflammatory rheumatism, which prostrated me for eleven months. At times I was in intense agony. I could sleep in one position for only about two hours, then I had to be moved so that I could lie in another position. My rubber air mattress gave me very little relief, and I passed through periods of great suffering.

But in spite of this I did not cease my work. My right arm, from the elbow to the finger tips, was free from pain; the rest of the arm, the whole of the left arm, and both shoulders, could not be moved voluntarily. A framework was devised, and by the aid of this, I could write. During these eleven months, I wrote twenty-five hundred pages of letter paper, to send across the broad waters of the Pacific for publication in America.

I feel so thankful to the Lord that He never disappoints me; that He gives me strength and grace. As I stood by the side of my dying husband, I placed my hand in his, and said, "Do you know me, husband?" He nodded. Said I: "All through the years I have allowed you to bear the business responsibilities, and to lead out in new enterprises. Now I promise you to be a pioneer myself." And I added, "If you realize what I say, grasp my hand a little more firmly." He did so; he could not speak.

After my husband had been laid away in the grave, his friends thought of putting up a broken shaft as a monument. "Never!" said I, "never! He has done, singlehanded, the work of three men. Never shall a broken monument be placed over his grave!" . . .

God has helped me. Today I glorify His name in the presence of His people. I spent nearly ten years in Australia. A wonderful work has been done there; but more than twice as much could have been accomplished, if we had had the men and the means that we should have had. We thank God, nevertheless, for His sustaining presence, and for what we can now see in that field as the result of the efforts put forth.—Manuscript 8, 1904.

Earnest, Untiring Activity

Camp meetings should be held in our large cities. And if the speakers are careful in all they say, hearts will be reached as the truth is proclaimed in the power of the Spirit. The love of Christ received into the heart will banish the love of error. The love and benevolence manifested in the life of Christ is to be manifested in the lives of those who work for Him. The earnest, untiring activity that marked His life is to mark their lives. The character of the Christian is to be a reproduction of the character of Christ.

Let us never forget that we are not our own, that we have been bought with a price. Our powers are to be regarded as sacred trusts, to be used to the glory of God and the good of our fellow men. We are a part of the cross of Christ. With earnest, unwearying fidelity we are to seek to save the lost.—Manuscript 6, 1902.

12.

Angels Are Amazed *

~~~~~~~~~~~~~

Angels are amazed that men regard so lightly and indifferently the vital truths which mean so much to the sinner, and continue willing subjects under the captivity of Satan and sin, when so much has been endured in the divine person of the Son of God. O that we may cultivate habits of contemplation of the self-denial and self-sacrifice of the life of Christ, until we shall have a deep sense of the aggravating character of sin, and hate it as the vile thing it is.

Let the mind awaken to gratitude that through Christ Jesus, the Father is faithful to fulfill the promise to forgive all sin. His mercy and His love are forever an assurance as we look upon Christ uplifted upon the cross of Calvary. Will we individually rise to the appreciation as far as we have capacity to comprehend the truth, that God Jehovah loves and forgives us if we believe in and love Jesus?

O what a glorious truth! God is waiting to forgive all who come unto Him with repentance. Preach it. Lift up Jesus high that the people may behold Him. . . .

The Jews saw in the sacrificial offerings the symbol of Christ whose blood was shed for the salvation of the

---

* Appeared in *Notebook Leaflets*, Methods, No. 11.

world. All these offerings were to typify Christ and to rivet the great truth in their hearts that the blood of Jesus Christ alone cleanseth from all sin, and without the shedding of blood there is no remission of sins. Some wonder why God desired so many sacrifices and appointed the offering of so many bleeding victims in the Jewish economy.

Every dying victim was a type of Christ, which lesson was impressed on mind and heart in the most solemn, sacred ceremony, and explained definitely by the priests. Sacrifices were explicitly planned by God Himself to teach this great and momentous truth, that through the blood of Christ alone there is forgiveness of sins.

This grand and saving truth is oft repeated in the hearing of believers and unbelievers, and yet it is with amazement that angels behold the indifference of men to whom these truths mean so much. How little is evidenced that the church feels the force of the wonderful plan of redemption. How few make this truth, that only through faith in the cleansing blood of Jesus Christ there is forgiveness of the sins that cling to human beings like the foul leprosy, a living reality.

What depths of thought should this awaken in every mind! He needed no suffering to atone for Himself. His was a depth of suffering proportionate to the dignity of His person and His sinless, exalted character.—Letter 43, 1892.

Spasmodic Repentance

"Behold, I stand at the door, and knock: if any man hear my voice, and open the door, I will come in to him, and will sup with him, and he with me. To him that overcometh will I grant to sit with me in my throne, even as I also overcame, and am set down with my Father in his throne" (Rev. 3:20, 21).

Some may say, Why is this message sounded so constantly in our ears? It is because you do not thoroughly repent. You do not live in Christ and have Christ abiding in you. When one idol is expelled from the soul, Satan has another prepared to supply its place. Unless you make an entire consecration to Christ and live in communion with Him, unless you make Him your Counselor, you will find that your heart, open to evil thoughts, is easily diverted from the service of God to the service of self.

At times you may have a desire to repent. But unless you decidedly reform and put into practice the truths you have learned, unless you have an active, working faith, a faith that is constantly increasing in strength, your repentance is as the morning dew. It will give no permanent relief to the soul. A repentance caused by a spasmodic exercise of the feelings is a repentance that needs to be repented of; for it is delusive. A violent exercise of the feelings, which does not produce in you the peaceable fruits of righteousness, leaves you in a worse state than you were in before.

Every day the tempter will be on your track with some delusive, plausible excuse for your self-serving, your self-pleasing, and you will fall back into your old practices, neglecting the work of serving God, by which you would gain hope and comfort and assurance.

God calls for willing service—a service inspired by the love of Jesus in the heart. God is never satisfied with halfhearted, selfish service. He requires the whole heart, the undivided affections, and a complete faith and trust in His power to save from sin. . . .

God will honor and uphold every truehearted, earnest soul who is seeking to walk before Him in the perfection of the grace of Christ. The Lord Jesus will never leave nor forsake one humble, trembling soul. Shall we believe that God will work in our hearts? that if we allow Him to do so, He will make us pure and holy, by His rich grace qualifying us to be laborers together with Him? Can we with keen, sanctified perception appreciate the strength of the promises of God, and appropriate them to our individual selves, not because we are worthy, but because Christ is worthy, not because we are righteous, but because by living faith we claim the righteousness of Christ in our behalf?—Manuscript 125, 1901.

13.

Importance of Receiving the Holy Spirit

~~~~~~~~~~~~~~~~~~~~

During the night of the first Sabbath of the Newcastle meeting, I seemed to be in meeting, presenting the necessity and importance of our receiving the Spirit. This was the burden of my labor—the opening of our hearts to the Holy Spirit. On one occasion Christ told His disciples, "I have yet many things to say unto you, but ye cannot bear them now." Their limited comprehension put a restraint on Him. He could not open to them the truths He longed to unfold; for while their hearts were closed to them, His unfolding of these truths would be labor lost. They must receive the Spirit before they could fully understand Christ's lessons. "The Comforter, which is the Holy Ghost," Christ said, "whom the Father will send in my name, he shall teach you all things, and bring all things to your remembrance, whatsoever I have said unto you."

In my dream a sentinel stood at the door of an important building, and asked every one who came for entrance, "Have ye received the Holy Ghost?" A measuring-line was in his hand, and only very, very few were admitted into the building. "Your size as a human being is nothing," he said. "But if you have reached the full stature of a man in Christ Jesus, according to the knowledge you have had, you will receive an appointment to sit with Christ at the marriage supper of the Lamb; and through the eternal ages, you will never cease to learn of the blessings granted in the banquet prepared for you.

"You may be tall and well-proportioned in self, but you cannot enter here. None can enter who are grown-up children, carrying with them the disposition, the habits, and the characteristics which pertain to children. If you have nurtured suspicions, criticism, temper, self-dignity, you cannot be admitted; for you would spoil the feast. All who go in through this door have on the wedding garment, woven in the loom of heaven. Those who educate themselves to pick flaws in the characters of others, reveal a deformity that makes families unhappy, that turns souls from the truth to choose fables. Your leaven of distrust, your want of confidence, your power of accusing, closes against you the door of admittance. Within this door nothing can enter that could possibly mar the happiness of the dwellers by marring their perfect trust in one another. You cannot join the happy family in the heavenly courts; for I have wiped all tears from their eyes. You can never see the King in His beauty if you are not yourself a representative of His character.

"When you give up your own will, your own wisdom, and learn of Christ, you will find admittance into the kingdom of God. He requires entire, unreserved surrender. Give up your life for Him to order, mold, and fashion. Take upon your neck His yoke. Submit to be led and taught by Him. Learn that unless you become as a little child, you can never enter the kingdom of heaven.

"Abiding in Christ is choosing only the disposition of Christ, so that His interests are identified with yours. Abide in Him, to be and to do only what He wills. These are the conditions of discipleship, and unless they are complied with, you can never find rest. Rest is in Christ; it cannot be as something apart from Him.

"The moment His yoke is adjusted to your neck, that moment it is found easy; then the heaviest spiritual labor can be performed, the heaviest burdens borne, because the Lord gives the strength and the power, and He gives gladness in doing the work. Mark the points: 'Learn of me; for I am meek and lowly in heart' (Matt. 11:29). Who is it that speaks thus?—The Majesty of heaven, the King of glory. He desires that your conception of spiritual things shall be purified from the dross of selfishness, the defilement of a crooked, coarse, unsympathetic nature. You must have an inward, higher experience. You must obtain a growth in grace by abiding in Christ. When you are converted, you will not be a hindrance, but will strengthen your brethren."

As these words were spoken, I saw that some turned sadly away and mingled with the scoffers. Others, with tears, all broken in heart, made confession to those whom they had bruised and wounded. They did not think of maintaining their own dignity, but asked at every step, "What must I do to be saved?" (Acts 16:30). The answer was, "Repent, and be converted, that your sins may go beforehand to judgment, and be blotted out." Words were spoken which rebuked spiritual pride. This God will not tolerate. It is inconsistent with His Word and with our profession of faith. Seek the Lord, all ye who are ministers of His. Seek Him while He may be found, call upon Him while He is near. "Let the wicked forsake his way, and the unrighteous man his thoughts: and let him return unto the Lord, and he will have mercy upon him; and to our God, for he will abundantly pardon" (Isa. 55:7).

As I presented these principles to the people in the Sabbath meeting, all seemed to feel that the Lord had spoken through the feeble instrument.—*The Review and Herald,* April 11, 1899.

The time has come when we must expect the Lord to do great things for us. Our efforts must not flag or weaken. We are to grow in grace and in the knowledge of the Lord. Before the work is closed up and the sealing of God's people is finished, we shall receive the outpouring of the Spirit of God. Angels from heaven will be in our midst. The present is a fitting-up time for heaven when we must walk in full obedience to all the commands of God.—Letter 30, 1907.

14.

*In Every Place**

~~~~~~~~~~~~~~~~~

Christ was the great Medical Missionary to our world. He calls for volunteers who will cooperate with Him in the great work of sowing the world with truth. God's workers are to plant the standards of truth in every place to which they can gain access. The world needs restoring. It is lying in wickedness and the greatest peril. God's work for those out of Christ should broaden and extend. God calls upon His people to labor diligently for Him, so that Christian efficiency shall become widespread. His kingdom is to be enlarged. Memorials for Him are to be raised in America and in foreign countries.

The work of health reform connected with the present truth for this time, is a power for good. It is the right hand of the gospel, and often opens fields for the entrance of the gospel. But let it ever be remembered that the work must move solidly and in complete harmony with God's plan of organization. Churches are to be organized, and in no case are these churches to divorce themselves from the medical missionary work. Neither is the medical missionary work to be divorced from the gospel ministry. When

---

* Appeared in *Notebook Leaflets*, Christian Experience, No. 8.

this is done, both are one-sided. Neither is a complete whole.

The work for this time is to appeal to the Christian's mind as the most important work that can be done. It is the question of cultivating the Lord's vineyard. In this vineyard every man has a lot and a place, which the Lord has assigned him. And the success of each depends on his individual relationship to the one Divine Head.

The grace and love of our Lord Jesus Christ and His tender relationship to His church on earth are to be revealed by the growth of His work and the evangelization of people in many places. The heavenly principles of truth and righteousness are to be seen more and still more plainly in the lives of Christ's followers. More unselfishness and uncovetousness is to be seen in business transactions than has been seen in the churches since the pouring out of the Holy Spirit on the day of Pentecost. Not a vestige of the influence of selfish, worldly monopolies is to make the slightest impression on the people who are watching and working and praying for the second coming of our Lord and Saviour Jesus Christ in the clouds of heaven with power and great glory.

As a people we are not ready for the Lord's appearing. If we would close the windows of the soul earthward and open them heavenward, every institution established would be a bright and shining light in the world. Each member of the church, if he lived the great, elevated, ennobling truths for this time, would be a bright, shining light. God's people cannot please Him unless they are surcharged with the Holy Spirit's efficiency. So pure and true is to be their relationship to one another that by their words, their affections, their attributes, they will show that they are one with Christ. They are to be as signs and wonders in our world, carrying forward intelligently every line of the work. And the different parts of the work are to be so harmoniously related to one another that all will move like well-regulated machinery. Then will the joy of Christ's salvation be understood. There will then be none of the representation now made by those who have been given the light of truth to communicate, but who have not revealed the principles of truth in their association with one another, who have not done the Lord's work in a way that glorifies Him. . . .

After Christ rose from the dead, He proclaimed over the sepulcher, "I am the resurrection and the life." Christ, the risen Saviour, is our life. As Christ becomes the life of the soul, the change is felt, but language cannot describe it. All claims to knowledge, to influence, to power, are worthless without the perfume of Christ's character. Christ must be the very life of the soul, as the blood is the life of the body. . . .

Cleansed From All Selfishness

Those who are connected with the service of God must be purified from every thread of selfishness. All is to be done in accordance with the injunction, "Whatsoever ye do in word or deed, do all" (Col. 3:17) "to the glory of God" (1 Cor. 10:31). God's laws of justice and equity must be strictly obeyed in the transactions between neighbor and neighbor, brother and brother. We are to seek for perfect order and perfect righteousness, after God's own similitude. On these grounds alone will our works bear the test of the judgment. . . .

Christianity is the revealing of the tenderest affection for one another. The Christian life is made up of Christian duties and Christian privileges. Christ in His wisdom gave to His church in its infancy a system of sacrifices and offerings, of which He Himself was the foundation, and by which His death was prefigured. Every sacrifice pointed to Him as the Lamb slain from the foundation of the world, that all might understand that the wages of sin is death. In Him was no sin, yet He died for our sins.

The symbolic system of ceremonies worked to one end —the vindication of the law of God, that all who believe in Christ might come "in the unity of the faith, and of the knowledge of the Son of God, unto a perfect man, unto the measure of the stature of the fulness of Christ" (Eph. 4: 13). In Christian work there is ample room for the activity of all the gifts God has given. All are to be united in carrying out God's requirements, revealing at every advance step that faith which works by love and purifies the soul.

Christ is to receive supreme love from the beings He has created. And He requires also that man shall cherish a sacred regard for his fellow beings. Every soul saved will be saved through love, which begins with God. True conversion is a change from selfishness to sanctified affection for God and for one another. Will Seventh-day Adventists now make a thorough reformation, that their sin-stained souls may be cleansed from the leprosy of selfishness?

I must speak the truth to all. Those who have accepted the light from God's Word are never, never to leave an impression upon human minds that God will serve with their sins. His Word defines sin as the transgression of the law.—Manuscript 16, 1901.

In Hard Places

Often God's soldiers find themselves brought into hard and difficult places, they know not why. But are they to relax their hold because difficulties arise? Is their faith to diminish because they cannot see their way through the darkness? God forbid. They are to cherish an abiding sense of God's power to uphold them in their work. They cannot perish, neither can they lose their way if they will follow His guidance, and strive to uphold His law.—Undated manuscript 145.

15.

*When the Church Awakes**

~~~~~~~~~~~~~~~~~~~~

Prayer is needed in the home life, in the church life, in the missionary life. The efficiency of earnest prayer is but feebly understood. Were the church faithful in prayer, she would not be found remiss in so many things; for faithfulness in calling upon God will bring rich returns.

When the church awakes to the sense of her holy calling, many more fervent and effective prayers will ascend to heaven for the Holy Spirit to point out the work and duty of God's people regarding the salvation of souls. We have a standing promise that God will draw near to every seeking soul.

The church needs to be begotten again unto a lively hope "by the resurrection of Jesus from the dead, to an inheritance incorruptible, and undefiled, and that fadeth not away" (1 Peter 1:3, 4). When the church awakes to a sense of what must be done in our world, the members will have travail of soul for those who know not God and who in their spiritual ignorance cannot understand the truth for this time. Self-denial, self-sacrifice, is to be woven into all our experience. We are to pray and watch unto prayer, that there may be no inconsistency in our

---

* Appeared in *Notebook Leaflets*, Christian Experience, No. 16.

lives. We must not fail to show others that we understand that watching unto prayer means living our prayers before God, that He may answer them.

The church will not retrograde while the members seek help from the throne of grace, that they may not fail to cooperate in the great work of saving the souls that are on the brink of ruin. The members of a church that is an active, working church, will have a realization that they are wearing Christ's yoke, and drawing with Him.

The heavenly universe is waiting for consecrated channels, through which God can communicate with His people, and through them with the world. God will work through a consecrated, self-denying church, and He will reveal His Spirit in a visible and glorious manner, especially in this time, when Satan is working in a masterly manner to deceive the souls of both ministers and people. If God's ministers will cooperate with Him, He will be with them in a remarkable manner, even as He was with His disciples of old.

Will not the church awake to her responsibility? God is waiting to impart the Spirit of the greatest missionary the world has ever known to those who will work with self-denying, self-sacrificing consecration. When God's people receive this Spirit, power will go forth from them. —Manuscript 59, 1898.

The Passive Graces

The Lord permits circumstances to come that call for the exercise of the passive graces, which increase in purity and efficiency as we endeavor to give back to the Lord His own in tithes and offerings. You know something of what it means to pass through trials. These have given you the opportunity of trusting in God, of seeking Him in earnest prayer, that you may believe in Him, and rely upon Him with simple faith. It is by suffering that our virtues are tested, and our faith tried. It is in the day of trouble that we feel the preciousness of Jesus. You will be given opportunity to say, "Though he slay me, yet will I trust in him" (Job 13:15). Oh, it is so precious to think that opportunities are afforded us to confess our faith in the face of danger, and amid sorrow, sickness, pain, and death. . . .

With us, everything depends on how we accept the Lord's terms. As is our spirit, so will be the moral result upon our future life and character. Each individual soul has victories to gain, but he must realize that he cannot have things just as he wants them. We are to observe carefully every lesson Christ has given throughout His life and teaching. He does not destroy; He improves whatever He touches.—Letter 135, 1897.

Humility and Faith

In the work for this time, it is not money or talent or learning or eloquence that are needed so much as faith graced with humility. No opposition can prevail against truth presented in faith and humility, by workers who willingly bear toil and sacrifice and reproach for the Master's sake. We must be co-workers with Christ if we would see our efforts crowned with success. We must weep as He wept for those who will not weep for themselves, and plead as He pleaded for those who will not plead for themselves. —Manuscript 24, 1903.

A Quick Work

When divine power is combined with human effort, the work will spread like fire in the stubble. God will employ agencies whose origin man will be unable to discern; angels will do a work which men might have had the blessing of accomplishing, had they not neglected to answer the claims of God.—*The Review and Herald,* Dec. 15, 1885.

SECTION III

Revival and Reformation

INTRODUCTION

~~~~~~~~~~~~~~~~~~~~

One of the most outstanding appeals made by Ellen G. White for revival and reformation was published in the *Review and Herald* of March 22, 1887, under the title "The Church's Need." This article was drawn from heavily in the compilation of materials prepared by Elder A. G. Daniells, for *Christ Our Righteousness*. In the initial printings (1926 and 1937) the article also appeared in its entirety in the Appendix. For mechanical reasons in later printings (1941 and onward), the article, selections from which had appeared in the text of the book itself, was not included in the Appendix. This much-sought-after article in its entirety now opens this stirring section.

The spiritual contest immediately following a revival, which rages between the forces of righteousness and the forces of evil for the souls of those who have begun a new experience, is vividly portrayed in this section. In the setting of the great revival at Battle Creek College, and the events that followed in succeeding months, Ellen White deals with this vital question. The elements of this struggle are those that are present in every revival effort of the church.

This section closes with the presentation of experiences in audience response in a number of revivals in which Ellen White herself participated. These help to show how she carried into her work the instruction concerning soul winning that distinguished her counsels to gospel workers. Many of these experiences recorded by Mrs. White mainly in her daily journal appear in terse, diary style. The word pictures she paints of making appeals for public response, begin with the early years in Battle Creek and carry over into Europe and Australia, then back again to the United States. There is a certain amount of repetition in the accounts, but enough of singular interest in each item to prove of value to the reader.—WHITE TRUSTEES

16.

Calls for a Revival

~~~~~~~~~~~~~~~~

THE CHURCH'S GREAT NEED *

A revival of true godliness among us is the greatest and most urgent of all our needs. To seek this should be our first work. There must be earnest effort to obtain the blessing of the Lord, not because God is not willing to bestow His blessing upon us, but because we are unprepared to receive it. Our heavenly Father is more willing to give His Holy Spirit to them that ask Him, than are earthly parents to give good gifts to their children. But it is our work, by confession, humiliation, repentance, and earnest prayer, to fulfill the conditions upon which God has promised to grant us His blessing. A revival need be expected only in answer to prayer. While the people are so destitute of God's Holy Spirit, they cannot appreciate the preaching of the Word; but when the Spirit's power touches their hearts, then the discourses given will not be without effect. Guided by the teachings of God's Word, with the manifestation of His Spirit, in the exercise of sound discretion, those who attend our meetings will gain a precious experience, and returning home, will be prepared to exert a healthful influence.

---

* Article appearing in Appendix to first edition of *Christ Our Righteousness,* but omitted for mechanical reasons from the second reset edition.—COMPILERS.

The old standard bearers knew what it was to wrestle with God in prayer, and to enjoy the outpouring of His Spirit. But these are passing off from the stage of action; and who are coming up to fill their places? How is it with the rising generation? Are they converted to God? Are we awake to the work that is going on in the heavenly sanctuary, or are we waiting for some compelling power to come upon the church before we shall arouse? Are we hoping to see the whole church revived? That time will never come.

There are persons in the church who are not converted, and who will not unite in earnest, prevailing prayer. We must enter upon the work individually. We must pray more, and talk less. Iniquity abounds, and the people must be taught not to be satisfied with a form of godliness without the spirit and power. If we are intent upon searching our own hearts, putting away our sins, and correcting our evil tendencies, our souls will not be lifted up unto vanity; we shall be distrustful of ourselves, having an abiding sense that our sufficiency is of God.

We have far more to fear from within than from without. The hindrances to strength and success are far greater from the church itself than from the world. Unbelievers have a right to expect that those who profess to be keeping the commandments of God and the faith of Jesus, will do more than any other class to promote and honor, by their consistent lives, by their godly example and their active influence, the cause which they represent. But how often have the professed advocates of the truth proved the greatest obstacle to its advancement! The unbelief indulged, the doubts expressed, the darkness cherished, encourage the presence of evil angels, and open the way for the accomplishment of Satan's devices.

Opening the Door to the Adversary

The adversary of souls is not permitted to read the thoughts of men; but he is a keen observer, and he marks the words; he takes account of actions, and skillfully adapts his temptations to meet the cases of those who place

themselves in his power. If we would labor to repress
sinful thoughts and feelings, giving them no expression in
words or actions, Satan would be defeated; for he could
not prepare his specious temptations to meet the case.

But how often do professed Christians, by their lack
of self-control, open the door to the adversary of souls!
Divisions, and even bitter dissensions which would disgrace any worldly community, are common in the churches,
because there is so little effort to control wrong feelings,
and to repress every word that Satan can take advantage of.
As soon as an alienation of feeling arises, the matter is
spread before Satan for his inspection, and the opportunity
given for him to use his serpentlike wisdom and skill in
dividing and destroying the church. There is great loss in
every dissension. Personal friends of both parties take
sides with their respective favorites, and thus the breach
is widened. A house divided against itself cannot stand.
Criminations and recriminations are engendered and multiplied. Satan and his angels are actively at work to secure
a harvest from seed thus sown.

Worldlings look on, and jeeringly exclaim, "Behold
how these Christians hate one another! If this is religion,
we do not want it." And they look upon themselves and
their irreligious characters with great satisfaction. Thus
they are confirmed in their impenitence, and Satan exults at
his success.

The great deceiver has prepared his wiles for every
soul that is not braced for trial and guarded by constant
prayer and living faith. As ministers, as Christians, we
must work to take the stumbling blocks out of the way. We
must remove every obstacle. Let us confess and forsake
every sin, that the way of the Lord may be prepared, that
He may come into our assemblies and impart His rich
grace. The world, the flesh, and the devil must be overcome.

We cannot prepare the way by gaining the friendship
of the world, which is enmity with God; but by His help
we can break its seductive influence upon ourselves and
upon others. We cannot individually or as a body secure

ourselves from the constant temptations of a relentless and determined foe; but in the strength of Jesus we can resist them.

From every member of the church a steady light may shine forth before the world, so that they shall not be led to inquire, What do these people more than others? There can be and must be a withdrawal from conformity to the world, a shunning of all appearance of evil, so that no occasion shall be given for gainsayers. We cannot escape reproach; it will come; but we should be very careful that we are not reproached for our own sins or follies, but for Christ's sake.

There is nothing that Satan fears so much as that the people of God shall clear the way by removing every hindrance, so that the Lord can pour out His Spirit upon a languishing church and an impenitent congregation. If Satan had his way, there would never be another awakening, great or small, to the end of time. But we are not ignorant of his devices. It is possible to resist his power. When the way is prepared for the Spirit of God, the blessing will come. Satan can no more hinder a shower of blessing from descending upon God's people than he can close the windows of heaven that rain cannot come upon the earth. Wicked men and devils cannot hinder the work of God, or shut out His presence from the assemblies of His people, if they will, with subdued, contrite hearts, confess and put away their sins, and in faith claim His promises. Every temptation, every opposing influence, whether open or secret, may be successfully resisted, "not by might, nor by power, but by my spirit, saith the Lord of hosts" (Zech. 4:6).

We Are in the Day of Atonement

We are in the great day of atonement, when our sins are, by confession and repentance, to go beforehand to judgment. God does not now accept a tame, spiritless testimony from His ministers. Such a testimony would not be present truth. The message for this time must be meat in due season to feed the church of God. But Satan has been seeking gradually to rob this message of its power, that the people may not be prepared to stand in the day of the Lord.

In 1844 our great High Priest entered the most holy place of the heavenly sanctuary, to begin the work of the investigative judgment. The cases of the righteous dead have been passing in review before God. When that work shall be completed, judgment is to be pronounced upon the living. How precious, how important are these solemn moments! Each of us has a case pending in the court of heaven. We are individually to be judged according to the deeds done in the body. In the typical service, when the work of atonement was performed by the high priest in the most holy place of the earthly sanctuary, the people were required to afflict their souls before God, and confess their sins, that they might be atoned for and blotted out. Will any less be required of us in this antitypical day of atonement, when Christ in the sanctuary above is pleading in behalf of His people, and the final, irrevocable decision is to be pronounced upon every case?

What is our condition in this fearful and solemn time? Alas, what pride is prevailing in the church, what hypocrisy, what deception, what love of dress, frivolity, and amusement, what desire for the supremacy! All these sins have clouded the mind, so that eternal things have not been discerned. Shall we not search the Scriptures, that we may know where we are in this world's history? Shall we not become intelligent in regard to the work that is being accomplished for us at this time, and the position that we as sinners should occupy while this work of atonement is going forward? If we have any regard for our souls' salvation, we must make a decided change. We must seek the Lord with true penitence; we must with deep contrition of soul confess our sins, that they may be blotted out.

We must no longer remain upon the enchanted ground. We are fast approaching the close of our probation. Let every soul inquire, How do I stand before God? We know not how soon our names may be taken into the lips of Christ, and our cases be finally decided. What, oh, what will these decisions be! Shall we be counted with the right-eous, or shall we be numbered with the wicked?

The Church to Arise and Repent

Let the church arise, and repent of her backslidings before God. Let the watchmen awake, and give the trumpet a certain sound. It is a definite warning that we have to proclaim. God commands His servants, "Cry aloud, spare not, lift up thy voice like a trumpet, and shew my people their transgression, and the house of Jacob their sins" (Isa. 58:1). The attention of the people must be gained; unless this can be done, all effort is useless; though an angel from heaven should come down and speak to them, his words would do no more good than if he were speaking into the cold ear of death.

The church must arouse to action. The Spirit of God can never come in until she prepares the way. There should be earnest searching of heart. There should be united, persevering prayer, and through faith a claiming of the promises of God. There should be, not a clothing of the body with sackcloth, as in ancient times, but a deep humiliation of soul. We have not the first reason for self-congratulation and self-exaltation. We should humble ourselves under the mighty hand of God. He will appear to comfort and bless the true seekers.

The work is before us; will we engage in it? We must work fast, we must go steadily forward. We must be pre-paring for the great day of the Lord. We have no time to lose, no time to be engaged in selfish purposes. The world is to be warned. What are we doing as individuals to bring the light before others? God has left to every man his work; every one has a part to act, and we cannot neglect this work except at the peril of our souls.

O my brethren, will you grieve the Holy Spirit, and cause it to depart? Will you shut out the blessed Saviour, because you are unprepared for His presence? Will you leave souls to perish without the knowledge of the truth, because you love your ease too well to bear the burden that Jesus bore for you? Let us awake out of sleep. "Be sober, be vigilant; because your adversary the devil, as a roaring lion, walketh about, seeking whom he may devour" (1 Peter 5:8).—*The Review and Herald,* March 22, 1887.

REFORMATION ACCOMPANIES REVIVAL

In many hearts there seems to be scarcely a breath of spiritual life. This makes me very sad. I fear that aggressive warfare against the world, the flesh, and the devil has not been maintained. Shall we cheer on, by a half-dead Christianity, the selfish, covetous spirit of the world, sharing its ungodliness and smiling on its falsehood?—Nay! By the grace of God let us be steadfast to the principles of truth, holding firm to the end the beginning of our confidence. We are to be "not slothful in business; fervent in spirit; serving the Lord" (Rom. 12:11). One is our Master, even Christ. To Him we are to look. From Him we are to receive our wisdom. By His grace we are to preserve our integrity, standing before God in meekness and contrition, and representing Him to the world.

Sermons have been in great demand in our churches. The members have depended upon pulpit declamations instead of on the Holy Spirit. Uncalled for and unused, the spiritual gifts bestowed on them have dwindled into feebleness. If the ministers would go forth into new fields, the members would be obliged to bear responsibilities, and by use their capabilities would increase.

God brings against ministers and people the heavy charge of spiritual feebleness, saying, "I know thy works, that thou art neither cold nor hot: I would thou wert cold or hot. So then because thou art lukewarm, and neither cold nor hot, I will spue thee out of my mouth. Because thou sayest, I am rich, and increased with goods, and have need of nothing; and knowest not that thou art wretched, and miserable, and poor, and blind, and naked: I counsel thee to buy of me gold tried in the fire, that thou mayest be rich; and white raiment, that thou mayest be clothed, and that the shame of thy nakedness do not appear; and anoint thine eyes with eyesalve, that thou mayest see" (Rev. 3:15-

18). God calls for a spiritual revival and a spiritual reformation. Unless this takes place, those who are lukewarm will continue to grow more abhorrent to the Lord, until He will refuse to acknowledge them as His children.

A revival and a reformation must take place, under the ministration of the Holy Spirit. Revival and reformation are two different things. Revival signifies a renewal of spiritual life, a quickening of the powers of mind and heart, a resurrection from spiritual death. Reformation signifies a reorganization, a change in ideas and theories, habits and practices. Reformation will not bring forth the good fruit of righteousness unless it is connected with the revival of the Spirit. Revival and reformation are to do their appointed work, and in doing this work they must blend.—*The Review and Herald,* Feb. 25, 1902.

Simple Agencies Will Be Used

Representations have been made to me, showing that the Lord will carry out His plans through a variety of ways and instruments. It is not alone the most talented, not alone those who hold high positions of trust, or are the most highly educated from a worldly point of view, whom the Lord uses to do His grand and holy work of soulsaving. He will use simple means; He will use many who have had few advantages to help in carrying forward His work. He will, by the use of simple means, bring those who possess property and lands to a belief of the truth, and these will be influenced to become the Lord's helping hand in the advancement of His work.—Letter 62, 1909.

17.

Safeguarding the New Experience

~~~~~~~~~~~~~~~~

THE CONTEST FOLLOWING THE REVIVAL

[In 1893 there was a marked revival in our institutions at our Battle Creek headquarters, with large evidence of the work of the Spirit of God. Much of the blessing was lost in events which followed in quick succession. In this experience and the counsel given in connection with it may be found lessons which are of value today.—COMPILERS.]

After the outpouring of the Spirit of God in Battle Creek it was proved in the college that a time of great spiritual light is also a time of corresponding spiritual darkness. Satan and his legions of satanic agencies are on the ground, pressing their powers upon every soul to make of none effect the showers of grace that have come from heaven to revive and quicken the dormant energies into decided action to impart that which God has imparted. Had all the many souls, then enlightened, gone to work at once to impart to others that which God had given to them for that very purpose, more light would have been given, more power bestowed. God does not give light merely for one person but that he may diffuse light, and God be glorified. Its influence is felt.

In every age seasons of spiritual revival and the outpouring of the Holy Spirit have been followed by spiritual darkness and prevailing corruptions. Taking into account that which God has done in opportunities and privileges and blessings in Battle Creek, the church has not made honorable progress in doing her work, and God's blessing will not rest upon the church in advancing still more light until they use the light as God has directed in His Word. The light that would shine in clear and distinct rays will grow dim amid the moral darkness. The aggressive power of the truth of God is dependent upon the cooperation of the human agent with God in piety, in zeal, in unselfish efforts to get the light of truth before others.—Manuscript 45, 1893.

PERIL OF CONFUSING THE SPIRIT'S WORK WITH FANATICISM

There have been things written to me in regard to the movings of the Spirit of God at the last conference [1893], and at the college, which clearly indicate that because these blessings were not lived up to, minds have been confused, and that which was light from heaven has been called excitement. I have been made sad to have this matter viewed in this light. We must be very careful not to grieve the Holy Spirit of God, in pronouncing the ministration of His Holy Spirit a species of fanaticism. How shall we understand the workings of the Spirit of God if it was not revealed in clear and unmistakable lines, not only in Battle Creek but in many places?

I am not surprised that anyone should be confused at the after result. But in my experience of the past forty-nine years I have seen much of these things, and I have known that God has wrought in a marked manner; and let no one venture to say this is not the Spirit of God. It is just that which we are authorized to believe and pray for, for God is more willing to give the Holy Spirit to them that ask Him than parents are to give good gifts unto their children. But the Holy Spirit is not for the human agent to work; it is to work and use the human agent. That God did abundantly bless the students in the school and the church, I have not one doubt; but a period of great light and the outpouring of the Spirit is quite generally followed by a time of great darkness. Why? Because the enemy works with all his deceiving energies to make of none effect the deep movings of the Spirit of God on the human subject.

When the students at the school went into their match games and football playing, when they became absorbed in the amusement question, Satan saw it a good time to step in and make of none effect the Holy Spirit of God in molding and using the human subject. Had the teachers to a man done their duty, had they realized their accountability, had they stood in moral independence before God, had they used the ability which God had given them according to the sanctification of the spirit through the love of the truth, they would have had spiritual strength and divine enlightenment to press on and on and upward on the ladder of progress reaching heavenward. The fact is evident that they did not appreciate or walk in the light or follow the Light of the world.

It is an easy matter to idle away, talk and play away, the Holy Spirit's influence. To walk in the light is to keep moving onward in the direction of light. If the one blessed becomes negligent and inattentive and does not watch unto prayer, if he does not lift the cross and bear the yoke of Christ, if his love of amusements and strivings for the mastery absorb his power or ability, then God is not made the first and best and last in everything, and Satan comes in to act his part in playing the game of life for his soul. He can play much more earnestly than they can play, and make deep-laid plots for the ruin of the soul. . . .

The results after the working of the Spirit of God in Battle Creek are not because of fanaticism, but because those who were blessed did not show forth the praises of Him who called them out of darkness into His marvelous light; and when the earth is lightened with the glory of God, some will not know what it is, and from whence it came, because they misapplied and misinterpreted the Spirit shed upon them. God is a jealous God of His own glory. He will not honor those who dishonor Him. Some persons living in the light ought to have instructed these

souls young in experience to walk in the light after they
had received the light. I wish I had time to write more
fully, but I fear I have not.—Letter 58, 1893.

Easy Ways to Lose the Blessing

Some things have been urged upon my mind with great
force of late, and I feel constrained by the Spirit of God to
write in reference to them.* Has the Lord graciously
opened to you the windows of heaven and poured you out a
blessing? Oh! Then, that was the very time to educate the
teachers and students how to retain the precious favor of
God by working in accordance with increased light, and
send its precious rays to others. Has Heaven's light been
given? And for what purpose has it been given? That the
light should shine forth in practical works of righteousness.
When those so abundantly blessed shall be seen with
deeper and more fervent piety, having a sense that they
have been bought with the precious blood of the Lamb of
God, and are clothed with the garments of His salvation,
will they not represent Christ?

Have not the playing of games, and rewards, and the
using of the boxing glove been educating and training
after Satan's direction to lead to the possession of his attributes? What if they could see Jesus, the Man of Calvary
looking upon them in sorrow, as was represented to me.
Things are certainly receiving a wrong mold, and are
counteracting the work of the divine power which has
been graciously bestowed. (The work of every true Christian
is to represent Christ, to reflect light, to elevate the standard of morals, and by words and influence consecrated to
God, to compel the careless and reckless to think of God and
eternity. The world would gladly drop eternity out of their
reckoning, but they cannot succeed so long as there are
those who represent Christ in their practical life.)

Every believer forms a link in the golden chain connecting the soul to Jesus Christ, and is the channel of communication of that light to those who are in darkness. Let

---

* Addressed to the president of Battle Creek College.

one lose his connection with Christ, and Satan seizes the opportunity to lead him to dishonor Christ by words, by spirit, by action, and thus Christ's character is misinterpreted. I ask you, my brother, if the religion of Jesus Christ is not by the excess of the amusements misunderstood. When the Lord gave to Battle Creek the riches of His grace, were there those in responsibility who could have directed these souls as to how to improve upon the endowment given, in doing good, useful work that would give a change from their studies, other than the excitement and emotions caused by their games? This kind of pastime is not improving mind or spirit or manners for the preparation for the scenes of trial that they must soon enter. The superficial piety that passes for religion will be consumed when tried in the furnace.

The Lord would have the teachers consider the contagion of their own example. They need to pray much more and consider that the convictions which flow out from a well-ordered life and a godly conversation, from a living, decided Christianity, are the preparation of the garden of the heart for the seeds of truth to be planted for a fruitful harvest, and for the Sun of Righteousness when He comes with healing in His beams. Let your righteousness so shine before men, "that they may see your good works, and glorify your Father which is in heaven" (Matt. 5:16). "Ye are," said Christ to His disciples, "the salt of the earth: but if the salt have lost his savour, wherewith shall it be salted? it is thenceforth good for nothing, but to be cast out, and to be trodden under foot of men" (Matt. 5:13). The church illuminates the world, not by their profession of godliness, but by their manifestation of the transforming, sanctifying power of the truth on life and character. . . .

The time is altogether too full of tokens of the coming conflict to be educating the youth in fun and games.—Letter 46, 1893.

DANGER OF LIGHT BECOMING DARKNESS

The Lord has condescended to give you an outpouring of His Holy Spirit. At the camp meetings, and in our various institutions, a great blessing has been showered upon you. You have been visited by the heavenly messengers of light and truth and power, and it should not be thought a strange thing that God should thus bless you. How does Christ subdue His chosen people to Himself?—It is by the power of His Holy Spirit; for the Holy Spirit, through the Scriptures, speaks to the mind, and impresses truth upon the hearts of men. Before His crucifixion, Christ promised that the Comforter should be sent to His disciples. He said: "It is expedient for you that I go away: for if I go not away, the Comforter will not come unto you; but if I depart, I will send him unto you. And when he is come, he will reprove the world of sin, and of righteousness, and of judgment. . . . When he, the Spirit of truth, is come, he will guide you into all truth: for he shall not speak of himself; but whatsoever he shall hear, that shall he speak: and he will shew you things to come. He shall glorify me: for he shall receive of mine, and shall shew it unto you" (John 16:7, 8, 13-15).

This promise of Christ has been made little enough of, and because of a dearth of the Spirit of God, the spirituality of the law and its eternal obligations have not been comprehended. Those who have professed to love Christ, have not comprehended the relation which exists between them and God, and it is still but dimly outlined to their understanding. They but vaguely comprehend the amazing grace of God in giving His only-begotten Son for the salvation of the world. They do not understand how far reaching are the claims of the holy law, how intimately the precepts of the law are to be brought into practical life. They do not realize what a great privilege and necessity are prayer, repentance, and the doing of the words of Christ. It is the office of the Holy Spirit to reveal to the mind the character of the consecration that God will accept. Through the agency of the Holy Spirit, the soul is enlightened, and the character is renewed, sanctified, and uplifted.

Through the deep movings of the Spirit of God, I have had opened before me the character of the work of the visitation of the Spirit of God. I have had opened before me the danger in which souls would be placed who had been thus visited; for afterward, they would have to meet fiercer assaults of the enemy, who would press upon them his temptations to make of none effect the workings of the Spirit of God, and cause that the momentous truths presented and witnessed by the Holy Spirit, should not purify and sanctify those who had received the light of heaven, and thus cause that Christ should not be glorified in them.

The period of great spiritual light, if that light is not sacredly cherished and acted upon, will be turned into a time of corresponding spiritual darkness. The impression made by the Spirit of God, if men do not cherish the sacred impression, and occupy holy ground, will fade from the mind. Those who would advance in spiritual knowledge must stand by the very fount of God, and drink again and again from the wells of salvation so graciously opened unto them. They must never leave the source of refreshment; but with hearts swelling with gratitude and love at the display of the goodness and compassion of God, they must be continually partakers of the living water.

Oh, how much this means to every soul—"I am the light of the world"; "I am the bread of life: he that cometh to me shall never hunger [for anything more satisfying]; and he that believeth on me shall never thirst" (John 8:12; 6: 35). To come to this condition means that you have found the Source of light and love, and have learned when and how you may be replenished, and may make use of the promises of God by continually applying them to your souls.

"But I said unto you, That ye also have seen me, and believe not" (John 6:36). This has been literally fulfilled in the cases of many; for the Lord gave them a deeper insight into truth, into His character of mercy and compassion and love; and yet after being thus enlightened, they have turned from Him in unbelief. They saw the deep movings of the Spirit of God; but when the insidious temptations of Satan came in, as they always will come after a season of revival, they did not resist unto blood, striving against sin; and those who might have stood on vantage

ground, had they made a right use of the precious enlightenment that they had, were overcome by the enemy. They
should have reflected the light that God gave to them upon
the souls of others; they should have worked and acted in
harmony with the sacred revealings of the Holy Spirit; and
in not doing so, they suffered loss.

Spiritual Victory Lost to the Passions for Games

Among the students the spirit of fun and frolic was
indulged. They became so interested in playing games that
the Lord was crowded out of their minds; and Jesus stood
among you in the playground, saying, O that thou hadst
known, "even thou, at least in this thy day, the things
which belong unto thy peace!" (Luke 19:42). "Ye also
have seen me, and believe not" (John 6:36). Yes; Christ
revealed Himself to you, and deep impressions were made
as the Holy Spirit moved upon your hearts; but you pursued
a course by which you lost these sacred impressions, and
failed to maintain the victory. "All that the Father giveth
me shall come to me; and him that cometh to me I will in
no wise cast out" (John 6:37). You began to come to
Christ, but you did not abide in Christ. You forsook Him,
and the realization you had had of the great favors and
blessings He had given you, was lost from your heart. The
question of amusement occupied so large a place in your
minds, that after the solemn visitation of the Spirit of God,
you entered into its discussion with such great zeal that all
barriers were broken down; and through your passion for
games, you neglected to heed the word of Christ: "Watch
ye and pray, lest ye enter into temptation" (Mark 14:38).
The place that should have been occupied by Jesus was
usurped by your passion for games. You chose your amusements instead of the comfort of the Holy Spirit. You did
not follow the example of Jesus, who said, "I came down
from heaven, not to do mine own will, but the will of him
that sent me" (John 6:38).

The minds of many are so bewildered with their own
human desires and inclinations, and they have been so in
the habit of indulging them, that they cannot comprehend

the true sense of the Scriptures. Many suppose that in following Christ they will be obliged to be gloomy and disconsolate, because they are required to deny themselves the pleasures and follies that the world indulge in. The living Christian will be filled with cheerfulness and peace, because he lives as seeing Him who is invisible; and those who seek Christ in His true character have within them the elements of everlasting life, because they are partakers of the divine nature, having escaped the corruptions that are in the world through lust. Jesus said, "This is the Father's will which hath sent me, that of all which he hath given me, I should lose nothing, but should raise it up again at the last day. And this is the will of him that sent me, that every one which seeth the Son, and believeth on him, may have everlasting life: and I will raise him up at the last day" (John 6:39, 40).

The Child of God a Laborer With God

All spiritual life is derived from Jesus Christ. "As many as received him, to them gave he power to become the sons of God" (John 1:12). But what is the sure result of becoming a child of God? The result is that we become laborers together with God. There is a great work to be done for your own soul's salvation, and to qualify you to win others from unbelief to a life sustained by faith in Christ Jesus: "Verily, verily, I say unto you, He that believeth on me [with a casual faith?—No, with an abiding faith that works by love and purifies the soul] hath everlasting life. I am that bread of life. . . . I am the living bread which came down from heaven: if any man eat of this bread, he shall live for ever: and the bread that I will give is my flesh, which I will give for the life of the world. . . . Except ye eat the flesh of the Son of man, and drink his blood, ye have no life in you. Whoso eateth my flesh, and drinketh my blood, hath eternal life; and I will raise him up at the last day. . . . It is the Spirit that quickeneth; the flesh profiteth nothing: the words that I speak unto you, they are spirit, and they are life. But there are some of you that believe not. For Jesus knew from the beginning who they were that believed not, and who should betray him. And he said, Therefore said I unto you, that no man can come unto me, except it were given unto him of my Father" (John 6:47, 48, 51, 53, 54, 63-65).

When Jesus spoke these words, He spoke them with authority, assurance, and power. At times He manifested Himself in such a way that the deep movings of His Spirit were sensibly realized. But many who saw and heard and participated in the blessings of the hour, went their way, and soon forgot the light He had given them.

The treasures of eternity have been committed to the keeping of Jesus Christ, to give to whomsoever He will; but how sad it is that so many quickly lose sight of the precious grace that is proffered unto them through faith in Him. He will impart the heavenly treasures to those who will believe in Him, look to Him, and abide in Him. He thought it not robbery to be equal with God, and He knows no restraint nor control in bestowing the heavenly treasures upon whom He will. He does not exalt and honor the great ones of the world, who are flattered and applauded; but He calls upon His chosen, peculiar people who love and serve Him, to come unto Him and ask, and He will give them the bread of life, and endow them with the water of life, which shall be in them as a well of water springing up unto everlasting life.

Jesus brought to our world the accumulated treasures of God, and all who believe upon Him are adopted as His heirs. He declares that great shall be the reward of them who suffer for His name's sake. It is written, "Eye hath not seen, nor ear heard, neither have entered into the heart of man, the things which God hath prepared for them that love him" (1 Cor. 2:9).—*The Review and Herald,* Jan. 30, 1894.

WAS THE BLESSING CHERISHED?

In order to increase our spiritual endowment, it is necessary to walk in the light. In view of the event of Christ's soon coming, we must be vigilantly working to prepare our own souls, to keep our own lamps trimmed and burning, and to urge upon others the necessity of getting ready for the coming of the Bridegroom. Watching and working must go together; faith and works must be united, or our characters will not be symmetrical and well-balanced, perfect in Christ Jesus.

Should we give our lives up to prayerful meditation, our lights would grow dim, for light is given to us that we may impart it to others, and the more we impart light, the brighter our own light will become. If there is any one thing in the world in which we may manifest enthusiasm, it may be manifested in seeking the salvation of the souls for whom Christ died. Work of this kind will not cause us to neglect personal piety. The exhortation is given for us to be "not slothful in business; fervent in spirit; serving the Lord" (Rom. 12:11).

To have an eye single to the glory of God means to have singleness of purpose, to show forth the work that has been wrought in your heart, that subdues your will to the will of God, and brings into captivity every thought to the glory of God. The world has been looking upon you to see what would be the afterinfluence of the work of revival that came to the college, the sanitarium, the office of publication, and to the members of the church in Battle Creek. What testimony have you borne in your daily life and character?

God expected you all to do your best, not to please, amuse, and glorify yourselves, but to honor Him in all your ways, returning unto Him according to the light and privileges that He had given you through the endowment of His grace. He expected you to testify before heavenly intelligences, and to be living witnesses to the world, of the power of the grace of Christ. The Lord tested you, to see if you would treat His rich blessing as a cheap, light matter, or regard it as a rich treasure to be handled with reverent awe. If all had treated the gift of God in this manner—for the work was of God—then, according to the measure of each one's responsibility, the grace given would have been doubled, as were the talents of him who traded diligently with his lord's money.

A Blessing Turned Into a Curse

God has been testing the fidelity of His people, proving them to see what use they would make of His intrusted precious blessing. This blessing came from our Intercessor and Advocate in the heavenly courts; but Satan was ready to enter any avenue that was open for him, in order that he might turn the light and blessing into darkness and cursing.

How may the blessing be turned into a curse? By persuading the human agent not to cherish the light, or not to reveal to the world that it has been effective in transforming the character. Imbued with the Holy Spirit, the human agent consecrates himself to cooperate with divine agencies. He bears the yoke of Christ, lifts his burdens, and works in Christ's line to gain precious victories. He walks in the light as Christ is in the light. The scripture is fulfilled to him, "We all, with open face beholding as in a glass the glory of the Lord, are changed into the same image from glory to glory even as by the Spirit of the Lord" (2 Cor. 3:18).

Another year has now passed into eternity with its burden of record; and the light which shone from heaven upon you was to prepare you to arise and shine, to show forth the praises of God to the world as His commandment-keeping people. You were to be living witnesses; but if no special endeavor of a high and holy character bears testimony before the world, if no higher effort has been made than that which is seen in the popular churches of the day, then the name of God has not been honored, and His truth has not been magnified before the world, by presenting divine credentials in the people who have received great light. If they have had no greater appreciation of the manifest power of God than to eat and drink, and rise up to play, as did ancient Israel, then how can the Lord trust His people with rich and gracious manifestations? If they act directly contrary in almost every respect to the known will of God, and are found in carelessness, in levity, in selfishness, in ambition and pride, corrupting their way before the Lord, how can He give them another outpouring of the Holy Spirit?

God has the richest blessing for His people; but He cannot bestow it until they know how to treat the precious gift in showing forth the praises of Him who has called them out of darkness into His marvelous light. "Wherefore seeing we also are compassed about with so great a cloud of witnesses, let us lay aside every weight, and the sin which doth so easily beset us, and let us run with patience the race that is set before us, looking unto Jesus the author and finisher of our faith; who for the joy that was set before him endured the cross, despising the shame, and is set down at the right hand of the throne of God" (Heb. 12:1, 2). A portion of the joy which was set before Christ, was the joy of seeing His truth armed with the omnipotent power of the Holy Spirit, impressing His image upon the life and character of His followers.

Divine intelligences cooperate with human agencies as they seek to magnify the law and make it honorable. The law of the Lord is perfect, converting the soul. It is in the converted soul that the world sees a living testimony. Then shall the Lord of heaven have room to work? Shall He find a place in the hearts of those who claim to believe the truth? Shall His pure, disinterested benevolence meet with a response from the human agent? Shall the world see a display of the glory of Christ in the characters of those who profess to be His disciples? Shall Christ be favored and glorified in seeing His own sympathy and love pouring forth in streams of goodness and truth from His human agents? In implanting His gospel in the heart, He is pouring out the resources of heaven for the blessing of the world. "We are labourers together with God: ye are God's husbandry, ye are God's building" (1 Cor. 3:9).

What has the rich blessing of God done for those who were humble and contrite in heart to receive it? Has the blessing been cherished? Have the receivers been showing forth the praises of Him who has called them out of darkness into His marvelous light? There are some who are already questioning the work that was so good, and that

should have been most highly appreciated. They are looking upon it as a certain species of fanaticism.

Be Exceedingly Careful

It would be surprising if there were not some, who, not
being well-balanced in mind, have spoken and acted indis-
creetly; for whenever and wherever the Lord works in giving a genuine blessing, a counterfeit is also revealed, in
order to make of none effect the true work of God. Therefore we need to be exceedingly careful, and walk humbly
before God, that we may have spiritual eyesalve that we
may distinguish the working of the Holy Spirit of God
from the working of that spirit that would bring in wild
license and fanaticism. "By their fruits ye shall know them"
(Matt. 7:20). Those who are really beholding Christ will
be changed into His image, even by the Spirit of the Lord,
and will grow up to the full stature of men and women in
Christ Jesus. The Holy Spirit of God will inspire men with
love and purity; and refinement will be manifest in their
characters.

But because some have misappropriated the rich blessing of heaven, shall others deny that Jesus, the Saviour of
the world, has passed through our churches, and that to
bless? Let not doubt and unbelief question this; for in so
doing, you are treading on dangerous ground. God has
given the Holy Spirit to those who have opened the door of
their hearts to receive the heavenly gift. But let them not
yield to the temptation afterward to believe that they have
been deceived. Let them not say, "Because I feel darkness,
and am oppressed with doubt, and never saw Satan's power
so manifest as now, therefore I was mistaken." I warn you
to be careful. Sow not one expression of doubt. God has
wrought for you, bringing sound doctrines of truth into actual contact with the heart. Blessing was given you, that it
might produce fruit in sound practices and upright character.

The Sin of Rejecting Evidence

The sin for which Christ reproved Chorazin and Beth-
saida was the sin of rejecting evidence that would have con-

vinced them of the truth, had they yielded to its power. The sin of the scribes and Pharisees was the sin of placing the heavenly work which had been wrought before them in the darkness of unbelief, so that the evidence which should have led them into a settled faith was questioned, and the sacred things which should have been cherished were regarded as of no value. I fear that the people have permitted the enemy to work along these very lines, so that the good which emanated from God, the rich blessing which He has given, have come to be regarded by some as fanaticism.

If this attitude is preserved, then when the Lord shall again let His light shine upon the people, they will turn from the heavenly illumination, saying, "I felt the same in 1893, and some in whom I have had confidence, said that the work was fanaticism." Will not those who have received the rich grace of God, and who take the position that the working of the Holy Spirit was fanaticism, be ready to denounce the operations of the Spirit of God in the future, and the heart thus be proof against the solicitations of the still, small voice? The love of Jesus may be presented to those who thus barricade themselves against it, and exercise no constraining power upon them. The riches of the grace of heaven may be bestowed and yet rejected, instead of being cherished and gratefully recognized. With the heart men did believe unto righteousness, and for a time confession was made unto salvation; but, sad to relate, the receiver did not cooperate with heavenly intelligences, and cherish the light by working the works of righteousness.—*The Review and Herald,* Feb. 6, 1894.

18.

Special Appeals in Public Ministry

~~~~~~~~~~~~~~~~~~

[Ellen G. White, in her public ministry effectively employed the appeal which called for a response. Presented here are accounts of a number of instances which reveal her use of such methods under varying circumstances.—COMPILERS.]

At Battle Creek in Early Days

Attended meeting at the church at Battle Creek. Spoke to the people about one hour with freedom, in regard to the fall of Adam bringing misery and death, Christ bringing life and immortality to light through His humiliation and death. Felt to urge upon the people the necessity of entire consecration to God—the sanctification of the entire being, soul, body, and spirit. Spoke upon the death of Moses and the view he had of the promised land of Canaan. There was a depth of feeling in the congregation. . . . In meeting that evening we called those forward who had a desire to be Christians. Thirteen came forward. All bore testimony for the Lord. It was a good work.—Diary, Jan. 12, 1868.

Earnest Work at Tittabawassee, Michigan

Meetings were held all through the day. My husband spoke in forenoon; Brother Andrews in the afternoon. I followed with remarks quite at length, entreating those who had been interested through the meetings to commence from that day to serve God. We called forward those who wished to start in the service of the Lord. Quite a number came forward. I spoke several times, beseeching souls to break the bands of Satan and start then. One mother went to her son and wept and entreated him. He seemed hard, stubborn, and unyielding. I then arose and addressed Brother D, begged him to not stand in the way of his children. He started, then arose, spoke, said he would commence from that day. This was heard with glad hearts by all. Brother D is a precious man.

Sister E's husband then arose, testified that he would be a Christian. He is an influential man—a lawyer. His daughter was upon the anxious seat. Brother D then added his entreaties to ours. Sister D's also to their children. We entreated and at last prevailed. All came forward. The fathers and all the sons and other fathers followed their example. It was a day of gladness. Sister E said it was the happiest day of her life.—Diary, Feb. 19, 1868.

A Good Response in Battle Creek

I spoke in the afternoon from 2 Peter. I had freedom in talking. After I had spoken one hour I invited those who wished to be Christians to come forward. Between thirty and forty came forward quietly without excitement and occupied the front seats. I spoke with them in regard to making an entire surrender to God. We had a praying season for those who came forward. We had a very precious season of prayer. Those who wished baptism were requested to signify it by rising. Quite a number arose.—Diary, June 9, 1873.

After Some Hesitancy a Response

I spoke in the afternoon [at Stanley, Va.] from John 17:3. The Lord gave me much of His Holy Spirit. The house was full. I called those forward who wished to seek the Lord more earnestly and for those who wished to give themselves to the Lord a whole sacrifice. For a time not one made a move, but after a while many came forward and bore testimonies of confession. We had a precious season of prayer and all felt broken down, weeping and confessing their sins. O that each may understand!—Diary, Nov. 9, 1890.

As She Begins Work in Switzerland

Sabbath and Sunday were precious seasons.* The Lord especially blessed [me] in speaking Sunday afternoon. At the close of the discourse an invitation was given for all who desired to be Christians, and all who felt that they had not a living connection with God, to come forward, that we might unite our prayers with theirs for the pardon of sin, and for grace to resist temptation.

This was a new experience for many, but they did not hesitate. It seemed that the entire congregation were on their feet, and the best they could do was to be seated, and all seek the Lord together. Here was an entire congregation manifesting their determination to put away sin, and to engage most earnestly in the work of seeking God. After prayer, one hundred and fifteen testimonies were borne. Many of these showed a genuine experience in the things of God.—*Historical Sketches of the Foreign Missions of the Seventh-day Adventists,* p. 173.

At Christiania [Oslo], Norway

We spent two weeks in Christiania, and labored earnestly for the church. The Spirit of the Lord moved me to bear a very plain testimony. At our last meeting especially, I presented before them the necessity of a thorough change in the character if they would be children of God. . . . I urged upon them the necessity of deep repentance, confession, and forsaking of the sins which had shut away the sweet spirit of Christ from the church. We then called for those to come forward who would take a decided position on the Lord's side. Many responded. Some good confessions were made, and earnest testimonies were borne.—*The Review and Herald,* Oct. 19, 1886.

---

* At the Swiss Conference held in Basel, Switzerland, in 1885.

Determination Indicated by Standing

A request was made [at Basel, Switzerland] for all who would from this time make most earnest efforts to reach a higher standard to arise. All arose. We hope this now will have the effect to win them to God and to heavenly reflections and make earnest efforts to be all that God has given them power to be—faithful and true devoted soldiers of the cross of Christ.—Diary, Nov. 22, 1885.

Backsliders Reclaimed in Basel

In the afternoon of the Sabbath we assembled again for social meeting. The blessing of the Lord rested upon me as I again addressed the people for a short time. Every seat was full and extra seats were brought in. All listened with deep interest.

I invited those who desired the prayers of the servants of God to come forward. All who had been backslidden, all who wished to return to the Lord and seek Him diligently, could improve the opportunity. Several seats were quickly filled and the whole congregation was on the move. We told them the best they could do was to be seated right where they were and we would all seek the Lord together by confessing our sins, and the Lord had pledged His word, "If we confess our sins, he is faithful and just to forgive us our sins, and to cleanse us from all unrighteousness" (1 John 1:9).

Many testimonies were borne in quick succession and with depth of feelings, showing that the hearts were touched by the Spirit of God. Our meetings continued from two o'clock P.M. to five, and then we were obliged to close, with several earnest prayers.—Diary, Feb. 20, 1887.

An Outstanding Experience in Australia

On Sabbath, May 25 [1895], we had a precious meeting in the hall where our people meet at North Fitzroy. For several days before the meeting, I knew that I was expected to speak in the church on Sabbath; but unfortunately I had a severe cold and was quite hoarse. I felt inclined to excuse myself from this appointment; but as it was my only opportunity, I said, "I will place myself before the people, and I believe the Lord will answer my earnest prayers, and remove the hoarseness so that I can present my message to the people." I presented to my heavenly Father the promise, "Ask, and it shall be given you; seek, and ye shall find; knock, and it shall be opened unto you. For every one that asketh receiveth; and he that seeketh findeth; and to him that knocketh it shall be opened. . . . If ye, then, being evil, know how to give good gifts unto your children: how much more shall your heavenly Father give the Holy Spirit to them that ask him?" (Luke 11:9-13). . . .

The word of God is sure. I had asked, and I believed that I would be enabled to speak to the people. I selected a portion of Scripture; but when I rose to speak, it was taken from my mind, and I felt impressed to speak from the first chapter of second Peter. The Lord gave me special freedom in presenting the value of the grace of God. . . . I was enabled by the aid of the Holy Spirit to speak with clearness and power.

At the close of my discourse, I felt impressed by the Spirit of God to extend an invitation for all those to come forward who desired to give themselves fully to the Lord. Those who felt the need of the prayers of the servants of God were invited to make it manifest. About thirty came forward. Among these were the wives of the Brethren F, who for the first time made manifest their desire to come near to God. My heart was filled with unspeakable gratitude because of the movement made by these two women.

I could then see why I was so earnestly moved to make this invitation. At first I had hesitated, wondering if it were best to do so when my son and I were the only ones whom I could see who would give us any help on that occasion. But as though someone had spoken to me, the thought passed through my mind, "Cannot you trust in the Lord?" I said, "I will, Lord." Although my son was much surprised that I should make such a call on this occasion, he was equal to the emergency. I never heard him speak with greater power or deeper feeling than at that time. He called upon Brethren Faulkhead and Salisbury to come forward, and we knelt in prayer. My son took the lead, and the Lord surely indited his petition; for he seemed to pray as though in the presence of God. Brethren Faulkhead and Salisbury also presented fervent petitions, and then the Lord gave me a voice to pray. I remembered the Sisters F, who, for the first time, were taking a public stand for the truth. The Holy Spirit was in the meeting, and many were stirred by its deep movings.

At the close of the meeting many pressed their way to the platform, and taking me by the hand, requested me with tears in their eyes to pray for them. I answered heartily, "I will." The Sisters F were introduced to me, and I found that their hearts were very tender. . . . The mother of one of the sisters who has now taken her position on the truth, has been a most bitter opposer, and has threatened that if her daughter did become a Sabbathkeeper, she would not allow her to enter her home; for the mother would look upon her as a disgrace to the family. Mrs. F had often made the statement that she would never join the Seventh-day Adventists. She had been brought up in the Presbyterian Church, and had been educated to think that it was very improper for women to speak in meeting, and that for a woman to preach was altogether beyond the bounds of propriety. She enjoyed hearing Elders Daniells and Corliss, and thought them very clever speakers, but she would not listen to a woman's preaching. Her husband had prayed that God would so arrange matters that she might be converted under the ministry of Sister White. When I made the appeal, and urged those to come forward who felt their need of drawing nearer to God, to the surprise of all, these sisters came forward. The sister who had lost her little one, said that she was determined that she would not move forward, but the Spirit of the Lord so forcibly impressed her mind that she dared not refuse. . . . I feel so grateful to my heavenly Father for His lovingkindness in bringing these two precious souls to unite with their husbands in obeying the truth.—*The Review and Herald,* July 30, 1895.

Non-Adventist Visitors Respond at Ashfield Church

I invited all who wanted to give themselves to God in a sacred covenant, and to serve Him with their whole hearts, to rise to their feet. The house was full, and nearly all rose. Quite a number not of our faith were present, and some of these arose. I presented them to the Lord in earnest prayer, and we know that we had the manifestation of the Spirit of God. We felt that a victory had indeed been gained.—Manuscript 30a, 1896.

The Special Call at the Battle Creek College

I have now spoken to the helpers, nursing class, and physicians five times during the Week of Prayer, and I am sure my talks are appreciated. I have spoken in the college twice. Last Thursday Professor Prescott wished me to come over there. I went and prayed and spoke to the large chapel filled with students. I had much freedom in speaking and in presenting before them the goodness and mercy of God and the great condescension and sacrifice of Jesus Christ and the heavenly reward purchased for us, the last final victory, and what a privilege it is to be Christians.

Professor Prescott arose and attempted to speak, but his heart was full and he did not utter a word for five minutes, but stood weeping before the people. Then he said a few words, "I am glad that I am a Christian." He talked for about five minutes, then he gave liberty for all to speak. Many testimonies were borne, but it seemed to me that there must be a company reached that we had not yet succeeded in reaching. We called all to come forward who felt that they were unready for Christ's coming and had not an evidence of their acceptance with God. I thought the whole house was in motion. We then gave opportunity for all to express their feelings, but we had after a little another season of prayer and the blessing of the Lord seemed to reach hearts.

Then we separated into divisions and continued the work for two hours longer, and the Lord's Spirit came into the meeting in a remarkable manner. Several of those who had known nothing of a religious faith, unbelievers from the world, have obtained a genuine experience in the religious life. And the work is going deeper and deeper. The Lord is at work and will work, as fast as we prepare the way for Him that He can safely reveal His power in our behalf. —Letter 75, 1888.

Called Forward in San Francisco

Friday, December 21 [1900], I went to San Francisco, where I was to spend the Week of Prayer. Sabbath afternoon I spoke to the church there, although I was so weak that I had to cling to the pulpit with both hands to steady myself. I asked the Lord to give me strength to speak to the people. He heard my prayer, and strengthened me. I had great freedom in speaking from Rev. 2:1-5.

The deep moving of the Spirit of God came upon me, and the people were strongly impressed with the message borne. After I had finished speaking, all who desired to give themselves to the Lord were invited to come forward. A large number responded, and prayer was offered for them. Several who came forward are persons who have recently heard the Advent message, and are in the valley of decision. May the Lord strengthen the good impression made upon them, and may they give themselves wholly to Him. Oh, how I long to see souls converted, and hear them sing a new song, even praise to our God!

Sunday afternoon I spoke to a large audience, many of whom are not of our faith. My strength was renewed, and I was able, without clinging to the desk, to stand before the people. The Lord's blessing rested upon us, and increased strength came to me as I spoke. As on Sabbath, those seeking spiritual help were invited to come forward, and we were glad to see the ready response. The Lord came very near as we sought Him in prayer.—*The Review and Herald*, Feb. 19, 1901.

A Similar Work in Every Church

Sabbath, November 10, I visited San Francisco, and spoke to a church full of people who had ears to hear and hearts to understand. . . . After I had finished speaking, Elder Corliss invited all who wished to give themselves to Jesus to come forward. There was a quick and happy response, and I was told that nearly two hundred persons came forward. Men and women, youth and children, pressed into the front seats. The Lord would be pleased to have a work similar to this done in every church.

Many could not come forward, because the house was so crowded, yet the animated countenances and tearful eyes testified to the determination, "I will be on the Lord's side. From this time I will seek earnestly to reach a higher standard."—*The Review and Herald,* Feb. 12, 1901.

Response at General Conference of 1909

My brethren and sisters, seek the Lord while He may be found. There is a time coming when those who have wasted their time and opportunities will wish they had sought Him. . . . He wants you to keep in the line of reason, and in the line of labor. He wants you to go forth to our churches to labor earnestly for Him. He wants you to institute meetings for those outside of the churches, that they may learn the truths of this last message of warning. There are places where you will be gladly received, where souls will thank you for coming to their help. May the Lord help you to take hold of this work as you have never yet taken hold of it. Will you do this? Will you here rise to your feet and testify that you will make God your trust and your helper? [Congregation rises.]

[Praying] I thank thee, Lord God of Israel. Accept this pledge of this Thy people. Put Thy Spirit upon them. Let Thy glory be seen in them. As they shall speak the word of truth, let us see the salvation of God. Amen.—*General Conference Bulletin,* May 18, 1909.

SECTION IV

"Preach the Word"

INTRODUCTION

~~~~~~~~~~~~~~~

As in the year 1933 the General Conference leadership made plans for strong evangelistic emphasis and effort throughout North America, it was realized that if large objectives were to be accomplished, the ministers who stood before the people must turn from subjects of minor importance to the presentation of the third angel's message in its broad and gripping phases. At the request of the General Conference a sixteen-page pamphlet entitled "Preach the Word," containing Ellen G. White counsels, was published. Great good was accomplished by the many thousands of copies distributed, charging the ministry anew with the solemn responsibility of proclaiming the last judgment-hour message to the world. Those portions not in other E. G. White books are included in permanent form here. The statements printed do not constitute an exhaustive compilation of what Ellen White has written on this subject. Additional counsel may be found in the books *Evangelism, Gospel Workers, Testimonies to Ministers,* and *Christian Service.*

Following the pamphlet items are a few related chapters. "The Peril of Extreme Views" is a communication addressed to one of our ministers, containing instruction of great service, which until now has been available only in *Notebook Leaflets.* The chapter on "Time Setting" is pertinent. The section closes with counsels drawn from *Special Testimonies,* Series B, No. 2, written during the crisis of 1903 and 1904 when certain pantheistic views were being pressed upon the denomination as new light which, it was asserted, would prove a great blessing to the church. The chief blessing that resulted from this crisis was in the lessons in truth so earnestly communicated by the Lord's messenger to the struggling church, found mainly in *Testimonies,* volume 8, and *The Ministry of Healing.*— WHITE TRUSTEES.

19.

What to Preach and Not to Preach*

~~~~~~~~~~~~~~~

Let Christ Appear

The object of all ministry is to keep self out of sight, and to let Christ appear. The exaltation of Christ is the great truth that all who labor in word and doctrine are to reveal.—Manuscript 109, 1897.

Laborers in the cause of truth should present the righteousness of Christ, not as new light, but as precious light that has for a time been lost sight of by the people. We are to accept of Christ as our personal Saviour, and He imputes unto us the righteousness of God in Christ. Let us repeat and make prominent the truth that John has portrayed, "Herein is love, not that we loved God, but that he loved us, and sent his Son to be the propitiation for our sins" (1 John 4:10).

In the love of God has been opened the most marvelous vein of precious truth, and the treasures of the grace of Christ are laid open before the church and the world. . . . What love is this, what marvelous, unfathomable love that would lead Christ to die for us while we were yet sinners.

What a loss it is to the soul who understands the strong claims of the law, and who yet fails to understand the grace of Christ which doth much more abound.

It is true that the law of God reveals the love of God when it is preached as the truth in Jesus, for the gift of Christ to this guilty world must be largely dwelt upon in every discourse. It is no wonder that hearts have not been melted by the truth, when it has been presented in a cold and lifeless manner. No wonder faith has staggered at the promises of God, when ministers and workers have failed to present Jesus in His relation to the law of God. How often should they have assured the people that "he that spared not his own Son, but delivered him up for us all, how shall he not with him also freely give us all things?" (Rom. 8:32).

Satan is determined that men shall not see the love of God which led Him to give His only-begotten Son to save a lost race; for it is the goodness of God that leads men to repentance. O how shall we succeed in setting forth before the world the deep, precious love of God? In no other way can we compass it except by exclaiming, "Behold, what manner of love the Father hath bestowed upon us, that we should be called the sons of God" (1 John 3:1). Let us say to sinners, "Behold the Lamb of God, which taketh away the sin of the world" (John 1:29). By presenting Jesus as the representative of the Father, we shall be able to dispel the shadow that Satan has cast upon our pathway, in order that we shall not see the mercy and inexpressible love of God as manifested in Jesus Christ. Look at the cross of Calvary. It is a standing pledge of the boundless love, the measureless mercy of the heavenly Father.—Manuscript 154, 1897.

The Holy Spirit

Christ, the Great Teacher, had an infinite variety of subjects from which to choose, but the one upon which He dwelt most largely was the endowment of the Holy Spirit. What great things He predicted for the church because of this endowment. Yet what subject is less dwelt upon

now? What promise is less fulfilled? An occasional discourse is given upon the Holy Spirit, and then the subject
is left for after consideration.—Manuscript 20, 1891.

Teach Steps in Conversion

Ministers need to have a more clear, simple manner in
presenting the truth as it is in Jesus. Their own minds need
to comprehend the great plan of salvation more fully. Then
they can carry the minds of the hearers away from earthly
things to the spiritual and eternal. There are many who
want to know what they must do to be saved. They want a
plain and clear explanation of the steps requisite in conversion, and there should not a sermon be given unless a
portion of that discourse is to especially make plain the way
that sinners may come to Christ and be saved. They should
point them to Christ, as did John, and with touching
simplicity, their hearts aglow with the love of Christ, say,
"Behold the Lamb of God, which taketh away the sin of
the world." Strong and earnest appeals should be made to
the sinner to repent and be converted.

Those who neglect this part of the work need to be converted themselves before venturing to give a discourse.
Those whose hearts are filled with the love of Jesus, with
the precious truths of His Word, will be able to draw from
the treasure house of God things new and old. They will
not find time to relate anecdotes; they will not strain to become orators, soaring so high that they cannot carry the
people with them; but in simple language, with touching
earnestness, they will present the truth as it is in Jesus.—
The Review and Herald, Feb. 22, 1887.

Revival of Old Advent Truths

There is a work of sacred importance for ministers and
people to do. They are to study the history of the cause and
people of God. They are not to forget the past dealing of
God with His people. They are to revive and recount the
truths that have come to seem of little value to those who
do not know by personal experience of the power and

brightness that accompanied them when they were first seen and understood. In all their original freshness and power these truths are to be given to the world.—Manuscript 22, 1890.

The Ministration of Angels

Over every man good and evil angels strive. It is the man himself who determines which shall win. I call upon the ministers of Christ to press home upon the understanding of all who come within the reach of their voice, the truth of the ministration of angels. Do not indulge in fanciful speculations. The written Word is our only safety. We must pray as did Daniel, that we may be guarded by heavenly intelligences.—Letter 201, 1899.

Argumentative Sermons

The many argumentative sermons preached, seldom soften and subdue the soul. . . . It should be the burden of every messenger to set forth the fullness of Christ. When the free gift of Christ's righteousness is not presented, the discourses are dry and spiritless; the sheep and lambs are not fed. Said Paul, "My speech and my preaching was not with enticing words of man's wisdom, but in demonstration of the Spirit and of power" (1 Cor. 2:4). There is marrow and fatness in the gospel. Jesus is the living center of everything. Put Christ into every sermon. Let the preciousness, mercy, and glory of Jesus Christ be dwelt upon; for Christ formed within is the hope of glory.—Letter 15, 1892.

Present Truth in Meekness

Be careful messengers. Do not be anxious to hear and accept new theories, for often they are such as should never be presented before any congregation. Speak no boastful, self-exalting words. Let the Word of God come forth from lips that are sanctified by the truth. Every minister is to preach the truth as it is in Jesus. He should be assured of that which he affirms, and should handle the Word of God under the direction of the Holy Spirit of God. Walk and work carefully before God, my brethren, that no soul may be led into deception by your example. It had been better for you never to have been born than that you should lead one soul astray.

Those who profess to be servants of God need to make diligent work for the obtaining of that life where sin and sickness and sorrow cannot enter. They are to be instant in season and out of season.

God is calling for reformers who will speak strong, uplifting words from our pulpits. It is when men speak their own words in their own strength, instead of preaching the Word of God in the power of the Spirit, that they are hurt and offended when their words are not received with enthusiasm. It is then that they are tempted to speak words that will arouse a spirit of bitterness and opposition in their hearers. My brethren, be advised. Such words are not to come from the lips of Christ's ambassadors. Sanctified lips will speak words that reform, but do not exasperate. The truth is to be presented in the meekness and love of Christ. —Letter 348, 1907.

A Device of the Enemy

We are to pray for divine enlightenment, but at the same time we should be careful how we receive everything termed new light. We must beware lest, under cover of searching for new truth, Satan shall divert our minds from Christ and the special truths for this time. I have been shown that it is the device of the enemy to lead minds to dwell upon some obscure or unimportant point, something that is not fully revealed or is not essential to our salvation. This is made the absorbing theme, the "present truth," when all their investigations and suppositions only serve to make matters more obscure than before, and to confuse the minds of some who ought to be seeking for oneness through sanctification of the truth.—Letter 7, 1891.

Human Suppositions and Conjectures

Let no one present beautiful, scientific sophistries to lull the people of God to sleep. Clothe not the solemn, sacred truth for this time in any fantastic dress of man's wisdom. Let those who have been doing this stop and cry unto God to save their souls from deceiving fables.

It is the living energy of the Holy Spirit that will move hearts, not pleasing, deceptive theories. Fanciful representations are not the bread of life; they cannot save the soul from sin.

Christ was sent from heaven to redeem humanity. He taught the doctrines that God gave Him to teach. The truths that He proclaimed, as found in the Old Testament and the New, we today are to proclaim as the word of the living God.

Let those who want the bread of life go to the Scriptures, not to the teaching of finite, erring man. Give the people the bread of life that Christ came from heaven to bring to us. Do not mix with your teaching human suppositions and conjectures. Would that all knew how much they need to eat the flesh and drink the blood of the Son of God—to make His words a part of their very lives.—Manuscript 44, 1904.

Our Faith Founded on Truth

I long daily to be able to do double duty. I have been pleading with the Lord for strength and wisdom to reproduce the writings of the witnesses who were confirmed in the faith and in the early history of the message. After the passing of the time in 1844 they received the light and walked in the light, and when the men claiming to have new light would come in with their wonderful messages regarding various points of Scripture, we had, through the moving of the Holy Spirit, testimonies right to the point, which cut off the influence of such messages as Elder G has been devoting his time to presenting.* This poor man has been working decidedly against the truth that the Holy Spirit has confirmed.

* Reference is here made to teachings on the sanctuary question— at variance with those held by Seventh-day Adventists through the years— which denied the fulfillment of prophecy in 1844 and repudiated the ministry of Christ in the investigative judgment.—COMPILERS.

When the power of God testifies as to what is truth, that truth is to stand forever as the truth. No after suppositions contrary to the light God has given are to be entertained. Men will arise with interpretations of Scripture which are to them truth, but which are not truth. The truth for this time God has given us as a foundation for our faith. He Himself has taught us what is truth. One will arise, and still another, with new light, which contradicts the light that God has given under the demonstration of His Holy Spirit. A few are still alive who passed through the experience gained in the establishment of this truth. God has graciously spared their lives to repeat, and repeat till the close of their lives, the experience through which they passed even as did John the apostle till the very close of his life. And the standard bearers who have fallen in death are to speak through the reprinting of their writings. I am instructed that thus their voices are to be heard. They are to bear their testimony as to what constitutes the truth for this time.

We are not to receive the words of those who come with a message that contradicts the special points of our faith. They gather together a mass of Scripture, and pile it as proof around their asserted theories. This has been done over and over again during the past fifty years. And while the Scriptures are God's word, and are to be respected, the application of them, if such application moves one pillar from the foundation that God has sustained these fifty years, is a great mistake. He who makes such an application knows not the wonderful demonstration of the Holy Spirit that gave power and force to the past messages that have come to the people of God.

Elder G's proofs are not reliable. If received, they would destroy the faith of God's people in the truth that has made us what we are.

We must be decided on this subject; for the points that he is trying to prove by Scripture, are not sound. They do not prove that the past experience of God's people was a fallacy. We had the truth; we were directed by the angels of God. It was under the guidance of the Holy Spirit that the presentation of the sanctuary question was given. It is eloquence for every one to keep silent in regard to the features of our faith in which they acted no part. God never contradicts Himself. Scripture proofs are misapplied if forced to testify to that which is not true. Another and still another will arise and bring in supposedly great light, and make their assertions. But we stand by the old landmarks. [1 John 1:1-10 quoted.]

I am instructed to say that these words we may use as appropriate for this time, for the time has come when sin must be called by its right name. We are hindered in our work by men who are not converted, who seek their own glory. They wish to be thought originators of new theories, which they present claiming that they are truth. But if these theories are received, they will lead to a denial of the truth that for the past fifty years God has been giving to His people, substantiating it by the demonstration of the Holy Spirit.—Letter 329, 1905.

The Truths That Have Been Revealed

"Study to shew thyself approved unto God, a workman that needeth not to be ashamed, rightly dividing the word of truth." Learn to take the truths that have been revealed, and to handle them in such a way that they will be food for the flock of God.

We shall meet those who allow their minds to wander into idle speculations about things of which nothing is said in the Word of God. God has spoken in the plainest language upon every subject that affects the salvation of the soul. But He desires us to avoid all day dreaming, and He says, Go work today in my vineyard. The night cometh wherein no man can work. Cease all idle curiosity; watch, and work, and pray. Study the truths that have been revealed. Christ desires to break up all vacant reveries, and He points us to the fields ripe for the harvest. Unless we work earnestly, eternity will overwhelm us with its burden of responsibility. . . .

In the days of the apostles the most foolish heresies were presented as truth. History has been and will be repeated. There will always be those who, though apparently conscientious, will grasp at the shadow, preferring it to the substance. They take error in the place of truth, because error is clothed with a new garment, which they think covers something wonderful. But let the covering be removed, and nothingness appears.—*The Review and Herald,* Feb. 5, 1901.

Questions of Eternal Import

Dwell upon the lessons that Christ dwelt upon. Present them to the people as He presented them. Dwell upon questions that concern our eternal welfare. Anything that the enemy can devise to divert the mind from God's Word, anything new and strange that he can originate to create a diversity of sentiment, he will introduce as something wonderfully important. But those things that we cannot clearly comprehend are not a tenth as important to us as are the truths of God's Word that we can clearly comprehend and bring into our daily life. We are to teach the people the lessons that Christ brought into His teachings from the Old Testament Scriptures. The language of divine truth is exceedingly plain.—Letter 16, 1903.

Points Unnecessary for Faith

There are many questions treated upon that are not necessary for the perfection of the faith. We have no time for their study. Many things are above finite comprehension. Truths are to be received not within the reach of our reason, and not for us to explain. Revelation presents them to us to be implicitly received as the words of an infinite God. While every ingenious inquirer is to search out the truth as it is in Jesus, there are things not yet simplified, statements that human minds cannot grasp and reason out, without being liable to make human calculation and explanations, which will not prove a savor of life unto life.

But every truth which is essential for us to bring into our practical life, which concerns the salvation of the soul, is made very clear and positive.—Letter 8, 1895.

20.

Our Attitude Toward Doctrinal Controversy

~~~~~~~~~~~~~~~

"THE DAILY" OF DANIEL EIGHT

I have words to speak to my brethren east and west, north and south. I request that my writings shall not be used as the leading argument to settle questions over which there is now so much controversy. I entreat of Elders H, I, J, and others of our leading brethren, that they make no reference to my writings to sustain their views of "the daily."

It has been presented to me that this is not a subject of vital importance. I am instructed that our brethren are making a mistake in magnifying the importance of the difference in the views that are held. I cannot consent that any of my writings shall be taken as settling this matter. The true meaning of "the daily" is not to be made a test question.

I now ask that my ministering brethren shall not make use of my writings in their arguments regarding this question ["the daily"]; for I have had no instruction on the point under discussion, and I see no need for the controversy. Regarding this matter under present conditions, silence is eloquence.

The enemy of our work is pleased when a subject of minor importance can be used to divert the minds of our brethren from the great questions that should be the burden of our message. As this is not a test question, I entreat of my brethren that they shall not allow the enemy to triumph by having it treated as such.

The True Testing Questions

The work that the Lord has given us at this time is to present to the people the true light in regard to the testing questions of obedience and salvation—the commandments of God and the testimony of Jesus Christ.

In some of our important books that have been in print for years, and which have brought many to a knowledge of the truth, there may be found matters of minor importance that call for careful study and correction. Let such matters be considered by those regularly appointed to have the oversight of our publications. Let not these brethren, nor our canvassers, nor our ministers magnify these matters in such a way as to lessen the influence of these good soul-saving books. Should we take up the work of discrediting our literature, we would place weapons in the hands of those who have departed from the faith and confuse the minds of those who have newly embraced the message. The less that is done unnecessarily to change our publications, the better it will be.

In the night seasons I seem to be repeating to my brethren in responsible positions, words from the First Epistle of John. [Chapter 1 is quoted.]

A Daily Conversion

Our brethren should understand that self needs to be humbled and brought under the control of the Holy Spirit. The Lord calls upon those of us who have had great light to be converted *daily*. This is the message I have to bear to our editors and to the presidents of all our conferences. We must walk in the light while we have the light, lest darkness come upon us.

All who are led by the Holy Spirit of God will have a message for this last time. With mind and heart they will be carrying a burden for souls, and they will bear the heavenly message of Christ to those with whom they associate: Those who in speech act as the Gentiles act, cannot be introduced into the heavenly courts. My brethren, receive the light, redeeming the time because the days are evil.

Satan is busily working with all who will give him encouragement. Those who have the light, but refuse to walk in it, will become confused, until darkness pervades their souls, and shapes their whole course of action. But the spirit of wisdom and goodness of God as revealed in His Word, will become brighter and brighter as they follow on in the path of true obedience. All the righteous demands of God will be met through sanctification of the Holy Spirit. . . .

There are great privileges and blessings for all who will humble themselves and fully consecrate their hearts to God. Great light will be given to them. When men are willing to be transformed, then they will be exercised unto godliness.

"And of his fulness have all we received, and grace for grace" (John 1:16). "My grace is sufficient for thee: for my strength is made perfect in weakness" (2 Cor. 12:9). Says the Saviour: "All power is given unto me in heaven and in earth. Go ye therefore, and teach all nations, baptizing them in the name of the Father, and of the Son, and of the Holy Ghost: teaching them to observe all things whatsoever I have commanded you: and, lo, I am with you alway, even unto the end of the world" (Matt. 28:18-20).

Shall this wealth of grace and power for service continue among us to be unappreciated and turned from without relish or appetite? The instruction I am bidden to give to our people now is the same as I gave while in Washington. The Lord calls for individual effort. One cannot do the work of another. Great light has been shining, but it has not been fully comprehended and received.

If our brethren will now consecrate themselves unreservedly to God, He will accept them. He will give them a transformation of mind, that they may be savors of life unto life. Wake up, brethren and sisters, that you may attain to your high calling through Christ Jesus our Lord.—Manuscript 11, 1910.

Not a Test Question

To My Brethren in the Ministry:

Dear Fellow Workers—

I have words to speak to . . . all who have been active in urging their views in regard to the meaning of "the daily" of Daniel 8. This is not to be made a test question, and the agitation that has resulted from its being treated as such has been very unfortunate. Confusion has resulted, and the minds of some of our brethren have been diverted from the thoughtful consideration that should have been given to the work that the Lord has directed should be done at this time in our cities. This has been pleasing to the great enemy of our work.

The light given me is that nothing should be done to increase the agitation upon this question. Let it not be brought into our discourses, and dwelt upon as a matter of great importance. We have a great work before us, and we have not an hour to lose from the essential work to be done. Let us confine our public efforts to the presentation of the important lines of truth on which we are united, and on which we have clear light.

I would bring to your attention the last prayer of Christ, as recorded in John 17. There are many subjects upon which we can speak—sacred, testing truths, beautiful in their simplicity. On these you may dwell with intense earnestness. But let not "the daily," or any other subject that will arouse controversy among brethren, be brought in at this time; for this will delay and hinder the work that the Lord would have the minds of our brethren centered upon just now. Let us not agitate questions that will reveal a marked difference of opinion, but rather let us bring from the Word the sacred truths regarding the binding claims of the law of God.

Our ministers should seek to make the most favorable presentation of truth. So far as possible, let all speak the same things. Let the discourses be simple, and treating upon vital subjects that can be easily understood. When all our ministers see the necessity of humbling themselves, then the Lord can work with them. We need now to be reconverted, that angels of God may cooperate with us, making a sacred impression upon the minds of those for whom we labor.

Draw in Even Cords

We must blend together in the bonds of Christlike unity; then our labors will not be in vain. Draw in even cords, and let no contentions be brought in. Reveal the unifying power of truth, and this will make a powerful impression on human minds. In unity there is strength.

This is not a time to make prominent unimportant points of difference. If some who have not had a strong living connection with the Master reveal to the world their weakness of Christian experience, the enemies of the truth, who are watching us closely, will make the most of it, and our work will be hindered. Let all cultivate meekness, and learn lessons from Him who is meek and lowly in heart.

The subject of "the daily" should not call forth such movements as have been made. As a result of the way this subject has been handled by men on both sides of the question, controversy has arisen and confusion has resulted. . . . While the present condition of difference of opinion regarding this subject exists let it not be made prominent. Let all contention cease. At such a time silence is eloquence.

The duty of God's servants at this time is to preach the Word in the cities. Christ came from the heavenly courts to this earth in order to save souls and we, as almoners of His grace, need to impart to the inhabitants of the great cities a knowledge of His saving truth.—Letter 62, 1910.

21.

Fanciful or Speculative Teachings

~~~~~~~~~~~~~~~~~~~~~~~

No Compromise

I must bear a decided message to our brethren. Let there be no compromise with evil. Meet boldly the dangerous influences that arise. Do not fear for the results of resisting the powers of the enemy.

In these days many deceptions are being taught as truth. Some of our brethren have taught views which we cannot endorse. Fanciful ideas, strained and peculiar interpretations of the Scripture are coming in. Some of these teachings may seem to be but jots and tittles now, but they will grow and become snares to the inexperienced.

We have a decided work to do. Let not the enemy cause us to swerve from the proclamation of the definite truth for this time, and turn our attention to fanciful ideas.

Unless we are individually wide awake to discern the workings of the Holy Spirit, we shall certainly stumble and fall into Satan's pitfalls of unbelief. I call upon our brethren to watch as faithful shepherds and guardians over the inexperienced, who are exposed to the wiles of seductive influences. Keep a continual lookout for rocks and quicksands that threaten to destroy faith in the messages that God has given for us at this time. Watch for souls as they that must give account. . . .

We need to search the Scriptures daily, that we may know the way of the Lord, and that we be not deceived by religious fallacies. The world is full of false theories and seductive spiritualistic ideas, which tend to destroy clear spiritual perception, and to lead away from truth and holiness. Especially at this time do we need to heed the warning, "Let no man deceive you with vain words" (Eph. 5:6).

We must be careful lest we misinterpret the Scriptures. The plain teachings of the Word of God are not to be so spiritualized that the reality is lost sight of. Do not overstrain the meaning of sentences in the Bible in an effort to bring forth something odd in order to please the fancy. Take the Scriptures as they read. Avoid idle speculation concerning what will be in the kingdom of heaven.— Manuscript 30, 1904.

A Life and Death Question

Letters have come to me, asking in regard to the teaching of some who say that nothing that has life should be killed, not even insects, however annoying or distressing they may be. Is it possible that anyone claims that God has given him this message to give to the people? The Lord has never given any human being such a message. God has told no one that it is a sin to kill the insects which destroy our peace and rest. In all His teaching, Christ gave no message of this character, and His disciples are to teach only what He commanded them.

There are those who are always seeking to engage in controversy. This is the sum of their religion. They are filled with a desire to produce something new and strange. They dwell upon matters of the smallest consequence, exercising upon these their sharp, controversial talents.

Idle tales are brought in as important truths, and by some they are actually set up as tests. Thus controversy is created, and minds are diverted from present truth. Satan knows that if he can get men and women absorbed in trifling details, greater questions will be left unheeded. He will furnish plenty of material for the attention of those who are willing to think upon trifling, unimportant subjects. The minds of the Pharisees were absorbed with questions of no moment. They passed by the precious truths of God's Word to discuss the traditionary lore handed down from generation to generation, which in no way concerned their salvation. And so today, while precious moments are passing into eternity, the great questions of salvation are overlooked for some idle tale.

I would say to my brethren and sisters, Keep close to the instruction found in the Word of God. Dwell upon the rich truths of the Scriptures. Thus only can you become one in Christ. You have no time to engage in controversy regarding the killing of insects. Jesus has not placed this burden upon you. "What is the chaff to the wheat?" (Jer. 23:28). These side issues which arise are as hay, wood, and stubble compared with the truth for these last days. Those who leave the great truths of God's Word to speak of such matters are not preaching the gospel. They are dealing with the idle sophistry which the enemy brings forward to divert minds from the truths that concern their eternal welfare. They have no word from Christ to vindicate their suppositions.

Do not spend your time in the discussion of such matters. If you have any question as to what you should teach, any question as to the subjects upon which you should dwell, go right to the discourses of the Great Teacher, and follow His instructions. . . .

Do not allow anything to draw your attention from the question, "What shall I do to inherit eternal life?" (Luke 10:25). This is a life and death question, which we must each settle for eternity. Let the mind be weighted with the importance of the solemn truth which we possess. Those who allow the mind to wander in search of cheap, unimportant theories need to be converted. . . .

Erroneous theories, with no authority from the Word of God, will come in on the right hand and the left, and to weaklings these theories will appear as truth which makes wise. But they are as nothingness. And yet many church members have become so well satisfied with cheap food that they have dyspeptic religion. Why will men and women belittle their experience by gathering up idle tales and presenting them as matters worthy of attention? The people of God have no time to dwell on the indefinite, frivolous questions which have no bearing on God's requirements.

God desires men and women to think soberly and candidly. They are to ascend to a higher and still higher grade, commanding a wider and still wider horizon. Looking unto Jesus, they are to be changed into His image. They are to spend their time in searching for the deep, everlasting truths of heaven. Then there will be nothing frivolous in their religious experience. As they study the grand truths of God's Word, they endure the seeing of Him who is invisible. They see that the most uplifting, ennobling truths are those most closely connected with the Source of all truth. And as they learn of Him, their motives and sympathies become firm and unchanging; for the impressions made by the All-wise are substantial and enduring. The living water, which Christ gives, is not like a surface spring, which babbles for a short time, and then dries up. The living water springs up unto everlasting life.

Let us follow the revealed will of God. Then we shall know that the light we receive comes from the divine Source of all true light. Those who cooperate with Christ are on safe ground. God richly blesses them as they consecrate their energies to the work of rescuing the world from corruption. Christ is our example. By beholding Him we are to be changed into His image, from glory to glory, from character to character. This is our work. God help us rightly to represent the Saviour to the world.—*The Review and Herald,* Aug. 13, 1901.

Conjectures Regarding the Future Life

There are men today who express their belief that there will be marriages and births in the new earth; but those who believe the Scriptures cannot accept such doctrines. The doctrine that children will be born in the new earth is not a part of the "sure word of prophecy" (2 Peter 1:19). The words of Christ are too plain to be misunderstood.

They should forever settle the question of marriages and births in the new earth. Neither those who shall be raised from the dead, nor those who shall be translated without seeing death, will marry or be given in marriage. They will be as the angels of God, members of the royal family.

I would say to those who hold views contrary to this plain declaration of Christ, Upon such matters silence is eloquence. It is presumption to indulge in suppositions and theories regarding matters that God has not made known to us in His Word. We need not enter into speculation regarding our future state.

To my ministering brethren I would say, "Preach the word; be instant in season, out of season" (2 Tim. 4:2). Do not bring to the foundation wood, and hay, and stubble —your own surmisings and speculations, which can benefit no one.

Christ withheld no truths essential to our salvation. Those things that are revealed are for us and our children, but we are not to allow our imagination to frame doctrines concerning things not revealed.

The Lord has made every provision for our happiness in the future life, but He has made no revelations regarding these plans, and we are not to speculate concerning them. Neither are we to measure the conditions of the future life by the conditions of this life.

Matters of vital importance have been plainly revealed in the Word of God. These subjects are worthy of our deepest thought. But we are not to search into matters on which God has been silent. Some have put forth the speculation that the redeemed will not have gray hair. Other foolish suppositions have been put forward, as though these were matters of importance. May God help His people to think rationally. When questions arise upon which we are uncertain, we should ask, "What saith the Scripture?"

Let those who wish for something new seek for that newness of life resulting from the new birth. Let them purify their souls by obeying the truth, and act in harmony with the instruction Christ gave to the lawyer who asked what he must do in order to inherit eternal life.

"Thou shalt love the Lord thy God with all thy heart, and with all thy soul, and with all thy strength, and with all thy mind; and thy neighbour as thyself. . . . This do, and thou shalt live" (Luke 10:27, 28). All who will conform their lives to the plain requirements of God's Word will inherit eternal life.—Manuscript 28, 1904.

Subjects Difficult to Understand

In this work there is danger of bringing before the people theories which, while they may be all truth, will create controversy, and will not lead men to the great supper prepared for them. We want the love of God formed within to subdue and soften our human nature and to bring us into conformity to His holy character. Then we shall spread before the people the unsearchable riches of Christ in all their abundance. The invitation is given by Christ Himself, and it is the work of all His followers to call attention to the board of provisions that has been made accessible to all. Then let not subjects difficult to be understood come first. Christ is calling men to the banquet, and let all who will, come.—Letter 89, 1898.

The One Hundred and Forty-four Thousand

Christ says that there will be those in the church who will present fables and suppositions, when God has given grand, elevating, ennobling truths which should ever be kept in the treasure house of the mind. When men pick up this theory and that theory, when they are curious to know something it is not necessary for them to know, God is not leading them. It is not His plan that His people shall present something which they have to suppose, which is not taught in the Word. It is not His will that they shall get into controversy over questions which will not help them spiritually, such as, Who is to compose the hundred and forty-four thousand? This those who are the elect of God will in a short time know without question.

My brethren and sisters, appreciate and study the truths God has given for you and your children. Spend not your time in seeking to know that which will be no spiritual help. "What shall I do to inherit eternal life?" (Luke 10: 25). This is the all-important question, and it has been clearly answered. "What is written in the law? how readest thou?"—Manuscript 26, 1901.

Christ Calls for Unity

Our church members see that there are differences of opinion among the leading men, and they themselves enter into controversy regarding the subjects under dispute. Christ calls for unity. But He does not call for us to unify on wrong practices. The God of heaven draws a sharp contrast between pure, elevating, ennobling truth and false, misleading doctrines. He calls sin and impenitence by the right name. He does not gloss over wrongdoing with a coat of untempered mortar. I urge our brethren to unify upon a true, scriptural basis.—Manuscript 10, 1905.

No Strife for Supremacy

When the laborers have an abiding Christ in their own souls, when all selfishness is dead, when there is no rivalry, no strife for the supremacy, when oneness exists, when they sanctify themselves, so that love for one another is seen and felt, then the showers of the grace of the Holy Spirit will just as surely come upon them as that God's promise will never fail in one jot or tittle. But when the work of others is discounted, that the workers may show their own superiority, they prove that their own work does not bear the signature it should. God cannot bless them.—*Manuscript* 24, 1896.

22.

*The Peril of Extreme Views**

~~~~~~~~~~~~~~~~~~~~~~

St. Helena, California
May 19, 1890

DEAR BROTHER K:

I expected ere this to see you and talk with you, or write to you; but I have not been able to do either, neither am I now able; but I feel a deep interest in you and am desirous that you shall not be separated from the work. I have not strength to do justice in conversation with you; your mind is so quick and your tongue so fluent, that I fear I should become very much wearied, and that which I might say would not remain distinct in your mind.

I see your danger; you can readily put your thoughts into words. You put things in a strong light; and your language is not guarded. Your views on some points are so expressed that you make your brethren afraid of you. This need not be. You should not try to get as far from your brethren as you can, making it appear that you do not see alike.

I have been shown that your influence for good is greatly lessened because you feel it your duty to express

---

* Appeared in *Notebook Leaflets*, Methods, No. 4.

your ideas on certain points which you do not fully comprehend yourself, and which, with all your efforts, you cannot make others comprehend. I have been shown that it was not necessary for you to feel that you must dwell upon these points. Some of your ideas are correct, others incorrect and erroneous.

If you would dwell on such subjects as Christ's willingness to forgive sins, to receive the sinner, to save that which is lost, subjects that inspire hope and courage, you would be a blessing. But while you strive to be original and take such extreme views, and use such strong language in presenting them, there is danger of doing much harm. Some may grasp your thought and seem to be benefited, but when tempted and overcome, they lose courage to fight the good fight of faith.

If you will dwell less on these ideas, which seem to you so important, and will restrain your extravagant expressions, you yourself will have more faith. I saw that your mind was at times unbalanced from trying very hard to study into and explain the mystery of godliness, which is just as great a mystery after your study and explanations as it was before.

Differing Experiences in Conversion

Lead the people to look to Jesus as their only hope and helper; leave the Lord room to work upon the mind, to speak to the soul, and to impress the understanding. It is not essential for you to know and tell others all the whys and wherefores as to what constitutes the new heart, or as to the position they can and must reach so as never to sin. You have no such work to do.

All are not constituted alike. Conversions are not all alike. Jesus impresses the heart, and the sinner is born again to new life. Often souls have been drawn to Christ when there was no violent conviction, no soul rending, no remorseful terrors. They looked upon an uplifted Saviour, they lived. They saw the soul's need, they saw the Saviour's sufficiency, and His claims, they heard His voice saying, "Follow Me," and they rose up and followed Him. This conversion was genuine, and the religious life was just as decided as was that of others who suffered all the agony of a violent process.

Our ministers must cease to dwell upon their peculiar ideas with the feeling, "You must see this point as I do, or you cannot be saved." Away with this egotism. The great work to be done in every case is to win souls to Christ. Men must see Jesus on the cross, they must look and live. It is not your ideas they must feed upon, but it is the flesh and blood of the Son of God. He says, "My flesh is meat indeed" (John 6:55). "The words that I speak unto you, they are spirit, and they are life" (John 6:63).

Leave Christ Room to Work

The soul that accepts Jesus places himself under the care of the Great Physician, and let men be careful how they come between the patient and the Physician who discerns all the needs of the soul. Christ, the physician of the soul, understands its defects and its maladies, and knows how to heal with the purchase of His own blood. What the soul lacks, He can best supply. But men are so officious, they want to do so much, that they overdo the matter, leaving Christ no room to work.

Whatever molding and fashioning needs to be wrought in the soul, Christ can best do. The conviction may not be deep, but if the sinner comes to Christ, viewing Him upon the cross, the just dying for the unjust, the sight will break every barrier down. Christ has undertaken the work of saving all who trust in Him for salvation. He sees the wrongs that need to be righted, the evils that need to be repressed. He came to seek and save that which was lost. "Him that cometh to me," He says, "I will in no wise cast out" (John 6:37).

Through the goodness and mercy of Christ the sinner is to be restored to the divine favor. God in Christ is daily beseeching men to be reconciled to God. With outstretched arms He is ready to receive and welcome not only the sinner but the prodigal. His dying love, manifested on Calvary, is the sinner's assurance of acceptance, peace, and love. Teach these things in the simplest form, that the sin-darkened soul may see the light shining from the cross of Calvary.

Satan is working in many ways, that the very men who ought to preach the message may be occupied with fine-drawn theories which he will cause to appear of such magnitude and importance as to fill the whole mind; and while they think they are making wonderful strides in experience, they are idolizing a few ideas, and their influence is injured, and tells but little on the Lord's side.

Let every minister make earnest efforts to ascertain what is the mind of Christ. Unless your mind becomes better balanced in regard to some things, your course will separate you from the work, and you will not know at what you stumble. You will advance ideas which you might better never have originated.

There are those who pick out from the Word of God, and also from the Testimonies, detached paragraphs or sentences that may be interpreted to suit their ideas, and they dwell upon these, and build themselves up in their own positions, when God is not leading them. Here is your danger.

You will take passages in the Testimonies that speak of the close of probation, of the shaking among God's people, and you will talk of a coming out from this people of a purer, holier people that will arise. Now all this pleases the enemy. We should not needlessly take a course that will make differences or create dissension. We should not give the impression that if our particular ideas are not followed, it is because the ministers are lacking in comprehension and in faith, and are walking in darkness.

Your mind has been on an unnatural strain for a long time. You have much truth, precious truth, but mingled with suppositions. Your extreme ideas and strong language often destroy the effect of your best efforts. Should many accept the views you advance, and talk and act upon them, we would see one of the greatest fanatical excitements that has ever been witnessed among Seventh-day Adventists. This is what Satan wants.

Leave Mysteries Alone

Now there are in the lessons of Christ, subjects in abundance that you can speak upon. And mysteries which neither you nor your hearers can understand or explain might better be left alone. Give the Lord Jesus Christ room Himself to teach; let Him by the influence of His Spirit open to the understanding the wonderful plan of salvation.

There is a time of trouble coming to the people of God, but we are not to keep that constantly before the people, and rein them up to have a time of trouble beforehand. There is to be a shaking among God's people, but this is not the present truth to carry to the churches. . . .

The ministers should not feel that they have some wonderful advanced ideas, and unless all receive these, they will be shaken out and a people will arise to go forward and upward to the victory. Some of those who are resisting the very principles of the message God has sent for this time, present just such cases as yourself. They point to your extreme views and teachings as an excuse for their neglect of receiving the Lord's messages.

Satan's object is accomplished just as surely when men run ahead of Christ and do the work He has never entrusted to their hand, as when they remain in the Laodicean state, lukewarm, feeling rich and increased with goods, and in need of nothing. The two classes are equally stumbling blocks.

Some zealous ones who are aiming and straining every energy for originality have made a grave mistake in trying to get something startling, wonderful, entrancing before the people, something that they think others do not comprehend; but they do not themselves know what they are talking about. They speculate upon God's Word, advancing ideas that are not a whit of help to themselves or to the churches. For the time being they may excite the imagination, but there is a reaction, and these very ideas become a hindrance. Faith is confounded with fancy, and their views may bias the mind in a wrong direction.

Let the plain, simple statements of the Word of God be food for the mind; this speculating upon ideas that are not clearly presented there is dangerous business.

You are naturally combative. You do not care much whether you harmonize with your brethren or not. You would like to enter into controversy, would like to fight for your particular ideas; but you should lay this aside, for this is not developing the Christian graces. Work with all your power to answer the prayer of Christ, that His disciples may be one, as He is one with the Father.

Not a soul of us is safe unless we learn of Jesus daily, His meekness, His lowliness of heart. When you go to any place to labor, do not be dictatorial, do not be severe, do not be antagonistic. Preach the love of Christ, and this will melt and subdue hearts. Seek to be of one mind and of one judgment, coming close in harmony with your brethren, and to speak the same things.

Talk Not of Divisions

This talking about divisions because all do not have the same ideas as present themselves to your mind, is not the work of God, but of the enemy. Talk the simple truths wherein you can agree. Talk of unity; do not become narrow and conceited; let your mind broaden.

Christ does not weigh character in scales of human judgment. He says, "I, if I be lifted up from the earth, will draw all men unto me" (John 12:32). Every soul who responds to this drawing will turn from iniquity. Christ is able to save to the uttermost all who come unto Him. He who comes to Jesus is setting his feet upon a ladder that reaches from earth to heaven. Teach it by pen, by voice, that God is above the ladder; the bright rays of His glory are shining upon every round of the ladder. He is looking graciously upon all who are climbing painfully upward, that He may send them help, divine help, when the hand seems to be relaxing and the foot trembling. Yes, tell it, tell it in words that will melt the heart, that not one who shall perseveringly climb the ladder will fail of an entrance into the everlasting kingdom of our Lord and Saviour

Jesus Christ; those who believe in Christ shall never perish, neither shall any pluck them out of His hand.

Tell the people in clear, hopeful language how they may escape the heritage of shame which is our deserved portion. But for Christ's sake do not present before them ideas that will discourage them, that will make the way to heaven seem very difficult. Keep all these overstrained ideas to yourself.

While we must often impress the mind with the fact that the Christian life is a life of warfare, that we must watch and pray and toil, that there is peril to the soul in relaxing the spiritual vigilance for one moment, the completeness of the salvation proffered us from Jesus who loves us and gave Himself that we should not perish but have everlasting life, is to be the theme.

Day by day we may walk with God, day by day following on to know the Lord, entering into the holiest by the blood of Jesus, laying hold on the hope set before us. If we reach heaven it must be by binding the soul to the Mediator, becoming partakers of the divine nature. Leaning on Christ, your life being hid with Christ in God and led by His Spirit, you have the genuine faith.

Believing fully in the efficacy of His atoning sacrifice, we shall be laborers together with God. Trusting in His merits, we are to work out our own salvation with fear and trembling; for it is God that worketh in us both to will and to do of His good pleasure. Always keeping hold of Christ, we are coming nearer and nearer to God. Jesus desires us to keep this always prominent. Do not arouse your combative spirit; the wisdom that is from above is first pure, then peaceable, easy to be entreated, full of mercy and good fruits. . . .

Harmonize With Your Brethren

Do not think that you must make prominent every idea your imagination receives. Jesus said to His disciples, "I have yet many things to say unto you, but ye cannot bear them now" (John 16:12). How much more should we, who are constantly liable to err, beware of urging upon others that which they are not prepared to receive. Constantly looking unto Jesus, restrain your strong, extravagant expressions. But while you should be cautious as to your words and ideas, it is not necessary that your labors should entirely cease. Seek to be in harmony with your brethren, and there will be plenty for you to do in the vineyard of the Lord. But exalt Christ, not your ideas and views. Put on the armor, and keep step with God's workers, shoulder to shoulder; press the battle against the enemy. Hide in Jesus. Dwell on the simple lessons of Christ, feed the flock of God, and you will become settled, strengthened, established; you will work to build up others in the most holy faith.

If you differ with your brethren as to your understanding of the grace of Christ and the operations of His Spirit, you should not make these differences prominent. You view the matter from one point; another, just as devoted to God, views the same question from another point, and speaks of the things that make the deepest impression on his mind; another viewing it from a still different point, presents another phase; and how foolish it is to get into contention over these things, when there is really nothing to contend about. Let God work on the mind and impress the heart.

The Lord is constantly at work to open the understanding, to quicken the perceptions, that man may have a right sense of sin and of the far-reaching claims of God's law. The unconverted man thinks of God as unloving, as severe, and even revengeful; His presence is thought to be a constant restraint, His character an expression of "Thou shalt not." His service is regarded as full of gloom and hard requirements. But when Jesus is seen upon the cross, as the gift of God because He loved man, the eyes are opened to see things in a new light. God as revealed in Christ is not a severe judge, an avenging tyrant, but a merciful and loving Father.

As we see Jesus dying upon the cross to save lost man, the heart echoes the words of John, "Behold, what manner of love the Father hath bestowed upon us, that we should be called the sons of God: therefore the world knoweth us not, because it knew him not" (1 John 3:1). There is nothing that more decidedly distinguishes the Christian from the worldly man than the estimate he has of God.

Some workers in the cause of God have been too ready to hurl denunciations against the sinner; the grace and love of the Father in giving His Son to die for the sinful race have been put in the background. The teacher needs the grace of Christ upon his own soul, in order to make known to the sinner what God really is—a Father waiting with yearning love to receive the returning prodigal, not hurling at him accusations in wrath, but preparing a festival of joy to welcome his return (Zeph. 3:14-17).

O that we might all learn the way of the Lord in winning souls to Christ! We should learn and teach the precious lessons in the light that shineth from the sacrifice upon the cross of Calvary. There is but one way that leads from ruin, and continuously ascends, faith all the time reaching beyond the darkness into the light, until it rests upon the throne of God. All who have learned this lesson have accepted the light which has come to their understanding. To them this upward way is not a dark, uncertain passage; it is not the way of finite minds, not a path cut out by human device, a path in which toll is exacted from every traveler.

You cannot gain an entrance by penance nor by any works that you can do. No, God Himself has the honor of providing a way, and it is so complete, so perfect, that man cannot, by any works he may do, add to its perfection. It is broad enough to receive the greatest sinner if he repents, and it is so narrow, so holy, lifted up so high, that sin cannot be admitted there.

When God is seen as He is, the blessed truth shines with a new and clearer light. That which kept the mind in perplexity is cleared away by the bright beams of the Sun of Righteousness. And yet there are many things we shall not comprehend; but we have the blessed assurance that what we know not now, we shall know hereafter.— Letter 15a, 1890.

23.

Beware of Any Time Setting

~~~~~~~~~~~~~~~~~~~~~~~

"IT IS NOT FOR YOU TO KNOW THE TIMES OR THE
SEASONS" *

"He shewed himself alive after his passion by many
infallible proofs, being seen of them forty days, and speaking of the things pertaining to the kingdom of God: and,
being assembled together with them, commanded them
that they should not depart from Jerusalem, but wait for
the promise of the Father, which, saith he, ye have heard
of me. For John truly baptized with water; but ye shall be
baptized with the Holy Ghost not many days hence. When
they therefore were come together, they asked of him,
saying, Lord, wilt thou at this time restore again the
kingdom to Israel? And he said unto them, It is not for
you to know the times or the seasons, which the Father
hath put in his own power" (Acts 1:3-7).

The disciples were anxious to know the exact time for
the revelation of the kingdom of God; but Jesus tells them
that they may not know the times and the seasons; for the
Father has not revealed them. To understand when the
kingdom of God should be restored, was not the thing of

---

* Sermon at Lansing, Michigan, Sept. 5, 1891.

most importance for them to know. They were to be found following the Master, praying, waiting, watching, and working. They were to be representatives to the world of the character of Christ. That which was essential for a successful Christian experience in the days of the disciples, is essential in our day. "And he said unto them, It is not for you to know the times or the seasons, which the Father hath put in his own power. But ye shall receive power, after that the Holy Ghost is come upon you." And after the Holy Ghost was come upon them, what were they to do? "And ye shall be witnesses unto me both in Jerusalem, and in all Judaea, and in Samaria, and unto the uttermost part of the earth" (Acts 1:7, 8).

Improve Present Opportunities

This is the work in which we also are to be engaged. Instead of living in expectation of some special season of excitement, we are wisely to improve present opportunities, doing that which must be done in order that souls may be saved. Instead of exhausting the powers of our mind in speculations in regard to the times and seasons which the Lord has placed in His own power, and withheld from men, we are to yield ourselves to the control of the Holy Spirit, to do present duties, to give the bread of life, unadulterated with human opinions, to souls who are perishing for the truth.

Satan is ever ready to fill the mind with theories and calculations that will divert men from the present truth, and disqualify them for the giving of the third angel's message to the world. It has ever been thus; for our Saviour often had to speak reprovingly to those who indulged in speculations and were ever inquiring into those things which the Lord had not revealed. Jesus had come to earth to impart important truth to men, and He wished to impress their minds with the necessity of receiving and obeying His precepts and instructions, of doing their present duty, and His communications were of an order that imparted knowledge for their immediate and daily use.

Jesus said: "This is life eternal, that they might know

thee the only true God, and Jesus Christ, whom thou hast sent" (John 17:3). All that was done and said had this one object in view—to rivet truth in their minds that they might attain unto everlasting life. Jesus did not come to astonish men with some great announcement of some special time when some great event would occur, but He came to instruct and save the lost. He did not come to arouse and gratify curiosity; for He knew that this would but increase the appetite for the curious and the marvelous. It was His aim to impart knowledge whereby men might increase in spiritual strength, and advance in the way of obedience and true holiness. He gave only such instruction as could be appropriated to the needs of their daily life, only such truth as could be given to others for the same appropriation.

He did not make new revelations to men, but opened to their understanding truths that had long been obscured or misplaced through the false teaching of the priests and teachers. Jesus replaced the gems of divine truth in their proper setting, in the order in which they had been given to patriarchs and prophets. And after giving them this precious instruction, He promised to give them the Holy Spirit whereby all things that He had said unto them should be brought to their remembrance.

We are in continual danger of getting above the simplicity of the gospel. There is an intense desire on the part of many to startle the world with something original, that shall lift the people into a state of spiritual ecstasy, and change the present order of experience. There is certainly great need of a change in the present order of experience; for the sacredness of present truth is not realized as it should be, but the change we need is a change of heart, and can only be obtained by seeking God individually for His blessing, by pleading with Him for His power, by fervently praying that His grace may come upon us, and that our characters may be transformed. This is the change we need today, and for the attainment of this experience we should exercise persevering energy and manifest heartfelt earnestness. We should ask with true sincerity,

"What shall I do to be saved?" We should know just what steps we are taking heavenward.

Warned in Regard to Time Setting

Christ gave to His disciples truths whose breadth and depth and value they little appreciated, or even comprehended, and the same condition exists among the people of God today. We too have failed to take in the greatness, to perceive the beauty of the truth which God has entrusted to us today. Should we advance in spiritual knowledge, we would see the truth developing and expanding in lines of which we have little dreamed, but it will never develop in any line that will lead us to imagine that we may know the times and the seasons which the Father hath put in His own power. Again and again have I been warned in regard to time setting. There will never again be a message for the people of God that will be based on time. We are not to know the definite time either for the outpouring of the Holy Spirit or for the coming of Christ.

I was searching through my writings, before coming to this meeting, to see what I should take with me to Australia, and I found an envelope on which was written, "Testimony given in regard to time setting, June 21, 1851. Preserve carefully." I opened it, and this is what I found. It reads:

"A copy of a vision the Lord gave Sister White, June 21, 1851, at Camden, N.Y. The Lord showed me that the message must go, and that it must not be hung on time; for time will never be a test again. I saw that some were getting a false excitement, arising from preaching time, that the third angel's message can stand on its own foundation, and that it needs not time to strengthen it, and that it will go with mighty power, and do its work, and will be cut short in righteousness.

"I saw some were making everything bend to this next fall; that is, making their calculations, and disposing of their property in reference to that time. I saw that this was wrong for this reason: instead of going to God daily, and earnestly desiring to know their present duty, they looked ahead, and made their calculations as though they knew that the work would end this fall, without inquiring their duty of God daily.—E. G. White.

"Copied at Milton, June 29, 1851, A. A. G."

This was the document I came upon last Monday in searching over my writings, and here is another which was written in regard to a man who was setting time in 1884, and sending broadcast his arguments to prove his theories. The report of what he was doing was brought to me at the Jackson [Michigan] camp meeting, and I told the people they need not take heed to this man's theory; for the event he predicted would not take place. The times and the seasons God has put in His own power. And why has not God given us this knowledge?—Because we would not make a right use of it if He did. A condition of things would result from this knowledge among our people that would greatly retard the work of God in preparing a people to stand in the great day that is to come. We are not to live upon time excitement. We are not to be engrossed with speculations in regard to the times and the seasons which God has not revealed. Jesus has told His disciples to "watch," but not for a definite time. His followers are to be in the position of those who are listening for the orders of their Captain; they are to watch, wait, pray, and work, as they approach the time for the coming of the Lord; but no one will be able to predict just when that time will come; for "of that day and hour knoweth no man." You will not be able to say that He will come in one, two, or five years, neither are you to put off His coming by stating that it may not be for ten or twenty years.

To Have Lamps Trimmed and Burning

It is the duty of the people of God to have their lamps trimmed and burning, to be as men that wait for the Bridegroom, when He shall return from the wedding. You have not a moment to lose in neglect of the great salvation that has been provided for you. The time of the probation of souls is coming to an end. From day to day the destiny

of men is being sealed, and even from this congregation
we know not how soon many shall close their eyes in
death and be habited for the tomb. We should now consider that our life is swiftly passing away, that we are not
safe one moment unless our life is hid with Christ in God.
Our duty is not to be looking forward to some special time
for some special work to be done for us, but to go forward
in our work of warning the world; for we are to be witnesses of Christ to the uttermost parts of the world.

All around us are the young, the impenitent, the unconverted, and what are we doing for them? Parents, in
the ardor of your first love, are you seeking for the conversion of your children, or are you engrossed with the things
of this life to such an extent that you are not making
earnest efforts to be laborers together with God? Do you
have an appreciation of the work and mission of the
Holy Spirit? Do you realize that the Holy Spirit is the
agency whereby we are to reach the souls of those around
us? When this meeting shall close, will you go from here
and forget the earnest appeals that have been made to
you? Will the messages of warning be left unheeded, and
the truth you have heard leak out of your heart as water
leaks out of a broken vessel?

The apostle says, "Therefore we ought to give the more
earnest heed to the things which we have heard, lest at
any time we should let them slip. For if the word spoken
by angels was stedfast, and every transgression and disobedience received a just recompence of reward; how shall
we escape, if we neglect so great salvation; which at the
first began to be spoken by the Lord, and was confirmed
unto us by them that heard him; God also bearing them
witness, both with signs and wonders, and with divers
miracles, and gifts of the Holy Ghost, according to his own
will?" (Heb. 2:1-4).

The third angel's message is swelling into a loud cry,
and you must not feel at liberty to neglect the present
duty, and still entertain the idea that at some future time
you will be the recipients of great blessing, when without
any effort on your part a wonderful revival will take

place. Today you are to give yourselves to God, that He may make of you vessels unto honor, and meet for His service. Today you are to give yourself to God, that you may be emptied of self, emptied of envy, jealousy, evil surmising, strife, everything that shall be dishonoring to God. Today you are to have your vessel purified that it may be ready for the heavenly dew, ready for the showers of the latter rain; for the latter rain will come, and the blessing of God will fill every soul that is purified from every defilement. It is our work today to yield our souls to Christ, that we may be fitted for the time of refreshing from the presence of the Lord—fitted for the baptism of the Holy Spirit.—*The Review and Herald,* March 22, 1892.

THE TIME NOT REVEALED

God has not revealed to us the time when this message will close, or when probation will have an end. Those things that are revealed we shall accept for ourselves and for our children; but let us not seek to know that which has been kept secret in the councils of the Almighty. It is our duty to watch and work and wait, to labor every moment for the souls of men that are ready to perish. We are to keep walking continually in the footsteps of Jesus, working in His lines, dispensing His gifts as good stewards of the manifold grace of God. Satan will be ready to give to anyone who is not learning every day of Jesus, a special message of his own creating, in order to make of no effect the wonderful truth for this time.

Letters have come to me asking me if I have any special light as to the time when probation will close; and I answer that I have only this message to bear, that it is now time to work while the day lasts, for the night cometh in which no man can work. Now, just now, it is time for us to be watching, working, and waiting. The Word of the Lord reveals the fact that the end of all things is at hand, and its testimony is most decided that it is necessary for every soul to have the truth planted in the heart so that it will control the life and sanctify the charac-

ter. The Spirit of the Lord is working to take the truth of
the inspired Word and stamp it upon the soul so that
professed followers of Christ will have a holy, sacred joy
that they will be able to impart to others. The opportune
time for us to work is now, just now, while the day lasts.
But there is no command for anyone to search the Scripture in order to ascertain, if possible, when probation will
close. God has no such message for any mortal lips. He
would have no mortal tongue declare that which He has
hidden in His secret councils.—*The Review and Herald,*
Oct. 9, 1894.

Watch and Pray

I have no specific time of which to speak when the
outpouring of the Holy Spirit will take place—when the
mighty angel will come down from heaven, and unite
with the third angel in closing up the work for this world;
my message is that our only safety is in being ready for the
heavenly refreshing, having our lamps trimmed and burning. Christ has told us to watch; "for in such an hour as ye
think not, the Son of man cometh." "Watch and pray" is
the charge that is given us by our Redeemer. Day by day
we are to seek the enlightenment of the Spirit of God, that
it may do its office work upon the soul and character. O,
how much time has been wasted through giving attention
to trifling things. Repent and be converted, that your sins
may be blotted out when the times of refreshing shall come
from the presence of the Lord.—*The Review and Herald,*
March 29, 1892.

24.

The Alpha and the Omega

~~~~~~~~~~~

[During the summer of 1904, at a critical point in the crisis over the promulgation by Dr. J. H. Kellogg of pantheistic theories, and at a time when he was advocating unsound policies relating to the management of our medical work, Ellen G. White sounded a number of warnings, which were assembled and "published for the author" in a sixty-page pamphlet, *Special Testimonies*, Series B, No. 2, entitled "Testimonies for the Church Containing Letters to Physicians and Ministers Giving Messages of Warning and Words of Counsel and Admonition Regarding Our Present Situation." In two of these communications she refers to "The Alpha and the Omega." Following are the two statements in their entirety as taken from the pamphlet. Further counsels making reference to pantheism may be found in *Testimonies*, volume 8, pages 255-318 and *The Ministry of Healing*, pages 427-438. For the background of the experience with pantheism, see A. G. Daniells' *The Abiding Gift of Prophecy*, pages 330-342, and L. H. Christian's *The Fruitage of Spiritual Gifts*, pages 277-296.—COMPILERS.]

TEACH THE WORD

Washington, D.C.

July 24, 1904

TO OUR LEADING PHYSICIANS:

Dear Fellow Workers: I am awakened at eleven o'clock. The representations passing before me are so vivid that I cannot sleep. The word of the Lord has come to me that there is a decided work to be done in warning our medical missionaries against the dangers and perils that surround them.

The Lord calls upon those connected with our sanitariums to reach a higher standard. No lie is of the truth. If we follow cunningly devised fables, we unite with the enemy's forces against God and Christ. God calls upon those who have been wearing a yoke of human manufacture to break this yoke, and no longer be the bond servants of men.

The battle is on. Satan and his angels are working with all deceivableness of unrighteousness. They are untiring in their efforts to draw souls away from the truth, away from righteousness, to spread ruin throughout the universe. They work with marvelous industry to furnish a multitude of deceptions to take souls captive. Their efforts are unceasing. The enemy is ever seeking to lead souls into infidelity and skepticism. He would do away with God, and with Christ, who was made flesh and dwelt among us to teach us that in obedience to God's will we may be victorious over sin.

Assailed by Every Form of Evil

Every form of evil is waiting for an opportunity to assail us. Flattery, bribes, inducements, promises of wonderful exaltation, will be most assiduously employed.

What are God's servants doing to raise the barrier of a "Thus saith the Lord" against this evil? The enemy's agents are working unceasingly to prevail against the truth. Where are the faithful guardians of the Lord's flocks? Where are His watchmen? Are they standing on the high tower, giving the danger signal, or are they allowing the peril to pass unheeded? Where are the medical missionaries? Are they co-workers with Christ, wearing His yoke, or are they wearing a yoke of human manufacture?

Satan and his angels are making every effort to obtain control of minds, that men may be swayed by falsehood and pleasing fables. Are our physicians lifting the danger signal? Are the men who have been placed in prominent positions in our sanitariums lifting the danger signal? Or are many of the watchmen asleep, while mischievous tongues and acute minds, sharpened by long practice in evading the truth, are continually at work to bring in confusion, and to carry out plans instigated by the enemy?

Please read Paul's exhortation to the Colossians. He speaks of his earnest desire that the hearts of the believers might be "knit together in love, and unto all riches of the full assurance of understanding, to the acknowledgment of the mystery of God, and of the Father, and of Christ; in whom are hid all the treasures of wisdom and knowledge" (Col. 2:2, 3). "And this I say," he declares, "lest any man should beguile you with enticing words. . . . As ye have therefore received Christ Jesus the Lord, so walk ye in him: rooted and built up in him, and stablished in the faith, as ye have been taught, abounding therein with thanksgiving. Beware lest any man spoil you through philosophy and vain deceit, after the tradition of men, after the rudiments of the world, and not after Christ. For in him dwelleth all the fulness of the Godhead bodily" (Col. 2:4-9).

Will the men in our institutions keep silent, allowing insidious fallacies to be promulgated to the ruin of souls? The sentiments of the enemy are being scattered everywhere. Seeds of discord, of unbelief, of infidelity, are being sown broadcast. Shall our medical missionaries raise no barrier against this evil? Is it not time that we asked ourselves, Shall we allow the adversary to lead us to give up the work of proclaiming the truth? Shall we allow him to keep us from being channels through which the blessings of the gospel, as a current of life, shall flow to the world? Let every man now arouse, and work as he has opportunity. Let him speak words in season and out of season, and look to Christ for encouragement and strength in welldoing.

Dangers Continually Increasing

The dangers coming upon us are continually increasing. It is high time that we put on the whole armor of God, and work earnestly to keep Satan from gaining any further advantage. Angels of God, that excel in strength, are waiting for us to call them to our aid, that our faith may not be eclipsed by the fierceness of the conflict. Renewed energy is now needed. Vigilant action is called for. Indifference and sloth will result in the loss of personal religion and of heaven.

At this time the Laodicean message is to be given, to arouse a slumbering church. Let the thought of the shortness of time stimulate you to earnest, untiring effort. Remember that Satan has come down with great power, to work with all deceivableness of unrighteousness in them that perish.

For years our physicians have been trained to think that they must not give expression to sentiments that differ from those of their chief.* O that they had broken the yoke! O that they had called sin by its right name! Then they would not be regarded in the heavenly courts as men who, though bearing weighty responsibilities, have failed of speaking the truth in reproof of that which has been in disobedience to God's Word.

Physicians, have you been doing the Master's business in listening to fanciful and spiritualistic interpretations of the Scriptures, interpretations which undermine the foundations of our faith, and holding your peace? God says, "Neither will I be with you any more, unless you awake, and vindicate your Redeemer."

Sophistries That Undermine the Pillars

My message to you is: No longer consent to listen without protest to the perversion of truth. Unmask the pretentious sophistries which, if received, will lead ministers and physicians and medical missionary workers to ignore the truth. Every one is now to stand on his guard. God calls upon men and women to take their stand under the blood-stained banner of Prince Emmanuel. I have been instructed to warn our people; for many are in danger

---

* Reference is here made to Dr. J. H. Kellogg, for many years the medical superintendent of the Battle Creek Sanitarium.—COMPILERS.

of receiving theories and sophistries that undermine the foundation pillars of the faith.

Sometimes our physicians talk for hours, when they are weary and perplexed, and in no fit condition to talk. Medical missionaries should refuse to hold long night sessions of conversation. These night talks have been times when Satan with his seductive influence has stolen away from one and then another the faith once delivered to the saints. Brilliant, sparkling ideas often flash from a mind that is influenced by the great deceiver. Those who listen and acquiesce will become charmed, as Eve was charmed by the serpent's words. They cannot listen to charming philosophical speculations, and at the same time keep the word of the living God clearly in mind.

Our physicians have lost a great deal out of their lives because they have seen wrong transactions and heard wrong words spoken, and seen wrong principles followed, and have not spoken in reproof, for fear that they would be repulsed.

I call upon those who have been connected with these binding influences to break the yoke to which they have long submitted, and stand as free men in Christ. Nothing but a determined effort will break the spell that is upon them.

The Alpha Now Seen

Be not deceived; many will depart from the faith, giving heed to seducing spirits and doctrines of devils. We have now before us the alpha of this danger. The omega will be of a most startling nature.

We need to study the words that Christ uttered in the prayer that He offered just before His trial and crucifixion. "These words spake Jesus, and lifted up his eyes to heaven, and said, Father, the hour is come; glorify thy Son, that thy Son also may glorify thee: as thou hast given him power over all flesh, that he should give eternal life to as many as thou hast given him. And this is life eternal, that they might know thee the only true God, and Jesus Christ, whom thou hast sent. I have glorified thee on the earth: I have finished the work which thou gavest me to do. And now, O Father, glorify thou me with thine own self with the glory which I had with thee before the world was. I have manifested thy name unto the men which thou gavest me out of the world: thine they were, and thou gavest them me; and they have kept thy word" (John 17:1-6).

Christians to Manifest Godliness

The righteousness of God is absolute. This righteousness characterizes all His works, all His laws. As God is, so must His people be. The life of Christ is to be revealed in the lives of His followers. In all His public and private acts, in every word and deed, practical godliness was seen, and this godliness is to be seen in the lives of His disciples.

Those who heed the light given them will bring the virtues of the character of Christ into the daily life. Christ did no sin, because there was no sin in Him. God has shown me that the lives of believers are to reveal practical righteousness.

Has not God spoken in His Word concerning the solemn events which must shortly take place? As you read these things, do you believe what He says? Or have you, through listening to specious philosophy, given up your faith in God? Can any power avert the punishment that must come upon you unless you humble your hearts before God and confess your sins? How is it, my brethren in the medical missionary work? Does not the living God speak to you from His Word concerning the events that are taking place in fulfillment of that Word? Soon the last great reckoning with man will take place. Have your lives been such that you can then be weighed in the balances of the sanctuary, and not be found wanting? Or has your faith been molded and restricted until it has become unbelief? Has your obedience to men become rebellion against God? "Examine yourselves, whether ye be in the faith; prove your own selves" (2 Cor. 13:5).—*Special Testimonies,* Series B, No. 2, pp. 12-17.

BEWARE

Washington, D.C.
August 7, 1904

MY DEAR BROTHER:

I am given a message to bear to you and the rest of our physicians who are connected with the Medical Missionary Association. Separate from the influence exerted by the book *Living Temple;** for it contains specious sentiments. There are in it sentiments that are entirely true, but these are mingled with error. Scriptures are taken out of their connection, and are used to uphold erroneous theories.

The thought of the errors contained in this book has given me great distress, and the experience that I have passed through in connection with the matter has nearly cost me my life.

It will be said that *Living Temple* has been revised. But the Lord has shown me that the writer has not changed, and that there can be no unity between him and the ministers of the gospel while he continues to cherish his present sentiments. I am bidden to lift my voice in warning to our people, saying, "Be not deceived; God is not mocked" (Gal. 6:7).

You have had access to *Testimonies for the Church,* volumes 7 and 8. In these *Testimonies* the danger signal is raised. But the light so clear and plain to minds that have not been influenced by deceptive theories, has not been discerned by some. While the misleading theories of this book are entertained by our physicians, there cannot be union between them and the ministers who are bearing the gospel message. There should be no union until there is a change.

When medical missionaries make their practice and example harmonize with the name they bear, when they feel their need of uniting firmly with the ministers of the gospel, then there can be harmonious action. But we must

---

* A 568-page book issued in 1903 by Dr. J. H. Kellogg in which pantheistic philosophies were promulgated.—COMPILERS.

firmly refuse to be drawn away from the platform of eternal truth, which since 1844 has stood the test.

Alpha Presented in "Living Temple"

I am instructed to speak plainly. "Meet it," is the word spoken to me. "Meet it firmly, and without delay." But it is not to be met by our taking our working forces from the field to investigate doctrines and points of difference. We have no such investigation to make. In the book *Living Temple* there is presented the alpha of deadly heresies. The omega will follow, and will be received by those who are not willing to heed the warning God has given.

Our physicians, upon whom important responsibilities rest, should have clear spiritual discernment. They are to stand constantly on guard. Dangers that we do not now discern will soon break upon us, and I greatly desire that they shall not be deceived. I have an intense longing to see them standing free in the Lord. I pray that they may have courage to stand firm for the truth as it is in Jesus, holding fast the beginning of their confidence unto the end.—*Special Testimonies,* Series B, No. 2, pp. 49, 50.

25.

*The Foundation of Our Faith**

~~~~~~~~~~~~~~~~~~~~

The Lord will put new, vital force into His work as human agencies obey the command to go forth and proclaim the truth. He who declared that His truth would shine forever will proclaim this truth through faithful messengers, who will give the trumpet a certain sound. The truth will be criticized, scorned, and derided; but the closer it is examined and tested, the brighter it will shine.

As a people, we are to stand firm on the platform of eternal truth that has withstood test and trial. We are to hold to the sure pillars of our faith. The principles of truth that God has revealed to us are our only true foundation. They have made us what we are. The lapse of time has not lessened their value. It is the constant effort of the enemy to remove these truths from their setting, and to put in their place spurious theories. He will bring in everything that he possibly can to carry out his deceptive designs. But the Lord will raise up men of keen perception, who will give these truths their proper place in the plan of God.

I have been instructed by the heavenly messenger that some of the reasoning in the book *Living Temple* is un-

* This article appeared in *Special Testimonies*, Series B, No. 2, pages 51-59, published in 1904.

sound, and that this reasoning would lead astray the minds of those who are not thoroughly established on the foundation principles of present truth. It introduces that which is nought but speculation in regard to the personality of God and where His presence is. No one on this earth has a right to speculate on this question. The more fanciful theories are discussed, the less men will know of God and of the truth that sanctifies the soul.

One and another come to me, asking me to explain the positions taken in *Living Temple*. I reply, "They are unexplainable." The sentiments expressed do not give a true knowledge of God. All through the book are passages of Scripture. These scriptures are brought in in such a way that error is made to appear as truth. Erroneous theories are presented in so pleasing a way that unless care is taken, many will be misled.

We need not the mysticism that is in this book. Those who entertain these sophistries will soon find themselves in a position where the enemy can talk with them, and lead them away from God. It is represented to me that the writer of this book is on a false track. He has lost sight of the distinguishing truths for this time. He knows not whither his steps are tending. The track of truth lies close beside the track of error, and both tracks may seem to be one to minds which are not worked by the Holy Spirit, and which, therefore, are not quick to discern the difference between truth and error.

A View of Approaching Danger

About the time that *Living Temple* was published, there passed before me in the night season, representations indicating that some danger was approaching, and that I must prepare for it by writing out the things God had revealed to me regarding the foundation principles of our faith. A copy of *Living Temple* was sent me, but it remained in my library, unread. From the light given me by the Lord, I knew that some of the sentiments advocated in the book did not bear the endorsement of God, and that they were a snare that the enemy had prepared for the last days. I thought that this would surely be discerned, and that it would not be necessary for me to say anything about it.

In the controversy that arose among our brethren regarding the teachings of this book, those in favor of giving it a wide circulation declared: "It contains the very sentiments that Sister White has been teaching." This assertion struck right to my heart. I felt heartbroken; for I knew that this representation of the matter was not true.

Finally my son said to me, "Mother, you ought to read at least some parts of the book, that you may see whether they are in harmony with the light that God has given you." He sat down beside me, and together we read the preface, and most of the first chapter, and also paragraphs in other chapters. As we read, I recognized the very sentiments against which I had been bidden to speak in warning during the early days of my public labors. When I first left the State of Maine, it was to go through Vermont and Massachusetts, to bear a testimony against these sentiments. *Living Temple* contains the alpha of these theories. I knew that the omega would follow in a little while; and I trembled for our people. I knew that I must warn our brethren and sisters not to enter into controversy over the presence and personality of God. The statements made in *Living Temple* in regard to this point are incorrect. The scripture used to substantiate the doctrine there set forth, is scripture misapplied.

I am compelled to speak in denial of the claim that the teachings of *Living Temple* can be sustained by statements from my writings. There may be in this book expressions and sentiments that are in harmony with my writings. And there may be in my writings many statements which, taken from their connection, and interpreted according to the mind of the writer of *Living Temple,* would seem to be in harmony with the teachings of this book. This may give apparent support to the assertion that the sentiments in *Living Temple* are in harmony with my writings. But God forbid that this sentiment should prevail.

Few can discern the result of entertaining the sophis-

tries advocated by some at this time. But the Lord has
lifted the curtain, and has shown me the result that would
follow. The spiritualistic theories regarding the personality
of God, followed to their logical conclusion, sweep away
the whole Christian economy. They estimate as nothing
the light that Christ came from heaven to give John to give
to His people. They teach that the scenes just before us
are not of sufficient importance to be given special attention. They make of no effect the truth of heavenly origin,
and rob the people of God of their past experience, giving
them instead a false science.

In a vision of the night I was shown distinctly that
these sentiments have been looked upon by some as the
grand truths that are to be brought in and made prominent
at the present time. I was shown a platform, braced by
solid timbers—the truths of the Word of God. Some one
high in responsibility in the medical work was directing
this man and that man to loosen the timbers supporting this
platform. Then I heard a voice saying, "Where are the
watchmen that ought to be standing on the walls of
Zion? Are they asleep? This foundation was built by the
Master Worker, and will stand storm and tempest. Will
they permit this man to present doctrines that deny the
past experience of the people of God? The time has come
to take decided action."

The enemy of souls has sought to bring in the supposi-
tion that a great reformation was to take place among
Seventh-day Adventists, and that this reformation would
consist in giving up the doctrines which stand as the pillars
of our faith, and engaging in a process of reorganization.
Were this reformation to take place, what would result?
The principles of truth that God in His wisdom has given
to the remnant church, would be discarded. Our religion
would be changed. The fundamental principles that have
sustained the work for the last fifty years would be accounted as error. A new organization would be established. Books of a new order would be written. A system
of intellectual philosophy would be introduced. The found-
ers of this system would go into the cities, and do a won-

derful work. The Sabbath of course, would be lightly regarded, as also the God who created it. Nothing would be allowed to stand in the way of the new movement. The leaders would teach that virtue is better than vice, but God being removed, they would place their dependence on human power, which, without God, is worthless. Their foundation would be built on the sand, and storm and tempest would sweep away the structure.

Who has authority to begin such a movement? We have our Bibles. We have our experience, attested to by the miraculous working of the Holy Spirit. We have a truth that admits of no compromise. Shall we not repudiate everything that is not in harmony with this truth?

I hesitated and delayed about the sending out of that which the Spirit of the Lord impelled me to write. I did not want to be compelled to present the misleading influence of these sophistries. But in the providence of God, the errors that have been coming in *must be met*.

An Iceberg! "Meet It"

Shortly before I sent out the testimonies regarding the efforts of the enemy to undermine the foundation of our faith through the dissemination of seductive theories, I had read an incident about a ship in a fog meeting an iceberg. For several nights I slept but little. I seemed to be bowed down as a cart beneath sheaves. One night a scene was clearly presented before me. A vessel was upon the waters, in a heavy fog. Suddenly the lookout cried, "Iceberg just ahead!" There, towering high above the ship, was a gigantic iceberg. An authoritative voice cried out, "Meet it!" There was not a moment's hesitation. It was a time for instant action. The engineer put on full steam, and the man at the wheel steered the ship straight into the iceberg. With a crash she struck the ice. There was a fearful shock, and the iceberg broke into many pieces, falling with a noise like thunder to the deck. The passengers were violently shaken by the force of the collision, but no lives were lost. The vessel was injured, but not beyond repair. She rebounded from the contact, trembling from stem to stern, like a living creature. Then she moved forward on her way.

Well I knew the meaning of this representation. I had my orders. I had heard the words, like a voice from our Captain, "Meet it!" I knew what my duty was, and that there was not a moment to lose. The time for decided action had come. I must without delay obey the command, "Meet it!"

That night I was up at one o'clock, writing as fast as my hand could pass over the paper. For the next few days I worked early and late, preparing for our people the instruction given me regarding the errors that were coming in among us.

I have been hoping that there would be a thorough reformation, and that the principles for which we fought in the early days, and which were brought out in the power of the Holy Spirit, would be maintained.

The Firm Foundation of Our Faith

Many of our people do not realize how firmly the foundation of our faith has been laid. My husband, Elder Joseph Bates, Father Pierce,* Elder [Hiram] Edson, and others who were keen, noble, and true, were among those who, after the passing of the time in 1844, searched for the truth as for hidden treasure. I met with them, and we studied and prayed earnestly. Often we remained together until late at night, and sometimes through the entire night, praying for light and studying the Word. Again and again these brethren came together to study the Bible, in order that they might know its meaning, and be prepared to teach it with power. When they came to the point in their study where they said, "We can do nothing more," the Spirit of the Lord would come upon me, I would be taken off in vision, and a clear explanation of the passages

---

* Older brethren among the pioneers are here thus reminiscently referred to. "Father Pierce" was Stephen Pierce, who served in ministerial and administrative work in the early days. "Father Andrews" was Edward Andrews, the father of J. N. Andrews.—COMPILERS.

we had been studying would be given me, with instruction
as to how we were to labor and teach effectively. Thus
light was given that helped us to understand the scriptures
in regard to Christ, His mission, and His priesthood. A
line of truth extending from that time to the time when
we shall enter the city of God, was made plain to me, and
I gave to others the instruction that the Lord had given me.

During this whole time I could not understand the
reasoning of the brethren. My mind was locked, as it
were, and I could not comprehend the meaning of the
scriptures we were studying. This was one of the greatest
sorrows of my life. I was in this condition of mind until
all the principal points of our faith were made clear to
our minds, in harmony with the Word of God. The
brethren knew that when not in vision, I could not understand these matters, and they accepted as light direct from
heaven the revelations given.

For two or three years my mind continued to be
locked to an understanding of the Scriptures. In the
course of our labors, my husband and I visited Father
Andrews,* who was suffering intensely with inflammatory rheumatism. We prayed for him. I laid my hands on
his head, and said, "Father Andrews, the Lord Jesus maketh thee whole." He was healed instantly. He got up, and
walked about the room, praising God, and saying, "I
never saw it on this wise before. Angels of God are in this
room." The glory of the Lord was revealed. Light seemed
to shine all through the house, and an angel's hand was
laid upon my head. From that time to this I have been able
to understand the Word of God.

What influence is it that would lead men at this stage
of our history to work in an underhand, powerful way to
tear down the foundation of our faith—the foundation
that was laid at the beginning of our work by prayerful
study of the Word and by revelation? Upon this foundation we have been building for the past fifty years. Do you
wonder that when I see the beginning of a work that

---

* See note on page 206.

would remove some of the pillars of our faith, I have something to say? I must obey the command, "Meet it!" . . .

I must bear the messages of warning that God gives me to bear, and then leave with the Lord the results. I must now present the matter in all its bearings; for the people of God must not be despoiled.

We are God's commandment-keeping people. For the past fifty years every phase of heresy has been brought to bear upon us, to becloud our minds regarding the teaching of the Word—especially concerning the ministration of Christ in the heavenly sanctuary, and the message of Heaven for these last days, as given by the angels of the fourteenth chapter of Revelation. Messages of every order and kind have been urged upon Seventh-day Adventists, to take the place of the truth which, point by point, has been sought out by prayerful study, and testified to by the miracle-working power of the Lord. But the waymarks which have made us what we are, are to be preserved, and they will be preserved, as God has signified through His Word and the testimony of His Spirit. He calls upon us to hold firmly, with the grip of faith, to the fundamental principles that are based upon unquestionable authority.

SECTION V

Christ and the Doctrines

INTRODUCTION

~~~~~~~~~~~~~~~~~~~~~~~

Over a period of more than sixty years about 2,000 E. G. White articles were published in the *Review and Herald*. Another 2,000 articles were furnished to the *Signs of the Times*. Hundreds of messages from her pen appeared in the *Youth's Instructor*, our health journals, the union conference papers, et cetera.

These articles covered a wide variety of subjects, including practical instruction, warnings and counsel for the church, accounts of travels and labors, instruction in soul-winning work, and perhaps most important, doctrinal presentations. The freedom of space offered by periodical form of presentation made possible varied and detailed treatment of many important doctrinal topics. The same subjects were dealt with again and again, each time with an emphasis on varying points of interest. In harmony with her instruction, these many articles have been drawn upon in the work of compiling certain Ellen G. White books that have been published since her death.

While there is not a general call for the republication of all of the articles in their entirety, there is a desire to have a choice group of articles devoted largely to doctrinal subjects reprinted in their completeness of coverage. Many of these are outstanding in their presentation of the central truths of the Advent message. These priceless messages are here presented for the most part in their entirety, giving the reader the benefit of each statement in its full setting. There are a few exceptions where there were large segments of an article that were not closely related to the doctrinal presentation, and in these cases deletions have been made and indicated in the usual way. The careful student of the Word of God will rejoice to see these choice doctrinal statements—all of which center in Christ our Lord—appear in this permanent form.—WHITE TRUSTEES.

26.

*The Perfect Law**

The law of God, as presented in the Scriptures, is broad in its requirements. Every principle is holy, just, and good. The law lays men under obligation to God; it reaches to the thoughts and feelings; and it will produce conviction of sin in every one who is sensible of having transgressed its requirements. If the law extended to the outward conduct only, men would not be guilty in their wrong thoughts, desires, and designs. But the law requires that the soul itself be pure and the mind holy, that the thoughts and feelings may be in accordance with the standard of love and righteousness.

In His teachings, Christ showed how far-reaching are the principles of the law spoken from Sinai. He made a living application of that law whose principles remain forever the great standard of righteousness—the standard by which all shall be judged in that great day when the judgment shall sit, and the books shall be opened. He came to fulfill all righteousness, and, as the head of humanity, to show man that he can do the same work, meeting every specification of the requirements of God. Through the measure of His grace furnished to the human agent, not

---

* This article appeared in *The Review and Herald,* April 5, 1898.

one need miss heaven. Perfection of character is attainable by every one who strives for it. This is made the very foundation of the new covenant of the gospel. The law of Jehovah is the tree; the gospel is the fragrant blossoms and fruit which it bears.

When the Spirit of God reveals to man the full meaning of the law, a change takes place in his heart. The faithful portrayal of his true state by the prophet Nathan made David acquainted with his own sins, and aided him in putting them away. He accepted the counsel meekly, and humbled himself before God. "The law of the Lord," he said, "is perfect, converting the soul: the testimony of the Lord is sure, making wise the simple. The statutes of the Lord are right, rejoicing the heart: the commandment of the Lord is pure, enlightening the eyes. The fear of the Lord is clean, enduring for ever: the judgments of the Lord are true and righteous altogether. More to be desired are they than gold, yea, than much fine gold: sweeter also than honey and the honeycomb. Moreover by them is thy servant warned: and in keeping of them there is great reward. Who can understand his errors? cleanse thou me from secret faults. Keep back thy servant also from presumptuous sins; let them not have dominion over me: then shall I be upright, and I shall be innocent from the great transgression. Let the words of my mouth, and the meditation of my heart, be acceptable in thy sight, O Lord, my strength, and my redeemer" (Ps. 19: 7-14).

Paul's Estimate of the Law

Paul's testimony of the law is: "What shall we say then? Is the law sin [the sin is in the man, not in the law]? God forbid. Nay, I had not known sin, but by the law: for I had not known lust, except the law had said, Thou shalt not covet. But sin, taking occasion by the commandment, wrought in me all manner of concupiscence. For without the law sin was dead. For I was alive without the law once: but when the commandment came, sin revived, and I died. And the commandment, which was ordained to life, I found to be unto death. For sin, taking occasion by the commandment, deceived me, and by it slew me" (Rom. 7:7-11).

Sin did not kill the law, but it did kill the carnal mind in Paul. "Now we are delivered from the law," he declares, "that being dead wherein we were held; that we should serve in newness of spirit, and not in the oldness of the letter" (Rom. 7:6). "Was that then which is good made death unto me? God forbid. But sin, that it might appear sin, working death in me by that which is good; that sin by the commandment might become exceeding sinful" (Rom. 7:13). "Wherefore the law is holy, and the commandment holy, and just, and good" (Rom. 7:12). Paul calls the attention of his hearers to the broken law, and shows them wherein they are guilty. He instructs them as a schoolmaster instructs his scholars, and shows them the way back to their loyalty to God.

There is no safety nor repose nor justification in transgression of the law. Man cannot hope to stand innocent before God, and at peace with Him through the merits of Christ, while he continues in sin. He must cease to transgress, and become loyal and true. As the sinner looks into the great moral looking glass, he sees his defects of character. He sees himself just as he is, spotted, defiled, and condemned. But he knows that the law cannot in any way remove the guilt or pardon the transgressor. He must go farther than this. The law is but the schoolmaster to bring him to Christ. He must look to his sin-bearing Saviour. And as Christ is revealed to him upon the cross of Calvary, dying beneath the weight of the sins of the whole world, the Holy Spirit shows him the attitude of God to all who repent of their transgressions. "For God so loved the world, that he gave his only begotten Son, that whosoever believeth in him should not perish, but have everlasting life" (John 3:16).

We need, individually, to take heed as we have never done before to a "Thus saith the Lord." There are men who are disloyal to God, who profane His holy Sabbath, who cavil over the plainest statements of the Word, who wrest the Scriptures from their true meaning, and who at the same time make desperate efforts to harmonize their disobedience with the Scriptures. But the Word condemns such practices, as it condemned the scribes and Pharisees in Christ's day. We need to know what is truth. Shall we do as did the Pharisees? Shall we turn from the greatest Teacher the world has ever known to the traditions and maxims and sayings of men?

Results of Transgressing the Law

There are many beliefs that the mind has no right to entertain. Adam believed the lie of Satan, the wily insinuations against the character of God. "And the Lord God commanded the man, saying, Of every tree of the garden thou mayest freely eat: but of the tree of the knowledge of good and evil, thou shalt not eat of it: for in the day that thou eatest thereof thou shalt surely die" (Gen. 2:16, 17). When Satan tempted Eve, he said, "Hath God said, Ye shall not eat of every tree of the garden? And the woman said unto the serpent, We may eat of the fruit of the trees of the garden: but of the fruit of the tree which is in the midst of the garden, God hath said, Ye shall not eat of it, neither shall ye touch it, lest ye die. And the serpent said unto the woman, Ye shall not surely die: for God doth know that in the day ye eat thereof, then your eyes shall be opened, and ye shall be as gods, knowing good and evil" (Gen. 3:1-5).

The knowledge which God did not want our first parents to have was a knowledge of guilt. And when they accepted the assertions of Satan, which were false, disobedience and transgression were introduced into our world. This disobedience to God's express command, this belief of Satan's lie, opened the floodgates of woe upon the world. Satan has continued the work begun in the Garden of Eden. He has worked vigilantly, that man might accept his assertions as proof against God. He has worked against Christ in His efforts to restore the image of God in man, and imprint in his soul the similitude of God.

The belief of a falsehood did not make Paul a kind,

tender, compassionate man. He was a religious zealot, exceedingly mad against the truth concerning Jesus. He went through the country, haling men and women, and committing them to prison. Speaking of this, he says: "I am verily a man which am a Jew, born in Tarsus, a city in Cilicia, yet brought up in this city at the feet of Gamaliel, and taught according to the perfect manner of the law of the fathers, and was zealous toward God, as ye all are this day. And I persecuted this way unto the death, binding and delivering into prisons both men and women" (Acts 22:3, 4).

The human family are in trouble because of their transgression of the Father's law. But God does not leave the sinner until He shows the remedy for sin. The only-begotten Son of God has died that we might live. The Lord has accepted this sacrifice in our behalf, as our substitute and surety, on the condition that we receive Christ and believe on Him. The sinner must come in faith to Christ, take hold of His merits, lay his sins upon the Sin Bearer, and receive His pardon. It was for this cause that Christ came into the world. Thus the righteousness of Christ is imputed to the repenting, believing sinner. He becomes a member of the royal family, a child of the heavenly King, an heir of God, and joint heir with Christ.

27.

The Character of the Law of God*

David says: "The law of the Lord is perfect" (Ps. 19: 7). "Concerning thy testimonies, I have known of old that thou hast founded them for ever" (Ps. 119:152). And Paul testifies: "The law is holy, and the commandment holy, and just, and good" (Rom. 7:12).

As the Supreme Ruler of the universe, God has ordained laws for the government not only of all living beings, but of all the operations of nature. Everything, whether great or small, animate or inanimate, is under fixed laws which cannot be disregarded. There are no exceptions to this rule; for nothing that the divine hand has made has been forgotten by the divine mind. But while everything in nature is governed by natural law, man alone, as an intelligent being, capable of understanding its requirements, is amenable to moral law. To man alone, the crowning work of His creation, God has given a conscience to realize the sacred claims of the divine law, and a heart capable of loving it as holy, just, and good; and of man prompt and perfect obedience is required. Yet God does not compel him to obey; he is left a free moral agent.

The subject of man's personal responsibility is under-

---

* This article appeared in *The Signs of the Times*, April 15, 1886.

stood by but few; and yet it is a matter of the greatest importance. We may each obey and live, or we may transgress God's law, defy His authority, and receive the punishment that is meet. Then to every soul the question comes home with force, Shall I obey the voice from heaven, the ten words spoken from Sinai, or shall I go with the multitude who trample on that fiery law? To those who love God it will be the highest delight to keep His commandments, and to do those things that are pleasing in His sight. But the natural heart hates the law of God, and wars against its holy claims. Men shut their souls from the divine light, refusing to walk in it as it shines upon them. They sacrifice purity of heart, the favor of God, and their hope of heaven, for selfish gratification or worldly gain.

Says the psalmist, "The law of the Lord is perfect" (Ps. 19:7). How wonderful in its simplicity, its comprehensiveness and perfection, is the law of Jehovah! It is so brief that we can easily commit every precept to memory, and yet so far-reaching as to express the whole will of God, and to take cognizance, not only of the outward actions, but of the thoughts and intents, the desires and emotions, of the heart. Human laws cannot do this. They can deal with the outward actions only. A man may be a transgressor, and yet conceal his misdeeds from human eyes; he may be a criminal—a thief, a murderer, or an adulterer—but so long as he is not discovered, the law cannot condemn him as guilty. The law of God takes note of the jealousy, envy, hatred, malignity, revenge, lust, and ambition that surge through the soul, but have not found expression in outward action, because the opportunity, not the will, has been wanting. And these sinful emotions will be brought into the account in the day when "God shall bring every work into judgment, with every secret thing, whether it be good, or whether it be evil" (Eccl. 12:14).

God's Law Is Simple

The law of God is simple, and easily understood. There are men who proudly boast that they believe only what they can understand, forgetting that there are mysteries in human life and in the manifestation of God's power in the works of nature—mysteries which the deepest philosophy, the most extensive research, is powerless to explain. But there is no mystery in the law of God. All can comprehend the great truths which it embodies. The feeblest intellect can grasp these rules; the most ignorant can regulate the life, and form the character after the divine standard. If the children of men would, to the best of their ability, obey this law, they would gain strength of mind and power of discernment to comprehend still more of God's purposes and plans. And this advancement would be continued, not only during the present life, but during eternal ages; for however far we may advance in the knowledge of God's wisdom and power, there is always an infinity beyond.

The divine law requires us to love God supremely and our neighbor as ourselves. Without the exercise of this love, the highest profession of faith is mere hypocrisy. "Thou shalt love the Lord thy God with all thy heart, and with all thy soul, and with all thy mind. This is the first and great commandment. And the second is like unto it, Thou shalt love thy neighbour as thyself. On these two commandments," says Christ, "hang all the law and the prophets" (Matt. 22:37-40).

The law demands perfect obedience. "Whosoever shall keep the whole law, and yet offend in one point, he is guilty of all" (James 2:10). Not one of those ten precepts can be broken without disloyalty to the God of heaven. The least deviation from its requirements, by neglect or willful transgression, is sin, and every sin exposes the sinner to the wrath of God. Obedience was the only condition upon which ancient Israel was to receive the fulfillment of the promises which made them the highly favored people of God; and obedience to that law will bring as great blessings to individuals and nations now as it would have brought to the Hebrews.

Obedience to the law is essential, not only to our salvation, but to our own happiness and the happiness of all with whom we are connected. "Great peace have they which love thy law: and nothing shall offend them" (Ps. 119:165), says the Inspired Word. Yet finite man will present to the people this holy, just, and good law, this law of liberty, which the Creator Himself has adapted to the wants of man, as a yoke of bondage, a yoke which no man can bear. But it is the sinner who regards the law as a grievous yoke; it is the transgressor that can see no beauty in its precepts. For the carnal mind "is not subject to the law of God, neither indeed can be" (Rom. 8:7).

"By the law is the knowledge of sin" (Rom. 3:20); for "sin is the transgression of the law" (1 John 3:4). It is through the law that men are convicted of sin; and they must feel themselves sinners, exposed to the wrath of God, before they will realize their need of a Saviour. Satan is continually at work to lessen man's estimate of the grievous character of sin. And those who trample the law of God under their feet are doing the work of the great deceiver; for they are rejecting the only rule by which they can define sin, and bring it home to the conscience of the transgressor.

The law of God reaches to those secret purposes, which, though they may be sinful, are often passed over lightly, but which are in reality the basis and the test of character. It is the mirror into which the sinner is to look if he would have a correct knowledge of his moral character. And when he sees himself condemned by that great standard of righteousness, his next move must be to repent of his sins, and seek forgiveness through Christ. Failing to do this, many try to break the mirror which reveals their defects, to make void the law which points out the blemishes in their life and character.

We are living in an age of great wickedness. Multitudes are enslaved by sinful customs and evil habits, and the fetters that bind them are difficult to break. Iniquity, like a flood, is deluding the earth. Crimes almost too fearful to be mentioned, are of daily occurrence. And yet men professing to be watchmen on the walls of Zion will teach that the law was designed for the Jews only, and passed away with the glorious privileges that ushered in

the gospel age. Is there not a relation between the prevailing lawlessness and crime, and the fact that ministers and
people hold and teach that the law is no longer of binding
force?

The condemning power of the law of God extends,
not only to the things we do, but to the things we do not
do. We are not to justify ourselves in omitting to do the
things that God requires. We must not only cease to do
evil, but we must learn to do well. God has given us
powers to be exercised in good works; and if these powers
are not put to use, we shall certainly be set down as wicked
and slothful servants. We may not have committed grievous sins; such offenses may not stand registered against us
in the book of God; but the fact that our deeds are not
recorded as pure, good, elevated, and noble, showing that
we have not improved our entrusted talents, places us under
condemnation.

The law of God existed before man was created. It
was adapted to the condition of holy beings; even angels
were governed by it. After the Fall, the principles of
righteousness were unchanged. Nothing was taken from
the law; not one of its holy precepts could be improved.
And as it has existed from the beginning, so will it continue to exist throughout the ceaseless ages of eternity.
"Concerning thy testimonies," says the psalmist, "I have
known of old that thou hast founded them for ever" (Ps.
119:152).

By this law, which governs angels, which demands
purity in the most secret thoughts, desires, and dispositions, and which shall "stand fast for ever" (Ps. 111:8),
all the world is to be judged in the rapidly approaching day
of God. Transgressors may flatter themselves that the
Most High does not know, that the Almighty does not
consider; He will not always bear with them. Soon they
will receive the reward of their doings, the death that is
the wages of sin; while the righteous nation, that have
kept the law, will be ushered through the pearly gates of
the celestial city, and will be crowned with immortal
life and joy in the presence of God and the Lamb.

28.

Satan's Enmity Toward the Law*

I awoke from my sleep last night with a great burden upon my mind. I was delivering a message to our brethren and sisters, and it was a message of warning and instruction concerning the work of some who are advocating erroneous theories as to the reception of the Holy Spirit, and its operation through human agencies.

I was instructed that fanaticism similar to that which we were called to meet after the passing of the time in 1844 would come in among us again in the closing days of the message, and that we must meet this evil just as decidedly now as we met it in our early experiences.

We are standing on the threshold of great and solemn events. Prophecies are fulfilling. Strange and eventful history is being recorded in the books of heaven—events which it was declared should shortly precede the great day of God. Everything in the world is in an unsettled state. The nations are angry, and great preparations for war are being made. Nation is plotting against nation, and kingdom against kingdom. The great day of God is hasting greatly. But although the nations are mustering their forces for war and bloodshed, the command to the angels is still

---

* This article appeared in *The Review and Herald*, Jan. 28, 1909.

in force, that they hold the four winds until the servants of God are sealed in their foreheads.

The world is now realizing the sure results of transgression of the law of God. His work of creation completed, the Lord rested on the seventh day, and sanctified the day of His rest, setting it apart as the day which man should devote to His worship. But today the world at large is utterly disregarding the law of Jehovah. Another day has been instituted in the place of God's day of rest. The human agent has set his way and his will against the positive teachings of the Word, and the world is plunged in rebellion and sin.

This work of opposition to the law of God had its beginning in the courts of heaven, with Lucifer, the covering cherub. Satan determined to be first in the councils of heaven, and equal with God. He began his work of rebellion with the angels under his command, seeking to diffuse among them the spirit of discontent. And he worked in so deceptive a way that many of the angels were won to his allegiance before his purposes were fully known. Even the loyal angels could not fully discern his character, nor see to what his work was leading. When Satan had succeeded in winning many angels to his side, he took his cause to God, representing that it was the desire of the angels that he occupy the position that Christ held.

The evil continued to work until the spirit of disaffection ripened into active revolt. Then there was war in heaven, and Satan, with all who sympathized with him, was cast out. Satan had warred for the mastery in heaven, and had lost the battle. God could no longer trust him with honor and supremacy, and these, with the part he had taken in the government of heaven, were taken from him.

Since that time Satan and his army of confederates have been the avowed enemies of God in our world, continually warring against the cause of truth and righteousness. Satan has continued to present to men, as he presented to the angels, his false representations of Christ and of God, and he has won the world to his side. Even the professedly Christian churches have taken sides with the first great apostate.

Satan represents himself as the prince of the kingdom of this world, and it was in this character that he approached Christ in the last of his three great temptations in the wilderness. "If thou wilt fall down and worship me," he said to the Saviour, "all these"—pointing to the kingdoms of the world which Satan had caused to pass before Jesus—"will I give thee."

Christ in the courts of heaven had known that the time would come when the power of Satan must be met and conquered if the human race was ever to be saved from his dominion. And when that time came, the Son of God laid off His kingly crown and royal robe, and clothing His divinity with humanity, came to the earth to meet the prince of evil, and to conquer him. In order to become the advocate of man before the Father, the Saviour would live His life on earth as every human being must, accepting its adversities and sorrows and temptations. As the Babe of Bethlehem, He would become one with the race, and by a spotless life from the manger to the cross He would show that man, by a life of repentance and faith in Him, might be restored to the favor of God. He would bring to man redeeming grace, forgiveness of sins. If men would return to their loyalty, and no longer transgress, they would receive pardon.

Christ in the weakness of humanity was to meet the temptations of one possessing the powers of the higher nature that God had bestowed on the angelic family. But Christ's humanity was united with divinity, and in this strength He would bear all the temptations that Satan could bring against Him, and yet keep His soul untainted by sin. And this power to overcome He would give to every son and daughter of Adam who would accept by faith the righteous attributes of His character.

God loved the world so dearly that He gave His only-begotten Son that whosoever would accept Him might have power to live His righteous life. Christ proved that it is possible for man to lay hold by faith on the power of God. He showed that the sinner, by repentance and the exercise of faith in the righteousness of Christ, can be reconciled to

God, and become a partaker of the divine nature, overcoming the corruption that is in the world through lust.

Today Satan presents the same temptations that he presented to Christ, offering us the kingdoms of the world in return for our allegiance. But upon him who looks to Jesus as the author and finisher of his faith, Satan's temptations have no power. He cannot cause to sin the one who will accept by faith the virtues of Him who was tempted in all points as we are, yet without sin.

"God so loved the world, that he gave his only begotten Son, that whosoever believeth in him should not perish, but have everlasting life." He who repents of his sin and accepts the gift of the life of the Son of God, cannot be overcome. Laying hold by faith of the divine nature, he becomes a child of God. He prays, he believes. When tempted and tried, he claims the power that Christ died to give, and overcomes through His grace. This every sinner needs to understand. He must repent of his sin, he must believe in the power of Christ, and accept that power to save and to keep him from sin. How thankful ought we to be for the gift of Christ's example!

Seek Not to Evade the Cross

Profound theories and speculations of human creation may abound, but he who would come off conqueror in the end, must be humble enough to depend upon divine power. When we thus grasp the power of Infinity, and come to Christ, saying, "In my hand no price I bring; simply to Thy cross I cling," then divine agencies can cooperate with us to sanctify and purify the life.

Let no one seek to evade the cross. It is through the cross that we are enabled to overcome. It is through affliction and trial that divine agencies can carry on a work in our lives that will result in the love and peace and kindness of Christ.

A great work is to be accomplished daily in the human heart by the study of the Word. We need to learn the simplicity of true faith. This will bring its returns. Let us seek for decided advancement in spiritual understanding. Let us make the precious Word the man of our counsel. We need to walk carefully every moment, keeping close to the side of Christ. The spirit and grace of Christ are needed in the life, and the faith that works by love and purifies the soul.

We need to understand clearly the divine requirements that God makes of His people. The law, which is the transcript of His character, no one need fail to understand. The words written by the finger of God on tables of stone so perfectly reveal His will concerning His people that none need make any mistake. The laws of His kingdom were definitely made known, to be afterward revealed to the people of all nations and tongues as the principles of His government. We would do well to study those laws recorded in Exodus 20 and in the thirty-first chapter, verses 12-18.

When the judgment shall sit, and the books shall be opened, and every man shall be judged according to the things written in the books, then the tables of stone, hidden by God until that day, will be presented before the world as the standard of righteousness. Then men and women will see that the prerequisite of their salvation is obedience to the perfect law of God. None will find excuse for sin. By the righteous principles of that law, men will receive their sentence of life or of death.

29.

*Christ Our Only Hope**

Before the foundations of the world were laid, Christ, the Only Begotten of God, pledged Himself to become the Redeemer of the human race, should Adam sin. Adam fell, and He who was partaker of the Father's glory before the world was, laid aside His royal robe and kingly crown, and stepped down from His high authority to become a Babe in Bethlehem, that by passing over the ground where Adam stumbled and fell, He might redeem fallen human beings. He subjected Himself to all the temptations that the enemy brings against men and women; and all the assaults of Satan could not make Him swerve from His loyalty to the Father. By living a sinless life He testified that every son and daughter of Adam can resist the temptations of the one who first brought sin into the world.

Christ brought men and women power to overcome. He came to this world in human form, to live a man amongst men. He assumed the liabilities of human nature, to be proved and tried. In His humanity He was a partaker of the divine nature. In His incarnation He gained in a new sense the title of the Son of God. Said the angel to Mary, "The power of the Highest shall overshadow

---

* This article appeared in *The Signs of the Times*, Aug. 2, 1905.

thee: therefore also that holy thing which shall be born of thee shall be called the Son of God" (Luke 1:35). While the Son of a human being, He became the Son of God in a new sense. Thus He stood in our world—the Son of God, yet allied by birth to the human race.

Christ came in human form to show the inhabitants of the unfallen worlds and of the fallen world that ample provision has been made to enable human beings to live in loyalty to their Creator. He endured the temptations that Satan was permitted to bring against Him, and resisted all his assaults. He was sorely afflicted, and hard beset, but God did not leave Him without recognition. When He was baptized of John in Jordan, as He came up out of the water, the Spirit of God, like a dove of burnished gold, descended upon Him, and a voice from heaven said, "This is my beloved Son, in whom I am well pleased" (Matt. 3:17). It was directly after this announcement that Christ was led by the Spirit into the wilderness. Mark says: "Immediately the spirit driveth him into the wilderness. And he was there in the wilderness forty days, tempted of Satan; and was with the wild beasts" (Mark 1:12, 13). "And in those days he did eat nothing" (Luke 4:2).

Meeting Temptation

When Jesus was led into the wilderness to be tempted, He was led by the Spirit of God. He did not invite temptation. He went to the wilderness to be alone, to contemplate His mission and work. By fasting and prayer He was to brace Himself for the bloodstained path He was to travel. How should He begin His work of freeing the captives held in torment by the destroyer? During His long fast, the whole plan of His work as man's deliverer was laid out before Him.

When Jesus entered the wilderness He was shut in by the Father's glory. Absorbed in communion with God, He was lifted above human weakness. But the glory departed, and He was left to battle with temptation. It was pressing upon Him every moment. His human nature shrank from the conflict that awaited Him. For forty days He fasted

and prayed. Weak and emaciated from hunger, worn and
haggard with mental agony, "his visage was so marred
more than any man, and his form more than the sons of
men" (Isa. 52:14). Now was Satan's opportunity. Now he
supposed that he could overcome Christ.

There came to the Saviour, as if in answer to His
prayers, one in the guise of an angel of light, and this was
the message that he bore: "If thou be the Son of God,
command that these stones be made bread" (Matt. 4:3).

Jesus met Satan with the words, "Man shall not live by
bread alone, but by every word that proceedeth out of the
mouth of God" (Matt. 4:4). In every temptation the
weapon of His warfare was the Word of God. Satan demanded of Christ a miracle as a sign of His divinity. But
that which is greater than all miracles, a firm reliance
upon a "Thus saith the Lord" was a sign that could not be
controverted. So long as Christ held to this position, the
tempter could gain no advantage.

A familiarity with the Word of God is our only hope.
Those who diligently search the Scriptures will not accept
Satan's delusions as the truth of God. No one need be
overcome by the speculations presented by the enemy of
God and of Christ. We are not to speculate regarding
points upon which the Word of God is silent. All that is
necessary for our salvation is given in the Word of God.
Day by day we are to make the Bible the man of our
counsel.

From all eternity Christ was united with the Father,
and when He took upon Himself human nature, He was
still one with God. He is the link that unites God with
humanity. "Forasmuch then as the children are partakers
of flesh and blood, he also himself likewise took part of
the same" (Heb. 2:14). Only through Him can we become children of God. To all who believe on Him, He
gives power to become the sons of God. Thus the heart becomes the temple of the living God. It is because Christ
took human nature that men and women become partakers
of the divine nature. He brings life and immortality to
light through the gospel.

30.

*The Law and the Gospel**

When the Jews rejected Christ they rejected the foundation of their faith. And, on the other hand, the Christian world of today who claim faith in Christ, but reject the law of God are making a mistake similar to that of the deceived Jews. Those who profess to cling to Christ, centering their hopes on Him, while they pour contempt upon the moral law, and the prophecies, are in no safer position than were the unbelieving Jews. They cannot understandingly call sinners to repentance, for they are unable to properly explain what they are to repent of. The sinner, upon being exhorted to forsake his sins, has a right to ask, What is sin? Those who respect the law of God can answer, Sin is the transgression of the law. In confirmation of this the apostle Paul says, I had not known sin but by the law.

Those only who acknowledge the binding claim of the moral law can explain the nature of the atonement. Christ came to mediate between God and man, to make man one with God by bringing him into allegiance to His law. There was no power in the law to pardon its transgressor. Jesus alone could pay the sinner's debt. But the

---
* This article appeared in *The Signs of the Times,* March 14, 1878.

fact that Jesus has paid the indebtedness of the repentant sinner does not give him license to continue in transgression of the law of God; but he must henceforth live in obedience to that law.

The law of God existed before the creation of man or else Adam could not have sinned. After the transgression of Adam the principles of the law were not changed, but were definitely arranged and expressed to meet man in his fallen condition. Christ, in counsel with His Father, instituted the system of sacrificial offerings; that death, instead of being immediately visited upon the transgressor, should be transferred to a victim which should prefigure the great and perfect offering of the Son of God.

The sins of the people were transferred in figure to the officiating priest, who was a mediator for the people. The priest could not himself become an offering for sin, and make an atonement with his life, for he was also a sinner. Therefore, instead of suffering death himself, he killed a lamb without blemish; the penalty of sin was transferred to the innocent beast, which thus became his immediate substitute, and typified the perfect offering of Jesus Christ. Through the blood of this victim, man looked forward by faith to the blood of Christ which would atone for the sins of the world.

Purpose of the Ceremonial Law

If Adam had not transgressed the law of God, the ceremonial law would never have been instituted. The gospel of good news was first given to Adam in the declaration made to him that the seed of the woman should bruise the serpent's head; and it was handed down through successive generations to Noah, Abraham, and Moses. The knowledge of God's law, and the plan of salvation were imparted to Adam and Eve by Christ Himself. They carefully treasured the important lesson, and transmitted it by word of mouth, to their children, and children's children. Thus the knowledge of God's law was preserved.

Men lived nearly a thousand years in those days, and angels visited them with instruction directly from Christ.

The worship of God through sacrificial offerings was established, and those who feared God acknowledged their sins before Him, and looked forward with gratitude and holy trust to the coming of the Day Star, which should guide the fallen sons of Adam to heaven, through repentance toward God and faith toward our Lord and Saviour Jesus Christ. Thus the gospel was preached in every sacrifice; and the works of the believers continually revealed their faith in a coming Saviour. Jesus said to the Jews: "For had ye believed Moses, ye would have believed me: for he wrote of me. But if ye believe not his writings, how shall ye believe my words?" (John 5:46, 47).

It was impossible, however, for Adam, by his example and precepts, to stay the tide of woe which his transgression had brought upon men. Unbelief crept into the hearts of men. The children of Adam present the earliest example of the two different courses pursued by men with regard to the claims of God. Abel saw Christ figured in the sacrificial offerings. Cain was an unbeliever in regard to the necessity of sacrifices; he refused to discern that Christ was typified by the slain lamb; the blood of beasts appeared to him without virtue. The gospel was preached to Cain as well as to his brother; but it was to him a savor of death unto death, because he would not recognize, in the blood of the sacrificial lamb, Jesus Christ the only provision made for man's salvation.

Our Saviour, in His life and death, fulfilled all the prophecies pointing to Himself, and was the substance of all the types and shadows signified. He kept the moral law, and exalted it by answering its claims as man's representative. Those of Israel who turned to the Lord, and accepted Christ as the reality shadowed forth by the typical sacrifices, discerned the end of that which was to be abolished. The obscurity covering the Jewish system as a veil, was to them as the veil which covered the glory upon the face of Moses. The glory upon the face of Moses was the reflection of that light which Christ came into the world to bring for the benefit of man.

While Moses was shut in the mount with God, the plan

of salvation, dating from the fall of Adam, was revealed to him in a most forcible manner. He then knew that the very angel who was conducting the travels of the children of Israel was to be revealed in the flesh. God's dear Son, who was one with the Father, was to make all men one with God who would believe on, and trust in Him. Moses saw the true significance of the sacrificial offerings. Christ taught the gospel plan to Moses, and the glory of the gospel, through Christ, illuminated the countenance of Moses so that the people could not look upon it.

Moses himself was unconscious of the beaming glory reflected upon his face, and knew not why the children of Israel fled from him when he approached them. He called them to him, but they dared not look upon that glorified face. When Moses learned that the people could not look upon his face, because of its glory, he covered it with a veil.

The glory upon the face of Moses was exceedingly painful to the children of Israel because of their transgression of God's holy law. This is an illustration of the feelings of those who violate the law of God. They desire to remove from its penetrating light which is a terror to the transgressor, while it seems holy, just, and good to the loyal. Those only who have a just regard for the law of God can rightly estimate the atonement of Christ which was made necessary by the violation of the Father's law.

Those who cherish the view that there was no Saviour in the old dispensation, have as dark a veil over their understanding as did the Jews who rejected Christ. The Jews acknowledged their faith in a Messiah to come in the offering of sacrifices which typified Christ. Yet when Jesus appeared, fulfilling all the prophecies regarding the promised Messiah, and doing works that marked Him as the divine Son of God, they rejected Him, and refused to accept the plainest evidence of His true character. The Christian church, on the other hand, who profess the utmost faith in Christ, in despising the Jewish system virtually deny Christ, who was the originator of the entire Jewish economy.

31.

The Law in Galatians

I am asked concerning the law in Galatians. What law is the schoolmaster to bring us to Christ? I answer: Both the ceremonial and the moral code of ten commandments.

Christ was the foundation of the whole Jewish economy. The death of Abel was in consequence of Cain's refusing to accept God's plan in the school of obedience to be saved by the blood of Jesus Christ typified by the sacrificial offerings pointing to Christ. Cain refused the shedding of blood which symbolized the blood of Christ to be shed for the world. This whole ceremony was prepared by God, and Christ became the foundation of the whole system. This is the beginning of its work as the schoolmaster to bring sinful human agents to a consideration of Christ the Foundation of the whole Jewish economy.

All who did service in connection with the sanctuary were being educated constantly in regard to the intervention of Christ in behalf of the human race. This service was designed to create in every heart a love for the law of God, which is the law of His kingdom. The sacrificial offering was to be an object lesson of the love of God revealed in Christ—in the suffering, dying victim, who took upon Himself the sin of which man was guilty, the innocent being made sin for us.

In the contemplation of this great theme of salvation we see Christ's work. Not only the promised gift of the Spirit, but also the nature and character of this sacrifice and intervention are subjects which should create in our hearts elevated, sacred, high ideas of the law of God, which holds its claims upon every human agency. The violation of that law in the small act of eating of the forbidden fruit, brought upon man and upon the earth the consequence of disobedience to the holy law of God. The nature of the intervention should ever make man afraid to do the smallest action in disobedience to God's requirement.

There should be a clear understanding of that which constitutes sin, and we should avoid the least approach to step over the boundaries from obedience to disobedience.

God would have every member of His creation understand the great work of the infinite Son of God in giving His life for the salvation of the world. "Behold, what manner of love the Father hath bestowed upon us, that we should be called the sons of God: therefore the world knoweth us not, because it knew him not" (1 John 3:1).

When he sees in Christ the embodiment of infinite and disinterested love and benevolence, there is awakened in the heart of the sinner a thankful disposition to follow where Christ is drawing.—Manuscript 87, 1900.

Especially the Moral Law

"The law was our schoolmaster to bring us unto Christ, that we might be justified by faith" (Gal. 3:24). In this scripture, the Holy Spirit through the apostle is speaking especially of the moral law. The law reveals sin to us, and causes us to feel our need of Christ and to flee unto Him for pardon and peace by exercising repentance toward God and faith toward our Lord Jesus Christ.

An unwillingness to yield up preconceived opinions, and to accept this truth, lay at the foundation of a large share of the opposition manifested at Minneapolis against the Lord's message through Brethren [E. J.] Waggoner and [A. T.] Jones. By exciting that opposition Satan succeeded in shutting away from our people, in a great measure, the special power of the Holy Spirit that God longed to impart to them. The enemy prevented them from obtaining that efficiency which might have been theirs in carrying the truth to the world, as the apostles proclaimed it after the day of Pentecost. The light that is to lighten the whole earth with its glory was resisted, and by the action of our own brethren has been in a great degree kept away from the world.

* * * * *

The law of ten commandments is not to be looked upon as much from the prohibitory side, as from the mercy side. Its prohibitions are the sure guarantee of happiness in obedience. As received in Christ, it works in us the purity of character that will bring joy to us through eternal ages. To the obedient it is a wall of protection. We behold in it the goodness of God, who by revealing to men the immutable principles of righteousness, seeks to shield them from the evils that result from transgression.

We are not to regard God as waiting to punish the sinner for his sin. The sinner brings the punishment upon himself. His own actions start a train of circumstances that bring the sure result. Every act of transgression reacts upon the sinner, works in him a change of character, and makes it more easy for him to transgress again. By choosing to sin, men separate themselves from God, cut themselves off from the channel of blessing, and the sure result is ruin and death.

The law is an expression of God's idea. When we receive it in Christ, it becomes our idea. It lifts us above the power of natural desires and tendencies, above temptations that lead to sin. "Great peace have they which love thy law: and nothing shall offend them" (Ps. 119:165)— cause them to stumble.

There is no peace in unrighteousness; the wicked are at war with God. But he who receives the righteousness of the law in Christ is in harmony with heaven. "Mercy and truth are met together; righteousness and peace have kissed each other" (Ps. 85:10).—Letter 96, 1896.

32.

The Righteousness of Christ
*in the Law**

The greatest difficulty Paul had to meet arose from the influence of Judaizing teachers. These made him much trouble by causing dissension in the church at Corinth. They were continually presenting the virtues of the ceremonies of the law, exalting these ceremonies above the gospel of Christ, and condemning Paul because he did not urge them upon the new converts.

Paul met them on their own ground. "If the ministration of death, written and engraven in stones, was glorious," he said, "so that the children of Israel could not stedfastly behold the face of Moses for the glory of his countenance; which glory was to be done away: how shall not the ministration of the spirit be rather glorious? For if the ministration of condemnation be glory, much more doth the ministration of righteousness exceed in glory" (2 Cor. 3:7-9).

The law of God, spoken in awful grandeur from Sinai, is the utterance of condemnation to the sinner. It is the province of the law to condemn, but there is in it no power

---

* This article appeared in *The Review and Herald*, April 22, 1902.

to pardon or to redeem. It is ordained to life; those who walk in harmony with its precepts will receive the reward of obedience. But it brings bondage and death to those who remain under its condemnation.

So sacred and so glorious is the law, that when Moses returned from the holy mount, where he had been with God, receiving from His hand the tables of stone, his face reflected a glory upon which the people could not look without pain, and Moses was obliged to cover his face with a veil.

The glory that shone on the face of Moses was a reflection of the righteousness of Christ in the law. The law itself would have no glory, only that in it Christ is embodied. It has no power to save. It is lusterless only as in it Christ is represented as full of righteousness and truth.

The types and shadows of the sacrificial service, with the prophecies, gave the Israelites a veiled, indistinct view of the mercy and grace to be brought to the world by the revelation of Christ. To Moses was unfolded the significance of the types and shadows pointing to Christ. He saw to the end of that which was to be done away when, at the death of Christ, type met antitype. He saw that only through Christ can man keep the moral law. By transgression of this law man brought sin into the world, and with sin came death. Christ became the propitiation for man's sin. He proffered His perfection of character in the place of man's sinfulness. He took upon Himself the curse of disobedience. The sacrifices and offerings pointed forward to the sacrifice He was to make. The slain lamb typified the Lamb that was to take away the sin of the world.

It was seeing the object of that which was to be done away, seeing Christ as revealed in the law, that illumined the face of Moses. The ministration of the law, written and engraved in stone, was a ministration of death. Without Christ, the transgressor was left under its curse, with no hope of pardon. The ministration had of itself no glory, but the promised Saviour, revealed in the types and shadows of the ceremonial law, made the moral law glorious.

Paul desires his brethren to see that the great glory of a

sin-pardoning Saviour gave significance to the entire Jewish economy. He desired them to see also that when Christ came to the world, and died as man's sacrifice, type met antitype.

After Christ died on the cross as a sin offering, the ceremonial law could have no force. Yet it was connected with the moral law, and was glorious. The whole bore the stamp of divinity, and expressed the holiness, justice, and righteousness of God. And if the ministration of the dispensation to be done away was glorious, how much more must the reality be glorious, when Christ was revealed, giving His life-giving, sanctifying Spirit to all who believe?

The proclamation of the law of ten commandments was a wonderful exhibition of the glory and majesty of God. How did this manifestation of power affect the people?— They were afraid. As they saw "the thunderings, and the lightnings, and the noise of the trumpet, and the mountain smoking," they "removed, and stood afar off. And they said unto Moses, Speak thou with us, and we will hear: but let not God speak with us, lest we die" (Ex. 20:18, 19). They desired Moses to be their mediator. They did not understand that Christ was their appointed mediator, and that, deprived of His mediation, they would certainly have been consumed.

"Moses said unto the people, Fear not: for God is come to prove you, and that his fear may be before your faces, that ye sin not. And the people stood afar off, and Moses drew near unto the thick darkness where God was" (Ex. 20:20, 21).

The pardon of sin, justification by faith in Jesus Christ, access to God only through a mediator because of their lost condition, their guilt and sin—of these truths the people had little conception. In a great measure they had lost a knowledge of God and of the only way to approach Him. They had lost nearly all sense of what constitutes sin and of what constitutes righteousness. The pardon of sin through Christ, the promised Messiah, whom their offerings typified, was but dimly understood.

Paul declared, "Seeing then that we have such hope, we

use great plainness of speech: and not as Moses, which put a vail over his face, that the children of Israel could not stedfastly look to the end of that which is abolished: but their minds were blinded: for until this day remaineth the same vail untaken away in the reading of the old testament; which vail is done away in Christ. But even unto this day, when Moses is read, the vail is upon their heart. Nevertheless when it shall turn to the Lord, the vail shall be taken away" (2 Cor. 3:12-16).

The Jews refused to accept Christ as the Messiah, and they cannot see that their ceremonies are meaningless, that the sacrifices and offerings have lost their significance. The veil drawn by themselves in stubborn unbelief is still before their minds. It would be removed if they would accept Christ, the righteousness of the law.

Many in the Christian world also have a veil before their eyes and heart. They do not see to the end of that which was done away. They do not see that it was only the ceremonial law which was abrogated at the death of Christ. They claim that the moral law was nailed to the cross. Heavy is the veil that darkens their understanding. The hearts of many are at war with God. They are not subject to His law. Only as they shall come into harmony with the rule of His government, can Christ be of any avail to them. They may talk of Christ as their Saviour; but He will finally say to them, I know you not. You have not exercised genuine repentance toward God for the transgression of His holy law, and you cannot have genuine faith in Me, for it was My mission to exalt God's law.

A Transcript of Christ's Character

Paul did not represent either the moral or the ceremonial law as ministers in our day venture to do. Some cherish such antipathy to the law of God that they will go out of the way to denounce and stigmatize it. Thus they despise and pour contempt on the majesty and glory of God.

The moral law was never a type or a shadow. It existed before man's creation, and will endure as long as

God's throne remains. God could not change nor alter one precept of His law in order to save man; for the law is the foundation of His government. It is unchangeable, unalterable, infinite, and eternal. In order for man to be saved, and for the honor of the law to be maintained, it was necessary for the Son of God to offer Himself as a sacrifice for sin. He who knew no sin became sin for us. He died for us on Calvary. His death shows the wonderful love of God for man, and the immutability of His law.

In the Sermon on the Mount, Christ declared, "Think not that I am come to destroy the law, or the prophets: I am not come to destroy, but to fulfil. For verily I say unto you, Till heaven and earth pass, one jot or one tittle shall in no wise pass from the law, till all be fulfilled" (Matt. 5:17, 18).

Christ bore the curse of the law, suffering its penalty, carrying to completion the plan whereby man was to be placed where he could keep God's law, and be accepted through the merits of the Redeemer; and by His sacrifice glory was shed upon the law. Then the glory of that which is not to be done away—God's law of ten commandments, His standard of righteousness—was plainly seen by all who saw to the end of that which was done away.

"We all, with open face beholding as in a glass the glory of the Lord, are changed into the same image from glory to glory, even as by the Spirit of the Lord" (2 Cor. 3:18). Christ is the sinner's advocate. Those who accept His gospel behold Him with open face. They see the relation of His mission to the law, and they acknowledge God's wisdom and glory as revealed by the Saviour. The glory of Christ is revealed in the law, which is a transcript of His character, and His transforming efficacy is felt upon the soul until men become changed to His likeness. They are made partakers of the divine nature, and grow more and more like their Saviour, advancing step by step in conformity to the will of God, till they reach perfection.

The law and the gospel are in perfect harmony. Each upholds the other. In all its majesty the law confronts the conscience, causing the sinner to feel his need of Christ as the propitiation for sin. The gospel recognizes the power and immutability of the law. "I had not known sin, but by the law," Paul declares (Rom. 7:7). The sense of sin, urged home by the law, drives the sinner to the Saviour. In his need man may present the mighty arguments furnished by the cross of Calvary. He may claim the righteousness of Christ; for it is imparted to every repentant sinner. God declares, "Him that cometh to me I will in no wise cast out" (John 6:37). "If we confess our sins, he is faithful and just to forgive us our sins, and to cleanse us from all unrighteousness" (1 John 1:9).

33.

"Search the Scriptures" *

It is of the highest importance that every human being endowed with reasoning powers should understand his relation to God. In our schools the work of redemption is not carefully studied. Many of the students have no real conception of what the plan of salvation means. God's word is pledged in our behalf. He who is touched with the feeling of our infirmities invites us: "Come unto me, all ye that labour and are heavy laden, and I will give you rest. Take my yoke upon you, and learn of me; for I am meek and lowly in heart: and ye shall find rest unto your souls. For my yoke is easy, and my burden is light" (Matt. 11:28-30).

Students, you are safe only as, in perfect submission and obedience, you connect yourselves with Christ. The yoke is easy, for Christ carries the weight. As you lift the burden of the cross, it will become light; and that cross is to you a pledge of eternal life. It is the privilege of each to follow gladly after Christ, exclaiming at every step, "Thy gentleness hath made me great" (2 Sam. 22:36). But if we would travel heavenward, we must take the Word of

---
* This article appeared in *The Youth's Instructor*, Oct. 13, 1898.

God as our lesson book. In the words of Inspiration we must read our lessons day by day.

The apostle Paul says: "Let this mind be in you, which was also in Christ Jesus: who, being in the form of God, thought it not robbery to be equal with God: but made himself of no reputation, and took upon him the form of a servant, and was made in the likeness of men: and being found in fashion as a man [as the representative of the human race], he humbled himself, and became obedient unto death, even the death of the cross. Wherefore God also hath highly exalted him, and given him a name which is above every name: that at the name of Jesus every knee should bow" (Phil. 2:5-10).

The humiliation of the man Christ Jesus is incomprehensible to the human mind; but His divinity and His existence before the world was formed can never be doubted by those who believe the Word of God. The apostle Paul speaks of our Mediator, the only-begotten Son of God, who in a state of glory was in the form of God, the Commander of all the heavenly hosts, and who, when He clothed His divinity with humanity, took upon Him the form of a servant. Isaiah declares: "Unto us a child is born, unto us a son is given: and the government shall be upon his shoulder: and his name shall be called Wonderful, Counsellor, The mighty God, The everlasting Father, The Prince of Peace. Of the increase of his government and peace there shall be no end, upon the throne of David, and upon his kingdom, to order it, and to establish it with judgment and with justice from henceforth even for ever" (Isa. 9:6, 7).

In consenting to become man, Christ manifested a humility that is the marvel of the heavenly intelligences. The act of consenting to be a man would be no humiliation were it not for the fact of Christ's exalted pre-existence. We must open our understanding to realize that Christ laid aside His royal robe, His kingly crown, His high command, and clothed His divinity with humanity, that He might meet man where he was, and bring to the human family moral power to become the sons and daughters of God. To redeem man, Christ became obedient unto death, even the death of the cross.

The humanity of the Son of God is everything to us. It is the golden chain that binds our souls to Christ, and through Christ to God. This is to be our study. Christ was a real man; He gave proof of His humility in becoming a man. Yet He was God in the flesh. When we approach this subject, we would do well to heed the words spoken by Christ to Moses at the burning bush, "Put off thy shoes from off thy feet, for the place whereon thou standest is holy ground" (Ex. 3:5). We should come to this study with the humility of a learner, with a contrite heart. And the study of the incarnation of Christ is a fruitful field, which will repay the searcher who digs deep for hidden truth.

The Scriptures Our Guide

The Bible is our guide in the safe paths that lead to eternal life. God has inspired men to write that which will present the truth to us, which will attract, and which, if practiced, will enable the receiver to obtain moral power to rank among the most highly educated minds. The minds of all who make the Word of God their study will enlarge. Far more than any other study, this is of a nature to increase the powers of comprehension, and endow every faculty with new vigor. It brings the mind in contact with broad, ennobling principles of truth. It brings us into close connection with all heaven, imparting wisdom, and knowledge, and understanding.

In dealing with commonplace productions, and feeding on the writings of uninspired men, the mind becomes dwarfed and cheapened. It is not brought into contact with deep, broad principles of eternal truth. The understanding unconsciously adapts itself to the comprehension of the things with which it is familiar; and in the consideration of these things the understanding is weakened, its powers contracted.

God designs that the Scriptures, the source of science that is above all human theory, shall be searched. He desires that man shall dig deep in the mines of truth, that he may gain the valuable treasure they contain. But too often human theories and wisdom are put in the place of the science of the Bible. Men engage in the work of remodeling God's purposes; they try to distinguish between the books of the Bible. Through their inventions they make the Scriptures testify to a lie.

Just What Man Needs

God has not made the reception of the gospel to depend upon human reasoning. The gospel is adapted for spiritual food, to satisfy man's spiritual appetite. In every case it is just what man needs. Those who have felt it necessary to have the students in our schools study many authors are themselves the most ignorant on the great themes of the Bible. The teachers themselves need to take up the Book of all books, and learn from the Scriptures that the gospel has power to prove its own divinity to the humble, contrite mind.

The gospel is the power of God and the wisdom of God. The character of Christ on earth revealed divinity, and the gospel which He has given is to be the study of His human heritage in all their educational departments, until teachers, children, and youth shall discern in the only true and living God the object of their faith and love and adoration. The Word is to be respected and obeyed. That Book which contains the record of Christ's life, His work, His doctrines, His sufferings, and final triumphs, is to be the source of our strength. We are granted the privileges of school life in this world that we may obtain a fitness for the higher life—the highest grade in the highest school, where, under God, our studies will continue through the ceaseless ages of eternity.

34.

*The Word Made Flesh**

"In the beginning was the Word, and the Word was with God, and the Word was God. The same was in the beginning with God. All things were made by him; and without him was not any thing made that was made. In him was life; and the life was the light of men. And the light shineth in darkness; and the darkness comprehended it not." "And the Word was made flesh, and dwelt among us, (and we beheld his glory, the glory as of the only begotten of the Father,) full of grace and truth" (John 1:1-5, 14).

This chapter delineates the character and importance of the work of Christ. As one who understands his subject, John ascribes all power to Christ, and speaks of His greatness and majesty. He flashes forth divine rays of precious truth, as light from the sun. He presents Christ as the only Mediator between God and humanity.

The doctrine of the incarnation of Christ in human flesh is a mystery, "even the mystery which hath been hid from ages and from generations" (Col. 1:26). It is the great and profound mystery of godliness. "The Word was made flesh, and dwelt among us" (John 1:14). Christ took upon

---

* This article appeared in *The Review and Herald,* April 5, 1906.

Himself human nature, a nature inferior to His heavenly nature. Nothing so shows the wonderful condescension of God as this. He "so loved the world, that he gave his only begotten Son" (John 3:16). John presents this wonderful subject with such simplicity that all may grasp the ideas set forth, and be enlightened.

Christ did not make believe take human nature; He did verily take it. He did in reality possess human nature. "As the children are partakers of flesh and blood, he also himself likewise took part of the same" (Heb. 2:14). He was the son of Mary; He was of the seed of David according to human descent. He is declared to be a man, even the Man Christ Jesus. "This man," writes Paul, "was counted worthy of more glory than Moses, inasmuch as he who hath builded the house hath more honour than the house" (Heb. 3:3).

Christ's Pre-existence

But while God's Word speaks of the humanity of Christ when upon this earth, it also speaks decidedly regarding His pre-existence. The Word existed as a divine being, even as the eternal Son of God, in union and oneness with His Father. From everlasting He was the Mediator of the covenant, the one in whom all nations of the earth, both Jews and Gentiles, if they accepted Him, were to be blessed. "The Word was with God, and the Word was God" (John 1:1). Before men or angels were created, the Word was with God, and was God.

The world was made by Him, "and without him was not any thing made that was made" (John 1:3). If Christ made all things, He existed before all things. The words spoken in regard to this are so decisive that no one need be left in doubt. Christ was God essentially, and in the highest sense. He was with God from all eternity, God over all, blessed forevermore.

The Lord Jesus Christ, the divine Son of God, existed from eternity, a distinct person, yet one with the Father. He was the surpassing glory of heaven. He was the commander of the heavenly intelligences, and the adoring homage of the angels was received by Him as His right. This was no robbery of God. "The Lord possessed me in the beginning of his way," He declares, "before his works of old. I was set up from everlasting, from the beginning, or ever the earth was. When there were no depths, I was brought forth; when there were no fountains abounding with water. Before the mountains were settled, before the hills was I brought forth: while as yet he had not made the earth, nor the fields, nor the highest part of the dust of the world. When he prepared the heavens, I was there: when he set a compass upon the face of the depth" (Prov. 8:22-27).

There are light and glory in the truth that Christ was one with the Father before the foundation of the world was laid. This is the light shining in a dark place, making it resplendent with divine, original glory. This truth, infinitely mysterious in itself, explains other mysterious and otherwise unexplainable truths, while it is enshrined in light, unapproachable and incomprehensible.

"Before the mountains were brought forth, or ever thou hadst formed the earth and the world, even from everlasting to everlasting, thou art God" (Ps. 90:2). "The people which sat in darkness saw great light; and to them which sat in the region and shadow of death light is sprung up" (Matt. 4:16). Here the pre-existence of Christ and the purpose of His manifestation to our world are presented as living beams of light from the eternal throne. "Now gather thyself in troops, O daughter of troops: he hath laid siege against us: they shall smite the judge of Israel with a rod upon the cheek. But thou, Beth-lehem Ephratah, though thou be little among the thousands of Judah, yet out of thee shall he come forth unto me that is to be ruler in Israel; whose goings forth have been from of old, from everlasting" (Micah 5:1, 2).

"We preach Christ crucified," declared Paul, "unto the Jews a stumblingblock, and unto the Greeks foolishness; but unto them which are called, both Jews and Greeks, Christ the power of God, and the wisdom of God" (1 Cor. 1:23, 24).

A Mystery

That God should thus be manifest in the flesh is indeed a mystery; and without the help of the Holy Spirit we cannot hope to comprehend this subject. The most humbling lesson that man has to learn is the nothingness of human wisdom, and the folly of trying, by his own unaided efforts, to find out God. He may exert his intellectual powers to the utmost, he may have what the world calls a superior education, yet he may still be ignorant in God's eyes. The ancient philosophers boasted of their wisdom; but how did it weigh in the scale with God? Solomon had great learning; but his wisdom was foolishness; for he did not know how to stand in moral independence, free from sin, in the strength of a character molded after the divine similitude. Solomon has told us the result of his research, his painstaking efforts, his persevering inquiry. He pronounces his wisdom altogether vanity.

By wisdom the world knew not God. Their estimation of the divine character, their imperfect knowledge of His attributes, did not enlarge and expand their mental conception. Their minds were not ennobled in conformity to the divine will, but they plunged into the grossest idolatry. "Professing themselves to be wise, they became fools, and changed the glory of the uncorruptible God into an image made like to corruptible man, and to birds, and fourfooted beasts, and creeping things" (Rom. 1:22, 23). This is the worth of all requirements and knowledge apart from Christ.

"I am the way, the truth, and the life," Christ declares: "no man cometh unto the Father, but by me" (John 14:6). Christ is invested with power to give life to all creatures. "As the living Father hath sent me," He says, "and I live by the Father: so he that eateth me, even he shall live by me." "It is the spirit that quickeneth; the flesh profiteth nothing: the words that I speak unto you, they are spirit, and they are life" (John 6:57, 63). Christ is not here referring to His doctrine, but to His person, the divinity of His character. "Verily, verily, I say unto you," He says again, "The hour is coming, and now is, when the dead shall hear the voice of the Son of God: and they that hear shall live. For as the Father hath life in himself; so hath he given to the Son to have life in himself; and hath given him authority to execute judgment also, because he is the Son of man" (John 5:25-27).

The Significance of Christ's Birth

God and Christ knew from the beginning, of the apostasy of Satan and of the fall of Adam through the deceptive power of the apostate. The plan of salvation was designed to redeem the fallen race, to give them another trial. Christ was appointed to the office of Mediator from the creation of God, set up from everlasting to be our substitute and surety. Before the world was made, it was arranged that the divinity of Christ should be enshrouded in humanity. "A body," said Christ, "hast thou prepared me" (Heb. 10:5). But He did not come in human form until the fullness of time had expired. Then He came to our world, a babe in Bethlehem.

No one born into the world, not even the most gifted of God's children, has ever been accorded such demonstration of joy as greeted the Babe born in Bethlehem. Angels of God sang His praises over the hills and plains of Bethlehem. "Glory to God in the highest," they sang, "and on earth peace, good will toward men" (Luke 2:14). O that today the human family could recognize this song! The declaration then made, the note then struck, the tune then started, will swell and extend to the end of time, and resound to the ends of the earth. It is glory to God, it is peace on earth, good will to men. When the Sun of Righteousness shall arise with healing in His wings, the song then started in the hills of Bethlehem will be re-echoed by the voice of a great multitude, as the voice of many waters, saying, "Alleluia: for the Lord God omnipotent reigneth" (Rev. 19:6).

By His obedience to all the commandments of God, Christ wrought out a redemption for men. This was not done by going out of Himself to another, but by taking humanity into Himself. Thus Christ gave to humanity an existence out of Himself. To bring humanity into Christ, to bring the fallen race into oneness with divinity, is the work of redemption. Christ took human nature that men might be one with Him as He is one with the Father, that God may love man as He loves His only-begotten Son, that men may be partakers of the divine nature, and be complete in Him.

The Holy Spirit, which proceeds from the only-begotten Son of God, binds the human agent, body, soul, and spirit, to the perfect, divine-human nature of Christ. This union is represented by the union of the vine and the branches. Finite man is united to the manhood of Christ. Through faith human nature is assimilated with Christ's nature. We are made one with God in Christ.

35.

*"Tempted in All Points Like as We Are"**

After the fall of man, Satan declared that human beings were proved to be incapable of keeping the law of God, and he sought to carry the universe with him in this belief. Satan's words appeared to be true, and Christ came to unmask the deceiver. The Majesty of heaven undertook the cause of man, and with the same facilities that man may obtain, withstood the temptations of Satan as man must withstand them. This was the only way in which fallen man could become a partaker of the divine nature. In taking human nature, Christ was fitted to understand man's trials and sorrows and all the temptations wherewith he is beset. Angels who were unacquainted with sin could not sympathize with man in his peculiar trials. Christ condescended to take man's nature, and was tempted in all points like as we, that He might know how to succor all who should be tempted.

In assuming humanity Christ took the part of every human being. He was the Head of humanity. A Being divine and human, with His long human arm He could encircle humanity, while with His divine arm He could lay hold of the throne of the Infinite.

---

* This article appeared in *The Signs of the Times*, June 9, 1898.

What a sight was this for Heaven to look upon! Christ, who knew not the least taint of sin or defilement, took our nature in its deteriorated condition. This was humiliation greater than finite man can comprehend. God was manifest in the flesh. He humbled Himself. What a subject for thought, for deep, earnest contemplation! So infinitely great that He was the Majesty of heaven, and yet He stooped so low, without losing one atom of His dignity and glory! He stooped to poverty and to the deepest abasement among men. For our sake He became poor, that we through His poverty might be made rich. "The foxes have holes," He said, "and the birds of the air have nests; but the Son of man hath not where to lay his head" (Matt. 8:20).

Christ submitted to insult and mockery, contempt and ridicule. He heard His message, which was fraught with love and goodness and mercy, misstated and misapplied. He heard Himself called the prince of demons, because He testified to His divine Sonship. His birth was supernatural, but by His own nation, those who had blinded their eyes to spiritual things, it was regarded as a blot and a stain. There was not a drop of our bitter woe which He did not taste, not a part of our curse which He did not endure, that He might bring many sons and daughters to God.

The fact that Jesus was on this earth as a man of sorrows and acquainted with grief, that in order to save fallen man from eternal ruin, He left His heavenly home, should lay in the dust all our pride, put to shame all our vanity, and reveal to us the sin of self-sufficiency. Behold Him making the wants, the trials, the griefs and sufferings of sinful men His own. Can we not take home the lesson that God endured these sufferings and bruises of soul in consequence of sin?

Christ came to the earth, taking humanity and standing as man's representative, to show in the controversy with Satan that man, as God created him, connected with the Father and the Son, could obey every divine requirement. Speaking through His servant He declares, "His commandments are not grievous" (1 John 5:3). It was sin that separated man from his God, and it is sin that maintains this separation.

The Prophecy in Eden

The enmity referred to in the prophecy in Eden was not to be confined merely to Satan and the Prince of life. It was to be universal. Satan and his angels were to feel the enmity of all mankind. "I will put enmity," said God, "between thee and the woman, and between thy seed and her seed; it shall bruise thy head, and thou shalt bruise his heel" (Gen. 3:15).

The enmity put between the seed of the serpent and the seed of the woman was supernatural. With Christ the enmity was in one sense natural; in another sense it was supernatural, as humanity and divinity were combined. And never was the enmity developed to such a marked degree as when Christ became an inhabitant of this earth. Never before had there been a being upon the earth who hated sin with so perfect a hatred as did Christ. He had seen its deceiving, infatuating power upon the holy angels, and all His powers were enlisted against it.

The purity and holiness of Christ, the spotless righteousness of Him who did no sin, was a perpetual reproach upon all sin in a world of sensuality and sin. In His life the light of truth was flashed amid the moral darkness with which Satan had enshrouded the world. Christ exposed Satan's falsehoods and deceiving character, and in many hearts destroyed his corrupting influence. It was this that stirred Satan with such intense hatred. With his hosts of fallen beings he determined to urge the warfare most vigorously; for there stood in the world One who was a perfect representative of the Father, One whose character and practices refuted Satan's misrepresentation of God. Satan had charged upon God the attribute he himself possessed. Now in Christ he saw God revealed in His true character—a compassionate, merciful Father, not willing that any should perish, but that all should come to Him in repentance, and have eternal life.

Intense worldliness has been one of Satan's most successful temptations. He designs to keep the hearts and minds of men so engrossed with worldly attractions that there will be no room for heavenly things. He controls their minds in their love of the world. Earthly things eclipse the heavenly, and put the Lord out of their sight and understanding. False theories and false gods are cherished in the place of the true. Men are charmed with the glitter and tinsel of the world. They are so attached to the things of the earth that many will commit any sin in order to gain some worldly advantage.

It was on this point that Satan thought to overthrow Christ. He thought that in His humanity He could be easily overcome. "The devil taketh him up into an exceeding high mountain, and sheweth him all the kingdoms of the world, and the glory of them; and saith unto him, All these things will I give thee, if thou wilt fall down and worship me" (Matt. 4:8, 9). But Christ was unmoved. He felt the strength of this temptation; but He met it in our behalf, and conquered. And He used only the weapons justifiable for human beings to use—the word of Him who is mighty in counsel—"It is written" (Matt. 4:4, 10).

With what intense interest was this controversy watched by the heavenly angels and the unfallen worlds, as the honor of the law was being vindicated. Not merely for this world, but for the universe of heaven, was the controversy to be forever settled. The confederacy of darkness was also watching for the semblance of a chance to triumph over the divine and human Substitute of the human race, that the apostate might shout, "Victory," and the world and its inhabitants forever become his kingdom.

But Satan reached only the heel; he could not touch the head. At the death of Christ, Satan saw that he was defeated. He saw that his true character was clearly revealed before all heaven, and that the heavenly beings and the worlds that God had created would be wholly on the side of God. He saw that his prospects of future influence with them would be entirely cut off. Christ's humanity would demonstrate for eternal ages the question which settled the controversy.

Sinlessness of Christ's Human Nature

In taking upon Himself man's nature in its fallen condition, Christ did not in the least participate in its sin. He was subject to the infirmities and weaknesses by which man is encompassed, "that it might be fulfilled which was spoken by Esaias the prophet, saying, Himself took our infirmities, and bare our sicknesses" (Matt. 8:17). He was touched with the feeling of our infirmities, and was in all points tempted like as we are. And yet He knew no sin. He was the Lamb "without blemish and without spot" (1 Peter 1:19). Could Satan in the least particular have tempted Christ to sin, he would have bruised the Saviour's head. As it was, he could only touch His heel. Had the head of Christ been touched, the hope of the human race would have perished. Divine wrath would have come upon Christ as it came upon Adam. Christ and the church would have been without hope.

We should have no misgivings in regard to the perfect sinlessness of the human nature of Christ. Our faith must be an intelligent faith, looking unto Jesus in perfect confidence, in full and entire faith in the atoning Sacrifice. This is essential that the soul may not be enshrouded in darkness. This holy Substitute is able to save to the uttermost; for He presented to the wondering universe perfect and complete humility in His human character, and perfect obedience to all the requirements of God. Divine power is placed upon man, that he may become a partaker of the divine nature, having escaped the corruption that is in the world through lust. This is why repenting, believing man can be made the righteousness of God in Christ.

36.

No Caste in Christ[*]

The highest angel in heaven had not the power to pay the ransom for one lost soul. Cherubim and seraphim have only the glory with which they are endowed by the Creator as His creatures, and the reconciliation of man to God could be accomplished only through a mediator who was equal with God, possessed of attributes that would dignify, and declare him worthy to treat with the infinite God in man's behalf, and also represent God to a fallen world. Man's substitute and surety must have man's nature, a connection with the human family whom he was to represent, and, as God's ambassador, he must partake of the divine nature, have a connection with the Infinite, in order to manifest God to the world, and be a mediator between God and man.

These qualifications were found alone in Christ. Clothing His divinity with humanity, He came to earth to be called the Son of man and the Son of God. He was the surety for man, the ambassador for God—the surety for man to satisfy by His righteousness in man's behalf the demands of the law, and the representative of God to make manifest His character to a fallen race.

---

[*] This article appeared in *The Review and Herald*, Dec. 22, 1891.

The world's Redeemer possessed the power to draw men to Himself, to quiet their fears, to dispel their gloom, to inspire them with hope and courage, to enable them to believe in the willingness of God to receive them through the merits of the divine Substitute. As subjects of the love of God we ever should be grateful that we have a mediator, an advocate, an intercessor in the heavenly courts, who pleads in our behalf before the Father.

We have everything we could ask to inspire us with faith and trust in God. In earthly courts, when a king would make his greatest pledge to assure men of his truth, he gives his child as a hostage, to be redeemed on the fulfillment of his promise; and behold what a pledge of the Father's faithfulness; for when He would assure men of the immutability of His council, He gave His only-begotten Son to come to earth, to take the nature of man, not only for the brief years of life, but to retain his nature in the heavenly courts, an everlasting pledge of the faithfulness of God. O the depth of the riches both of the wisdom and love of God! "Behold, what manner of love the Father hath bestowed upon us, that we should be called the sons of God" (1 John 3:1).

Through faith in Christ we become members of the royal family, heirs of God, and joint heirs with Jesus Christ. In Christ we are one. As we come in sight of Calvary, and view the royal Sufferer who in man's nature bore the curse of the law in his behalf, all national distinctions, all sectarian differences are obliterated; all honor of rank, all pride of caste is lost.

The light shining from the throne of God upon the cross of Calvary forever puts an end to man-made separations between class and race. Men of every class become members of one family, children of the heavenly King, not through earthly power, but through the love of God who gave Jesus to a life of poverty, affliction, and humiliation, to a death of shame and agony, that He might bring many sons and daughters unto glory.

It is not the position, not the finite wisdom, not the qualifications, not the endowments of any person that makes him rank high in the esteem of God. The intellect, the reason, the talents of men, are the gifts of God to be employed to His glory, for the upbuilding of His eternal kingdom. It is the spiritual and moral character that is of value in the sight of Heaven, and that will survive the grave and be made glorious with immortality for the endless ages of eternity. Worldly royalty so highly honored by men will never come forth from the sepulcher into which it enters. Riches, honor, the wisdom of men that have served the purposes of the enemy, can bring to their possessors no inheritance, no honor, no position of trust in the world which is to come. Only those who have appreciated the grace of Christ, which has made them heirs of God and joint heirs with Jesus, will rise from the grave bearing the image of their Redeemer.

All who are found worthy to be counted as the members of the family of God in heaven, will recognize one another as sons and daughters of God. They will realize that they all receive their strength and pardon from the same source, even from Jesus Christ who was crucified for their sins. They know that they are to wash their robes of character in His blood, to find acceptance with the Father in His name, if they would be in the bright assembly of the saints, clothed in the white robes of righteousness.

One in Christ

Then as the children of God are one in Christ, how does Jesus look upon caste, upon society distinctions, upon the division of man from his fellow man, because of color, race, position, wealth, birth, or attainments? The secret of unity is found in the equality of believers in Christ. The reason for all division, discord, and difference is found in separation from Christ. Christ is the center to which all should be attracted; for the nearer we approach the center, the closer we shall come together in feeling, in sympathy, in love, growing into the character and image of Jesus. With God there is no respect of persons.

Jesus knew the worthlessness of earthly pomp, and He gave no attention to its display. In His dignity of soul,

His elevation of character, His nobility of principle, He was far above the vain fashions of the world. Although the prophet describes Him as "despised and rejected of men; a man of sorrows and acquainted with grief" (Isa. 53:3), He might have been esteemed as the highest among the noble of the earth. The best circles of human society would have courted Him, had He condescended to accept their favor, but He desired not the applause of men, but moved independent of all human influence. Wealth, position, worldly rank in all its varieties and distinctions of human greatness, were all but so many degrees of littleness to Him who had left the honor and glory of heaven, and who possessed no earthly splendor, indulged in no luxury, and displayed no adornment but humility.

The lowly, those bound with poverty, pressed with care, burdened with toil, could find no reason in His life and example which would lead them to think that Jesus was not acquainted with their trials, knew not the pressure of their circumstances, and could not sympathize with them in their want and sorrow. The lowliness of His humble, daily life was in harmony with His lowly birth and circumstances. The Son of the infinite God, the Lord of life and glory, descended in humiliation to the life of the lowliest, that no one might feel himself excluded from His presence. He made Himself accessible to all. He did not select a favored few with whom to associate and ignore all others. It grieves the Spirit of God when conservatism shuts man away from his fellow man, especially when it is found among those who profess to be His children.

Christ came to give to the world an example of what perfect humanity might be when united with divinity. He presented to the world a new phase of greatness in His exhibition of mercy, compassion, and love. He gave to men a new interpretation of God. As head of humanity, He taught men lessons in the science of divine government, whereby He revealed the righteousness of the reconciliation of mercy and justice. The reconciliation of mercy and justice did not involve any compromise with sin, or ignore any claim of justice; but by giving to each divine attribute its ordained place, mercy could be exercised in the punishment of sinful, impenitent man without destroying its clemency or forfeiting its compassionate character, and justice could be exercised in forgiving the repenting transgressor without violating its integrity.

Christ Our High Priest

All this could be, because Christ laid hold of the nature of man, and partook of the divine attributes, and planted His cross between humanity and divinity, bridging the gulf that separated the sinner from God.

"For verily he took not on him the nature of angels; but he took on him the seed of Abraham. Wherefore in all things it behoved him to be made like unto his brethren, that he might be a merciful and faithful high priest in things pertaining to God, to make reconciliation for the sins of the people. For in that he himself hath suffered being tempted, he is able to succour them that are tempted" (Heb. 2:16-18).

"For we have not an high priest which cannot be touched with the feeling of our infirmities; but was in all points tempted like as we are, yet without sin" (Heb. 4:15).

"For every high priest taken from among men is ordained for men in things pertaining to God, that he may offer both gifts and sacrifices for sins: who can have compassion on the ignorant, and on them that are out of the way; for that he himself also is compassed with infirmity. And by reason hereof he ought, as for the people, so also for himself, to offer for sins. And no man taketh this honour unto himself, but he that is called of God, as was Aaron. So also Christ glorified not himself to be made an high priest; but he that said unto him, Thou art my Son, to day have I begotten thee. As he saith also in another place, Thou art a priest for ever after the order of Melchisedec. Who in the days of his flesh, when he had offered up prayers and supplications with strong crying and tears unto him that was able to save him from death, and was heard in that he feared; though he were a Son, yet learned he obedience by the things which he suffered; and being made perfect, he became the author of eternal salvation unto all them that obey him" (Heb. 5:1-9).

Jesus came to bring moral power to combine with human effort, and in no case are His followers to allow themselves to lose sight of Christ, who is their example in all things. He said, "For their sakes I sanctify myself, that they also might be sanctified through the truth" (John 17:19). Jesus presents the truth before His children that they may look upon it, and by beholding it, may become changed, being transformed by His grace from transgression to obedience, from impurity to purity, from sin to heart-holiness and righteousness of life.

A Special Class in Heaven

Some among the redeemed will have laid hold of Christ in the last hours of life, and in heaven instruction will be given to those who, when they died, did not understand perfectly the plan of salvation. Christ will lead the redeemed ones beside the river of life, and will open to them that which while on this earth they could not understand.—Undated manuscript 150.

37.

"Even So Send I You"*

"As my Father hath sent me, even so send I you" (John 20:21). We are to bear as definite a testimony to the truth as it is in Jesus, as did Christ and His apostles. Trusting in the efficiency of the Holy Spirit, we are to testify of the mercy, goodness, and love of a crucified and risen Saviour, and thus be agents through whom the darkness will be dispelled from many minds, and cause thanksgiving and praise to ascend from many hearts to God. There is a great work to be done by every son and daughter of God. Jesus says, "If ye love me, keep my commandments. And I will pray the Father, and he shall give you another Comforter, that he may abide with you for ever" (John 14:15, 16). In His prayer for His disciples, He says that He not only prayed for those in His immediate presence, but "for them also which shall believe on me through their word" (John 17:20). Again He said, "Ye have heard how I said unto you, I go away, and come again unto you. If ye loved me, ye would rejoice, because I said, I go unto the Father: for my Father is greater than I" (John 14:28). Thus we see that Christ has prayed for His people, and made them abundant promises to ensure

---

* This article appeared in *The Review and Herald*, June 25, 1895.

success to them as His colaborers. He said, "Greater works than these [those He did] shall he do; because I go unto my Father" (John 14:12).

O what great privileges belong to those who are believers and doers of the words of Christ! It is a knowledge of Christ as the sin bearer, as the propitiation for our iniquities, that enables us to live a life of holiness. This knowledge is the safeguard for the happiness of the human family. Satan knows that without this knowledge we should be thrown into confusion and divested of our strength. Our faith in God would be gone, and we should be left a prey to every artifice of the enemy. He has laid subtle plans by which to destroy man. It is his purpose to cast his hellish shadow, like the pall of death, between God and man, in order that he may hide Jesus from our view, so that he may cause us to forget the ministry of love and mercy, cut us off from further knowledge of God's great love and power to usward, and intercept every ray of light from heaven.

Christ alone was able to represent the Deity. He who had been in the presence of the Father from the beginning, He who was the express image of the invisible God, was alone sufficient to accomplish this work. No verbal description could reveal God to the world. Through a life of purity, a life of perfect trust and submission to the will of God, a life of humiliation such as even the highest seraph in heaven would have shrunk from, God Himself must be revealed to humanity. In order to do this, our Saviour clothed His divinity with humanity. He employed the human faculties, for only by adopting these could He be comprehended by humanity. Only humanity could reach humanity. He lived out the character of God through the human body which God had prepared for Him. He blessed the world by living out in human flesh the life of God, thus showing that He had the power to unite humanity to divinity.

Our Mission for Christ

Christ said: "No man knoweth the Son, but the Father; neither knoweth any man the Father, save the Son, and he to whomsoever the Son will reveal him" (Matt. 11:27). O how dimly the exalted work of the Son of God is comprehended! He held the salvation of the world in His hands. The commission given to the apostles is also given to His followers in this age. "Repentance and remission of sins should be preached in his name among all nations, beginning at Jerusalem" (Luke 24:47). Our Saviour has "all power . . . in heaven and in earth" (Matt. 28:18), and this power is promised unto us. "Ye shall receive power, after that the Holy Ghost is come upon you: and ye shall be witnesses unto me both in Jerusalem, and in all Judaea, and in Samaria, and unto the uttermost part of the earth" (Acts 1:8).

Even though a church may be composed of poor and uneducated and unknown persons, yet if they are believing, praying members, their influence will be felt for time and for eternity. If they go forth in simple faith, relying upon the promises of the Word of God, they may accomplish great good. If they let their light shine, Christ is glorified in them, and the interests of His kingdom are advanced. If they have a sense of their individual accountability to God, they will seek for opportunities to work, and will shine as lights in the world. They will be examples of sincerity and of zealous fervor in working out God's plan for the salvation of souls. The poor, the unlearned, if they choose, may become students in the school of Christ, and He will teach them true wisdom. The life of meek, childlike trust, of true piety, true religion, will be effective in its influence upon others. Persons who are highly educated are likely to depend more upon their book knowledge than upon God. Often they do not seek a knowledge of God's ways by wrestling earnestly with Him in secret prayer, laying hold upon the promises of God by faith. Those who have received the heavenly unction will go forth with a Christlike spirit, seeking an opportunity to engage others in conversation, and to reveal to them the knowledge of God and of Jesus Christ whom He has sent, whom to know is life eternal. They will become living epistles, revealing the Light of the world to mankind.

Christ has given "to every man his work" (Mark 13: 34). He expects every man to do his work with fidelity. High and low, rich and poor, all have a work to do for the Master. Every one is called to action. But if you do not obey the voice of the Lord, if you do not do His appointed work in firm reliance upon Christ as your sufficiency, if you do not follow His example, "unfaithful, slothful servant" will be registered against your name. Unless the light which has been given you is communicated to others, unless you let your light shine, it will go out in darkness, and your soul will be left in awful peril. God speaks to every one who knows the truth, "Let your light so shine before men, that they may see your good works, and glorify your Father which is in heaven" (Matt. 5:16). Communicate the knowledge of the truth to others. This is God's plan to enlighten the world. If you do not stand in your allotted place, if you do not let your light shine, you will become enshrouded in darkness. God calls upon all the sons and daughters of the heavenly family to be fully equipped, so that at any period they can step into the ranks ready for action. The heart made tender and sympathetic by the love of Jesus will find the precious pearls designed for the casket of the Lord Jesus.

38.

*The Temptation of Christ**

Christ was not in as favorable a position in the desolate wilderness to endure the temptations of Satan as was Adam when he was tempted in Eden. The Son of God humbled Himself and took man's nature after the race had wandered four thousand years from Eden, and from their original state of purity and uprightness. Sin had been making its terrible marks upon the race for ages; and physical, mental, and moral degeneracy prevailed throughout the human family.

When Adam was assailed by the tempter in Eden he was without the taint of sin. He stood in the strength of his perfection before God. All the organs and faculties of his being were equally developed, and harmoniously balanced.

Christ, in the wilderness of temptation, stood in Adam's place to bear the test he failed to endure. Here Christ overcame in the sinner's behalf, four thousand years after Adam turned his back upon the light of his home. Separated from the presence of God, the human family had been departing, every successive generation, farther from the original purity, wisdom, and knowledge which Adam possessed in Eden. Christ bore the sins and infirmities of

---

* This article appeared in *The Review and Herald*, July 28, 1874.

the race as they existed when He came to the earth to help
man. In behalf of the race, with the weaknesses of fallen
man upon Him, He was to stand the temptations of Satan
upon all points wherewith man would be assailed.

Adam was surrounded with everything his heart could
wish. Every want was supplied. There was no sin, and no
signs of decay in glorious Eden. Angels of God conversed
freely and lovingly with the holy pair. The happy songsters
caroled forth their free, joyous songs of praise to their
Creator. The peaceful beasts in happy innocence played
about Adam and Eve, obedient to their word. Adam was in
the perfection of manhood, the noblest of the Creator's
work. He was in the image of God, but a little lower than
the angels.

Christ as the Second Adam

In what contrast is the second Adam as He entered the
gloomy wilderness to cope with Satan singlehanded! Since
the Fall the race had been decreasing in size and physical
strength, and sinking lower in the scale of moral worth, up
to the period of Christ's advent to the earth. And in order
to elevate fallen man, Christ must reach him where he was.
He took human nature, and bore the infirmities and degeneracy of the race. He, who knew no sin, became sin for us.
He humiliated Himself to the lowest depths of human woe,
that He might be qualified to reach man, and bring him up
from the degradation in which sin had plunged him.

"For it became him, for whom are all things, and by
whom are all things, in bringing many sons unto glory, to
make the captain of their salvation perfect through sufferings" (Heb. 2:10). [Heb. 5:9; 2:17, 18 quoted.]

"For we have not an high priest which cannot be
touched with the feeling of our infirmities; but was in all
points tempted like as we are, yet without sin" (Heb. 4:
15).

Satan had been at war with the government of God,
since he first rebelled. His success in tempting Adam and
Eve in Eden, and introducing sin into the world, had em-
boldened this arch foe, and he had proudly boasted to the
heavenly angels that when Christ should appear, taking

man's nature, He would be weaker than himself, and he would overcome Him by his power. He exulted that Adam and Eve in Eden could not resist his insinuations when he appealed to their appetite. The inhabitants of the old world he overcame in the same manner, through the indulgence of lustful appetite and corrupt passions. Through the gratification of appetite he had overthrown the Israelites. He boasted that the Son of God Himself who was with Moses and Joshua was not able to resist his power, and lead the favored people of His choice to Canaan; for nearly all who left Egypt died in the wilderness. Also the meek man, Moses, he had tempted to take to himself glory which God claimed. David and Solomon, who had been especially favored of God, he had induced, through the indulgence of appetite and passion, to incur God's displeasure. And he boasted that he could yet succeed in thwarting the purpose of God in the salvation of man through Jesus Christ.

In the wilderness of temptation Christ was without food forty days. Moses had, on especial occasions, been thus long without food. But he felt not the pangs of hunger. He was not tempted and harassed by a vile and powerful foe, as was the Son of God. He was elevated above the human. He was especially sustained by the glory of God which enshrouded him.

Terrible Effects of Sin Upon Man

Satan had succeeded so well in deceiving the angels of God, and in the fall of noble Adam, that he thought that in Christ's humiliation he should be successful in overcoming Him. He looked with pleased exultation upon the result of his temptations and the increase of sin in the continued transgression of God's law for more than four thousand years. He had worked the ruin of our first parents, and brought sin and death into the world, and had led to ruin multitudes of all ages, countries, and classes. He had, by his power, controlled cities and nations until their sin provoked the wrath of God to destroy them by fire, water, earthquakes, sword, famine, and pestilence. By his subtlety and untiring efforts he had controlled the appetite and excited and strengthened the passions to so fearful a degree, that he had defaced, and almost obliterated the image of God in man. His physical and moral dignity were in so great a degree destroyed, that he bore but a faint resemblance in character, and noble perfection of form, to dignified Adam in Eden.

At the first advent of Christ, Satan had brought man down from his original, exalted purity, and had dimmed the fine gold with sin. He had transformed the man, created to be a sovereign in Eden, to a slave in the earth, groaning under the curse of sin. The halo of glory, which God had given holy Adam, covering him as a garment, departed from him after his transgression. The light of God's glory could not cover disobedience and sin. In the place of health and plenitude of blessings, poverty, sickness, and suffering of every type were to be the portion of the children of Adam.

Satan had, through his seductive power, led men through vain philosophy to question and finally to disbelieve in divine revelation and the existence of God. He could look abroad upon a world of moral wretchedness, and a race exposed to the wrath of a sin-avenging God, with fiendish triumph that he had been so successful in darkening the pathway of so many, and had led them to transgress the law of God. He clothed sin with pleasing attractions to secure the ruin of many.

But his most successful scheme in deceiving man has been to conceal his real purposes, and his true character, by representing himself as man's friend and a benefactor of the race. He flatters men with the pleasing fable that there is no rebellious foe, no deadly enemy that they need to guard against, and that the existence of a personal devil is all a fiction. While he thus hides his existence, he is gathering thousands under his control. He is deceiving them, as he tried to deceive Christ, that he is an angel from Heaven doing a good work for humanity. And the masses are so blinded by sin that they cannot discern the devices of Satan, and they honor him as they would a heavenly angel, while he is working their eternal ruin.

39.

First Temptation of Christ *

Christ has entered the world as Satan's destroyer, and the Redeemer of the captives bound by his power. He would leave an example in His own victorious life for man to follow and overcome the temptations of Satan. As soon as Christ entered the wilderness of temptation, His visage changed. The glory and splendor reflected from the throne of God which illuminated His countenance when the heavens opened before Him, and the Father's voice acknowledged Him as His Son in whom He was well pleased, was now gone. The weight of the sins of the world was pressing His soul, and His countenance expressed unutterable sorrow, a depth of anguish that fallen man had never realized. He felt the overwhelming tide of woe that deluged the world. He realized the strength of indulged appetite and of unholy passion that controlled the world, which had brought upon man inexpressible suffering. The indulgence of appetite had been increasing, and strengthening with every successive generation since Adam's transgression, until the race was so feeble in moral power that they could not overcome in their own strength. Christ, in behalf of the

---

* This article appeared in *The Review and Herald*, Aug. 4 and 18, 1874.

race, was to overcome appetite by standing the most powerful test upon this point. He was to tread the path of temptation alone, and there must be none to help Him, none to comfort or uphold Him. He was to wrestle with the powers of darkness.

As man could not, in his human strength, resist the power of Satan's temptations, Jesus volunteered to undertake the work, and bear the burden for man, and overcome the power of appetite in his behalf. He must show in man's behalf, self-denial and perseverance, and firmness of principle that is paramount to the gnawing pangs of hunger. He must show a power of control over appetite stronger than hunger and even death.

Significance of the Test

When Christ bore the test of temptation upon the point of appetite, He did not stand in beautiful Eden, as did Adam, with the light and love of God seen in everything His eye rested upon. But He was in a barren, desolate wilderness, surrounded with wild beasts. Everything around Him was repulsive, and [that] from which human nature would be inclined to shrink. With these surroundings He fasted forty days and forty nights, "and in those days he did eat nothing" (Luke 4:2). He was emaciated through long fasting, and felt the keenest sense of hunger. His visage was indeed marred more than the sons of men.

Christ thus entered upon His life of conflict to overcome the mighty foe, in bearing the very test Adam failed to endure, that, through successful conflict, He might break the power of Satan, and redeem the race from the disgrace of the Fall.

All was lost when Adam yielded to the power of appetite. The Redeemer, in whom was united both the human and the divine, stood in Adam's place, and endured a terrible fast of nearly six weeks. The length of this fast is the strongest evidence of the extent of the sinfulness and power of debased appetite upon the human family.

The humanity of Christ reached to the very depths of human wretchedness, and identified itself with the weaknesses and necessities of fallen man, while His divine nature grasped the Eternal. His work in bearing the guilt of man's transgression was not to give him license to continue to violate the law of God, which made man a debtor to the law, which debt Christ was Himself paying by His own suffering. The trials and sufferings of Christ were to impress man with a sense of his great sin in breaking the law of God, and to bring him to repentance and obedience to that law, and through obedience to acceptance with God. His righteousness He would impute to man, and thus raise him in moral value with God, so that his efforts to keep the divine law would be acceptable. Christ's work was to reconcile man to God through His human nature, and God to man through His divine nature.

As soon as the long fast of Christ commenced in the wilderness, Satan was at hand with his temptations. He came to Christ, enshrouded in light, claiming to be one of the angels from the throne of God, sent upon an errand of mercy to sympathize with Him, and to relieve Him of His suffering condition. He tried to make Christ believe that God did not require Him to pass through self-denial and the sufferings He anticipated; that he had been sent from heaven to bear to Him the message that God only designed to prove His willingness to endure.

Satan told Christ that He was only to set His feet in the bloodstained path, but not to travel it. Like Abraham He was tested to show His perfect obedience. He also stated that he was the angel that stayed the hand of Abraham as the knife was raised to slay Isaac, and he had now come to save His life; that it was not necessary for Him to endure the painful hunger and death from starvation; he would help Him bear a part of the work in the plan of salvation.

The Son of God turned from all these artful temptations, and was steadfast in His purpose to carry out in every particular, in the spirit and in the very letter, the plan which had been devised for the redemption of the fallen race. But Satan had manifold temptations prepared to ensnare Christ, and obtain advantage of Him. If he failed in one temptation, he would try another. He thought he would succeed, because Christ had humbled Himself as a man. He flattered himself that his assumed character, as one of the heavenly angels, could not be discerned. He feigned to doubt the divinity of Christ, because of His emaciated appearance and unpleasant surroundings.

Christ knew that in taking the nature of man He would not be in appearance equal to the angels of heaven. Satan urged that if He was indeed the Son of God He should give him evidence of His exalted character. He approached Christ with temptations upon appetite. He had overcome Adam upon this point and he had controlled his descendants, and through indulgence of appetite led them to provoke God by iniquity, until their crimes were so great that the Lord destroyed them from off the earth by the waters of the Flood.

Under Satan's direct temptations the children of Israel suffered appetite to control reason, and they were, through indulgence, led to commit grievous sins which awakened the wrath of God against them, and they fell in the wilderness. He thought that he should be successful in overcoming Christ with the same temptation. He told Christ that one of the exalted angels had been exiled to the world, and that His appearance indicated that, instead of His being the King of heaven, He was the angel fallen, and this explained His emaciated and distressed appearance.

Christ Did No Miracle for Himself

He then called the attention of Christ to his own attractive appearance, clothed with light and strong in power. He claimed to be a messenger direct from the throne of Heaven, and asserted that he had a right to demand of Christ evidences of His being the Son of God. Satan would fain disbelieve, if he could, the words that came from heaven to the Son of God at His baptism. He determined to overcome Christ, and, if possible, make his own kingdom and life secure. His first temptation to Christ was upon appetite. He had, upon this point, almost entire control of the world, and his temptations were adapted to the circumstances and surroundings of Christ, which made his temptations upon appetite almost over-powering.

Christ could have worked a miracle on His own account; but this would not have been in accordance with the plan of salvation. The many miracles in the life of Christ show His power to work miracles for the benefit of suffering humanity. By a miracle of mercy He fed five thousand at once with five loaves and two small fishes. Therefore He had power to work a miracle, and satisfy His own hunger. Satan flattered himself that he could lead Christ to doubt the words spoken from heaven at His baptism. And if he could tempt Him to question His sonship, and doubt the truth of the word spoken by His Father, he would gain a great victory.

He found Christ in the desolate wilderness without companions, without food, and in actual suffering. His surroundings were most melancholy and repulsive. Satan suggested to Christ that God would not leave His Son in this condition of want and real suffering. He hoped to shake the confidence of Christ in His Father, who had permitted Him to be brought into this condition of extreme suffering in the desert, where the feet of man had never trod. Satan hoped to insinuate doubts as to His Father's love that would find a lodgment in the mind of Christ, and that under the force of despondency and extreme hunger He would exert His miraculous power in His own behalf, and take Himself out of the hands of His heavenly Father. This was indeed a temptation to Christ. But He cherished it not for a moment. He did not for a single moment doubt His heavenly Father's love, although He seemed to be bowed down with inexpressible anguish. Satan's temptations, though skillfully devised, did not move the integrity of God's dear Son. His abiding confidence in His Father could not be shaken.

Christ Did Not Parley With Temptation

Jesus did not condescend to explain to His enemy how He was the Son of God, and in what manner, as such, He was to act. In an insulting, taunting manner Satan referred to the present weakness and the unfavorable appearance of Christ in contrast with his own strength and glory. He taunted Christ that He was a poor representative of the angels, much more of their exalted Commander, the acknowledged King in the royal courts. His present appearance indicated that He was forsaken of God and man. He said if Christ was indeed the Son of God, the monarch of heaven, He had power equal with God, and He could give him evidence by working a miracle and changing the stone just at His feet into bread, and relieve His hunger. Satan promised that, if Christ would do this, he would at once yield his claims of superiority, and that the contest between himself and Christ should there be forever ended.

Christ did not appear to notice the reviling taunts of Satan. He was not provoked to give him proofs of His power. He meekly bore his insults without retaliation. The words spoken from heaven at His baptism were very precious, evidencing to Him that His Father approved the steps He was taking in the plan of salvation as man's substitute and surety. The opening heavens, and descent of the heavenly dove, were assurances that His Father would unite His power in heaven with that of His Son upon the earth, to rescue man from the control of Satan, and that God accepted the effort of Christ to link earth to heaven, and finite man to the infinite.

These tokens, received from His Father, were inexpressibly precious to the Son of God through all His severe sufferings and terrible conflict with the rebel chief. And while enduring the test of God in the wilderness, and through His entire ministry, He had nothing to do in convincing Satan of His own power, and of His being the Saviour of the world. Satan had sufficient evidence of His exalted station. His unwillingness to ascribe to Jesus the honor due to Him, and manifest submission as a subordinate, ripened into rebellion against God, and shut him out of heaven.

It was not any part of the mission of Christ to exercise His divine power for His own benefit, to relieve Himself from suffering. This He had volunteered to take upon Himself. He had condescended to take man's nature, and He was to suffer the inconveniences, and ills, and afflictions of the human family. He was not to perform miracles on His own account. He came to save others. The object of His mission was to bring blessings, and hope, and life, to the afflicted and oppressed. He was to bear the burdens and griefs of suffering humanity.

Although Christ was suffering the keenest pangs of hunger, He withstood the temptations. He repulsed Satan with scripture, the same He had given Moses in the wilderness to repeat to rebellious Israel when their diet was restricted, and they were clamoring for flesh meats, "Man shall not live by bread alone, but by every word that proceedeth out of the mouth of God" (Matt. 4:4). In this declaration, and also by His example, Christ would show man that hunger for temporal food was not the greatest calamity that could befall him. Satan flattered our first parents that eating of the fruit of the tree of life* of which God had forbidden them would bring to them great good, and would ensure them against death, the very opposite of the truth which God had declared to them. "But of the tree of the knowledge of good and evil, thou shalt not eat of it: for in the day that thou eatest thereof thou shalt surely die" (Gen. 2:17). If Adam had been obedient, he would never have known want, sorrow, or death.

If the people who lived before the Flood had been obedient to the word of God, they would have been preserved, and would not have perished by the waters of the Flood. If the Israelites had been obedient to the words of God, He would have bestowed upon them special blessings. But they fell in consequence of the indulgence of appetite and passion. They would not be obedient to the words of God. Indulgence of perverted appetite led them

---

* The tree here referred to is obviously the tree of knowledge and not the tree of life. The phrase "of life" is patently a printer's error. It is not found in the first appearance of this article, in *The Signs of the Times* for July 9, 1874, nor in the reprint in pamphlet form, titled "Redemption or the Temptation of Christ," page 42.—COMPLIERS.

into numerous and grievous sins. If they had made the requirements of God their first consideration, and their physical wants secondary, in submission to God's choice of proper food for them, not one of them would have fallen in the wilderness. They would have been established in the goodly land of Canaan a holy, healthy people, with not a feeble one in all their tribes.

The Saviour of the world became sin for the race. In becoming man's substitute, Christ did not manifest His power as the Son of God. He ranked Himself among the sons of men. He was to bear the trial of temptation as a man, in man's behalf, under the most trying circumstances, and leave an example of faith and perfect trust in His heavenly Father. Christ knew that His Father would supply Him food when it would gratify Him to do so. He would not in this severe ordeal, when hunger pressed Him beyond measure, prematurely diminish one particle of the trial allotted to Him by exercising His divine power.

Fallen man, when brought into straightened places, could not have the power to work miracles on his own behalf, to save himself from pain or anguish, or to give himself victory over his enemies. It was the purpose of God to test and prove the race, and give them an opportunity to develop character by bringing them frequently into trying positions to test their faith and confidence in His love and power. The life of Christ was a perfect pattern. He was ever, by His example and precept, teaching man that God was his dependence, and that in God should be his faith and firm trust.

Christ knew that Satan was a liar from the beginning, and it required strong self-control to listen to the propositions of this insulting deceiver, and not instantly rebuke his bold assumptions. Satan expected to provoke the Son of God to engage in controversy with him; and he hoped that thus, in His extreme weakness and agony of spirit, he could obtain advantage over Him. He designed to pervert the words of Christ and claim advantage, and call to his aid his fallen angels to use their utmost power to prevail against and overcome Him.

The Saviour of the world had no controversy with Satan, who was expelled from heaven because he was no longer worthy of a place there. He who could influence the angels of God against their Supreme Ruler, and against His Son, their loved commander, and enlist their sympathy for himself, was capable of any deception. Four thousand years he had been warring against the government of God, and had lost none of his skill or power to tempt and deceive.

Victory Through Christ

Because man fallen could not overcome Satan with his human strength, Christ came from the royal courts of heaven to help him with His human and divine strength combined. Christ knew that Adam in Eden, with his superior advantages, might have withstood the temptations of Satan, and conquered him. He also knew that it was not possible for man, out of Eden, separated from the light and love of God since the Fall, to resist the temptations of Satan in his own strength. In order to bring hope to man, and save him from complete ruin, He humbled Himself to take man's nature, that, with His divine power combined with the human, He might reach man where he is. He obtains for the fallen sons and daughters of Adam that strength which it is impossible for them to gain for themselves, that in His name they may overcome the temptations of Satan.

The exalted Son of God in assuming humanity draws Himself nearer to man by standing as the sinner's substitute. He identifies Himself with the sufferings and afflictions of men. He was tempted in all points as man is tempted, that He might know how to succor those who should be tempted. Christ overcame on the sinner's behalf.

Jacob, in the night vision, saw earth connected with heaven by a ladder reaching to the throne of God. He saw the angels of God, clothed with garments of heavenly brightness, passing down from heaven and up to heaven upon this shining ladder. The bottom of this ladder rested

upon the earth, while the top of it reached to the highest
heavens, and rested upon the throne of Jehovah. The
brightness from the throne of God beamed down upon
this ladder, and reflected a light of inexpressible glory upon
the earth.

This ladder represented Christ, who had opened the
communication between earth and heaven. In Christ's
humiliation He descended to the very depth of human
woe in sympathy and pity for fallen man, which was
represented to Jacob by one end of the ladder resting upon
the earth, while the top of the ladder, reaching unto
heaven, represents the divine power of Christ, who grasps
the Infinite, and thus links earth to heaven and finite
man to the infinite God. Through Christ the communication
is opened between God and man. Angels may pass from
heaven to earth with messages of love to fallen man, and
to minister unto those who shall be heirs of salvation. It
is through Christ alone that the heavenly messengers
minister to men.

Adam and Eve in Eden were placed under most favorable circumstances. It was their privilege to hold communion with God and angels. They were without the
condemnation of sin. The light of God and angels was
with them, and around about them. The Author of their
existence was their teacher. But they fell beneath the
power and temptations of the artful foe. Four thousand
years had Satan been at work against the government of
God, and he had obtained strength and experience from
determined practice. Fallen men had not the advantages
of Adam in Eden. They had been separating from God for
four thousand years. The wisdom to understand, and
power to resist, the temptations of Satan had become less
and less, until Satan seemed to reign triumphant in the
earth. Appetite and passion, the love of the world and presumptuous sins, were the great branches of evil out of
which every species of crime, violence, and corruption
grew.

40.

Second Temptation of Christ*

Satan was defeated in his object to overcome Christ upon the point of appetite; and here in the wilderness Christ achieved a victory in behalf of the race upon the point of appetite, making it possible for man in all future time in His name to overcome the strength of appetite on his own behalf. Satan was not willing to cease his efforts until he had tried every means to obtain victory over the world's Redeemer. He knew that with himself all was at stake, whether he or Christ should be victor in the contest. And, in order to awe Christ with his superior strength, he carried Him to Jerusalem and set Him on a pinnacle of the Temple, and continued to beset Him with temptations.

He again demanded of Christ, if He was indeed the Son of God, to give him evidence by casting Himself from the dizzy height upon which he had placed Him. He urged Christ to show His confidence in the preserving care of His Father by casting Himself down from the Temple. In Satan's first temptation upon the point of appetite, he had tried to insinuate doubts in regard to God's love and care for Christ as His Son, by presenting His

---

* This article appeared in *The Review and Herald*, Aug. 18 and Sept. 1, 1874.

surroundings and His hunger as evidence that He was not in favor with God. He was unsuccessful in this. He next tried to take advantage of the faith and perfect trust Christ had shown in His heavenly Father to urge Him to presumption. "If thou be the Son of God, cast thyself down: for it is written, He shall give his angels charge concerning thee: and in their hands they shall bear thee up, lest at any time thou dash thy foot against a stone" (Matt. 4:6). Jesus promptly answered, "It is written again, Thou shalt not tempt the Lord thy God" (Matt. 4:7).

The Sin of Presumption

The sin of presumption lies close beside the virtue of perfect faith and confidence in God. Satan flattered himself that he could take advantage of the humanity of Christ to urge Him over the line of trust to presumption. Upon this point many souls are wrecked. Satan tried to deceive Christ through flattery. He admitted that Christ was right in the wilderness in His faith and confidence that God was His Father, under the most trying circumstances. He then urged Christ to give him one more proof of His entire dependence upon God, one more evidence of His faith that He was the Son of God, by casting Himself from the Temple. He told Christ that if He was indeed the Son of God He had nothing to fear; for angels were at hand to uphold Him. Satan gave evidence that he understood the Scriptures by the use he made of them.

The Redeemer of the world wavered not from His integrity and showed that He had perfect faith in His Father's promised care. He would not put the faithfulness and love of His Father to a needless trial, although He was in the hands of the enemy, and placed in a position of extreme difficulty and peril. He would not, at Satan's suggestion, tempt God by presumptuously experimenting on His providence. Satan had brought in scripture which seemed appropriate for the occasion, hoping to accomplish his designs by making the application to our Saviour at this special time.

Christ knew that God could indeed bear Him up if

He had required Him to throw Himself from the Temple. But to do this unbidden, and to experiment upon His Father's protecting care and love, because dared by Satan to do so, would not show His strength of faith. Satan was well aware that if Christ could be prevailed upon, unbidden by His Father, to fling Himself from the Temple to prove His claim to His heavenly Father's protecting care, He would in the very act show the weakness of His human nature.

Christ came off victor in the second temptation. He manifested perfect confidence and trust in His Father during His severe conflict with the powerful foe. Our Redeemer, in the victory here gained, has left man a perfect pattern, showing him that his only safety is in firm trust and unwavering confidence in God in all trials and perils. He refused to presume upon the mercy of His Father by placing Himself in peril that would make it necessary for His heavenly Father to display His power to save Him from danger. This would be forcing providence on His own account; and He would not then leave for His people a perfect example of faith and firm trust in God.

Satan's object in tempting Christ was to lead Him to daring presumption, and to show human weakness that would not make Him a perfect pattern for His people. Satan thought that should Christ fail to bear the test of his temptations, there could be no redemption for the race, and his power over them would be complete.

Christ Our Hope and Example

The humiliation and agonizing sufferings of Christ in the wilderness of temptation were for the race. In Adam all was lost through transgression. Through Christ was man's only hope of restoration to the favor of God. Man had separated himself at such a distance from God by transgression of His law, that he could not humiliate himself before God proportionate to his grievous sin. The Son of God could fully understand the aggravating sins of the transgressor, and in His sinless character He alone could make an acceptable atonement for man in suffering the agonizing sense of His Father's displeasure. The sorrow and anguish of the Son of God for the sins of the world were proportionate to His divine excellence and purity, as well as to the magnitude of the offense.

Christ was our example in all things. As we see His humiliation in the long trial and fast in the wilderness to overcome the temptations of appetite in our behalf, we are to take this lesson home to ourselves when we are tempted. If the power of appetite is so strong upon the human family, and its indulgence so fearful that the Son of God subjected Himself to such a test, how important that we feel the necessity of having appetite under the control of reason. Our Saviour fasted nearly six weeks, that He might gain for man the victory upon the point of appetite. How can professed Christians with an enlightened conscience, and Christ before them as their pattern, yield to the indulgence of those appetites which have an enervating influence upon the mind and heart? It is a painful fact that habits of self-gratification at the expense of health, and the weakening of moral power, are holding in the bonds of slavery at the present time a large share of the Christian world.

Many who profess godliness do not inquire into the reason of Christ's long period of fasting and suffering in the wilderness. His anguish was not so much from enduring the pangs of hunger as from His sense of the fearful result of the indulgence of appetite and passion upon the race. He knew that appetite would be man's idol, and would lead him to forget God, and would stand directly in the way of his salvation.

41.

Third Temptation of Christ *

Our Saviour showed perfect confidence in His heavenly Father, that He would not suffer Him to be tempted above what He should give Him strength to endure, and would bring Him óff conqueror if He patiently bore the test to which He was subjected. Christ had not, of His own will, placed Himself in danger. God had suffered Satan, for the time being, to have this power over His Son. Jesus knew that if He preserved His integrity in this extremely trying position, an angel of God would be sent to relieve Him if there was no other way. He had taken humanity, and was the representative of the race.

Satan saw that he prevailed nothing with Christ in his second great temptation. "And the devil, taking him up into an high mountain, shewed unto him all the kingdoms of the world in a moment of time. And the devil said unto him, All this power will I give thee, and the glory of them: for that is delivered unto me; and to whomsoever I will I give it. If thou therefore wilt worship me, all shall be thine" (Luke 4:5-7).

In the first two great temptations Satan had not revealed his true purposes or his character. He claimed to be

* This article appeared in *The Review and Herald,* Sept. 1, 1874.

an exalted messenger from the courts of heaven, but he
now throws off his disguise. In a panoramic view he presented before Christ all the kingdoms of the world in the
most attractive light, while he claimed to be the prince of
the world.

The Most Alluring Temptation

This last temptation was the most alluring of the three.
Satan knew that Christ's life must be one of sorrow, hard-
ship, and conflict. And he thought he could take advantage of this fact to bribe Christ to yield His integrity.
Satan brought all his strength to bear upon this last
temptation, for this last effort was to decide his destiny as
to who should be victor. He claimed the world as his
dominion, and he was the prince of the power of the air.
He bore Jesus to the top of an exceeding high mountain,
and then in a panoramic view presented before Him all the
kingdoms of the world that had been so long under his
dominion, and offered them to Him in one great gift. He
told Christ He could come into possession of the kingdoms
of the world without suffering or peril on His part. Satan
promises to yield his scepter and dominion, and Christ
shall be rightful ruler for one favor from Him. All he
requires in return for making over to Him the kingdoms
of the world that day presented before Him, is, that Christ
shall do him homage as to a superior.

The eye of Jesus for a moment rested upon the glory
presented before Him; but He turned away and refused to
look upon the entrancing spectacle. He would not endan-
ger His steadfast integrity by dallying with the tempter.
When Satan solicited homage, Christ's divine indignation
was aroused, and He could no longer tolerate the blas-
phemous assumption of Satan, or even permit him to remain in His presence. Here Christ exercised His divine
authority, and commanded Satan to desist. "Get thee
hence, Satan: for it is written, Thou shalt worship the
Lord thy God, and him only shalt thou serve" (Matt. 4:
10). Satan, in his pride and arrogance, had declared himself to be the rightful and permanent ruler of the world,

the possessor of all its riches and glory, claiming homage of all who lived in it, as though he had created the world and all things that were therein. Said he to Christ: "All this power will I give thee, and the glory of them: for that is delivered unto me; and to whomsoever I will I give it" (Luke 4:6). He endeavored to make a special contract with Christ, to make over to Him at once the whole of his claim, if He would worship him.

This insult to the Creator moved the indignation of the Son of God to rebuke and dismiss him. Satan had flattered himself in his first temptation that he had so well concealed his true character and purposes that Christ did not recognize him as the fallen rebel chief whom He had conquered and expelled from heaven. The words of dismissal from Christ, "Get thee hence, Satan," evidenced that he was known from the first, and that all his deceptive arts had been unsuccessful upon the Son of God. Satan knew that if Jesus should die to redeem man, his power must end after a season, and he would be destroyed. Therefore, it was his studied plan to prevent, if possible, the completion of the great work which had been commenced by the Son of God. If the plan of man's redemption should fail, he would retain the kingdom which he then claimed. And if he should succeed, he flattered himself that he would reign in opposition to the God of heaven.

When Jesus left heaven, and there left His power and glory, Satan exulted. He thought that the Son of God was placed in his power. The temptation took so easily with the holy pair in Eden, that he hoped he could with his satanic cunning and power overthrow even the Son of God, and thereby save his life and kingdom. If he could tempt Jesus to depart from the will of His Father, as he had done in his temptation with Adam and Eve, then his object would be gained.

The time was to come when Jesus should redeem the possession of Satan by giving His own life, and, after a season, all in heaven and earth should submit to Him. Jesus was steadfast. He chose His life of suffering, His

ignominious death, and, in the way appointed by His
Father, to become a lawful ruler of the kingdoms of the
earth, and have them given into His hands as an everlasting possession. Satan also will be given into His hands
to be destroyed by death, nevermore to annoy Jesus, or
the saints in glory.

Temptation Decidedly Resisted

Jesus said to this wily foe, "Get thee hence, Satan: for
it is written, Thou shalt worship the Lord thy God, and
him only shalt thou serve" (Matt. 4:10). Satan had asked
Christ to give him evidence that He was the Son of God,
and he had in this instance the proof he had asked. At the
divine command of Christ he was compelled to obey. He
was repulsed and silenced. He had no power to enable
him to withstand the peremptory dismissal. He was compelled without another word to instantly desist and to
leave the world's Redeemer.

The hateful presence of Satan was withdrawn. The
contest was ended. With immense suffering Christ's victory in the wilderness was as complete as was the failure of
Adam. And for a season He stood freed from the presence
of His powerful adversary, and from his legions of angels.

After Satan had ended his temptations he departed
from Jesus for a little season. The foe was conquered, but
the conflict had been long and exceedingly trying. And
after it was ended Christ was exhausted and fainting. He
fell upon the ground as though dying. Heavenly angels
who had bowed before Him in the royal courts, and who
had been with intense, yet painful, interest watching
their loved Commander, and with amazement had witnessed the terrible contest He had endured with Satan, now
came and ministered unto Him. They prepared Him food
and strengthened Him, for He lay as one dead. Angels
were filled with amazement and awe, as they knew the
world's Redeemer was passing through inexpressible suffering to achieve the redemption of man. He who was
equal with God in the royal courts, was before them
emaciated from nearly six weeks of fasting. Solitary and

alone He had been pursued by the rebel chief, who had been expelled from heaven. He had endured a more close and severe test than would ever be brought to bear upon man. The warfare with the power of darkness had been long and intensely trying to Christ's human nature in His weak and suffering condition. The angels brought messages of love and comfort from the Father to His Son, and also the assurance that all heaven triumphed in the full and entire victory He had gained in behalf of man.

The cost of the redemption of the race can never be fully realized until the redeemed shall stand with the Redeemer, by the throne of God. And as they have capacity to appreciate the value of immortal life, and the eternal reward, they will swell the song of victory and immortal triumph, "Saying with a loud voice, Worthy is the Lamb that was slain to receive power, and riches, and wisdom, and strength, and honour, and glory, and blessing" (Rev. 5:12). "And every creature," says John, "which is in heaven, and on the earth, and under the earth, and such as are in the sea, and all that are in them, heard I saying, Blessing, and honour, and glory, and power, be unto him that sitteth upon the throne, and unto the Lamb for ever and ever" (Rev. 5:13).

Although Satan had failed in his strongest efforts, and most powerful temptations, yet he had not given up all hope that he might, at some future time, be more successful in his efforts. He looked forward to the period of Christ's ministry, when he should have opportunities to try his power and artifices against Him. Satan laid his plans to blind the understanding of the Jews, God's chosen people, that they would not discern in Christ the world's Redeemer. He thought he could fill their hearts with envy, jealousy, and hatred against the Son of God, so that they would not receive Him, but make His life upon earth as bitter as possible.

42.

*The Revelation of God**

"God, who commanded the light to shine out of darkness, hath shined in our hearts, to give the light of the knowledge of the glory of God in the face of Jesus Christ" (2 Cor. 4:6).

Before the Fall, not a cloud rested upon the minds of our first parents to obscure their clear perception of the character of God. They were perfectly conformed to the will of God. For a covering, a beautiful light, the light of God, surrounded them. The Lord visited the holy pair, and instructed them through the works of His hands. Nature was their lesson book. In the Garden of Eden the existence of God was demonstrated in the objects of nature that surrounded them. Every tree of the garden spoke to them. The invisible things of God were clearly seen, being understood by the things which were made, even His eternal power and Godhead.

But while it is true that God could thus be discerned in nature, this does not favor the assertion that after the Fall a perfect knowledge of God was revealed in the natural world to Adam and his posterity. Nature could convey her lessons to man in his innocence; but transgression brought

---

* This article appeared in *The Review and Herald*, Nov. 8, 1898.

a blight upon nature, and intervened between nature and nature's God. Had Adam and Eve never disobeyed their Creator, had they remained in the path of perfect rectitude, they could have known and understood God. But when they listened to the voice of the tempter, and sinned against God, the light of the garments of heavenly innocence departed from them; and in parting with the garments of innocence, they drew about them the dark robes of ignorance of God. The clear and perfect light that had hitherto surrounded them had lightened everything they approached; but deprived of that heavenly light, the posterity of Adam could no longer trace the character of God in His created works.

The things of nature upon which we look today give us but a faint conception of Eden's beauty and glory; yet the natural world, with unmistakable voice, proclaims the glory of God. In the things of nature, marred as they are by the blight of sin, much that is beautiful remains. One omnipotent in power, great in goodness, in mercy, and love, has created the earth, and even in its blighted state it inculcates truths in regard to the skillful Master Artist. In this book of nature opened to us—in the beautiful, scented flowers, with their varied and delicate coloring— God gives to us an unmistakable expression of His love. After the transgression of Adam, God might have destroyed every opening bud and blooming flower, or He might have taken away their fragrance, so grateful to the senses. In the earth, seared and marred by the curse, in the briers, the thistles, the thorns, the tares, we may read the law of condemnation; but in the delicate color and perfume of the flowers, we may learn that God still loves us, that His mercy is not wholly withdrawn from the earth.

Nature is filled with spiritual lessons for mankind. The flowers die only to spring forth into new life; and in this we are taught the lesson of the resurrection. All who love God will bloom again in the Eden above. But nature cannot teach the lesson of the great and marvelous love of God. Therefore, after the Fall, nature was not the only teacher of man. In order that the world might not remain in darkness, in eternal spiritual night, the God of nature met us in Jesus Christ. The Son of God came to the world as the revelation of the Father. He was that "true Light, which lighteth every man that cometh into the world" (John 1:9). We are to behold "the light of the knowledge of the glory of God in the face of Jesus Christ" (2 Cor. 4:6).

In the person of His only-begotten Son, the God of heaven has condescended to stoop to our human nature. To the question of Thomas, Jesus said: "I am the way, the truth, and the life: no man cometh unto the Father, but by me. If ye had known me, ye should have known my Father also: and from henceforth ye know him, and have seen him. Philip saith unto him, Lord, shew us the Father, and it sufficeth us. Jesus saith unto him, Have I been so long time with you, and yet hast thou not known me, Philip? he that hath seen me hath seen the Father; and how sayest thou then, Shew us the Father? Believest thou not that I am in the Father, and the Father in me? the words that I speak unto you I speak not of myself: but the Father that dwelleth in me, he doeth the works. Believe me that I am in the Father, and the Father in me: or else believe me for the very works' sake" (John 14:6-11).

The most difficult and humiliating lesson that man has to learn is his own inefficiency in depending upon human wisdom, and the sure failure of his own efforts to read nature correctly. Sin has obscured his vision, and of himself he cannot interpret nature without placing it above God. He cannot discern in it God, or Jesus Christ, whom He has sent. He is in the same position as were the Athenians, who erected their altars for the worship of nature. Standing in the midst of Mars' Hill, Paul presented before the people of Athens the majesty of the living God in contrast with their idolatrous worship.

"Ye men of Athens," he said, "I perceive that in all things ye are too superstitious. For as I passed by, and beheld your devotions, I found an altar with this inscription, TO THE UNKNOWN GOD. Whom therefore ye ignorantly worship, him declare I unto you. God that made the world and all things therein, seeing that he is Lord of heaven and earth, dwelleth not in temples made with hands; neither is worshipped with men's hands, as though he needed any thing, seeing he giveth to all life, and breath, and all things; and hath made of one blood all nations of men for to dwell on all the face of the earth, and hath determined the times before appointed, and the bounds of their habitation; that they should seek the Lord, if haply they might feel after him, and find him, though he be not far from every one of us: for in him we live, and move, and have our being; as certain also of your own poets have said, For we are also his offspring. Forasmuch then as we are the offspring of God, we ought not to think that the Godhead is like unto gold, or silver, or stone, graven by art and man's device" (Acts 17:22-29).

Nature Is Not God

Those who have a true knowledge of God will not become so infatuated with the laws of matter or the operations of nature as to overlook, or refuse to acknowledge, the continual working of God in nature. Nature is not God, nor was it ever God. The voice of nature testifies of God, but nature is not God. As His created work, it simply bears a testimony to God's power. Deity is the author of nature. The natural world has, in itself, no power but that which God supplies. There is a personal God, the Father; there is a personal Christ, the Son. And "God, who at sundry times and in divers manners spake in time past unto the fathers by the prophets, hath in these last days spoken unto us by his Son, whom he hath appointed heir of all things, by whom also he made the worlds; who being the brightness of his glory, and the express image of his person, and upholding all things by the word of his power, when he had by himself purged our sins, sat down on the right hand of the Majesty on high" (Heb. 1:1-3).

The psalmist says: "The heavens declare the glory of God; and the firmament sheweth his handywork. Day unto day uttereth speech, and night unto night sheweth knowledge. There is no speech nor language, where their voice is not heard" (Ps. 19:1-3). Some may suppose that these grand things in the natural world are God. They are not God. All these wonders in the heavens are only doing the work appointed them. They are the Lord's agencies. God is the superintendent, as well as the Creator, of all things. The Divine Being is engaged in upholding the things that He has created. The same hand that holds the mountains and balances them in position, guides the worlds in their mysterious march around the sun.

There is scarcely an operation of nature to which we may not find reference in the Word of God. The Word declares that "he maketh his sun to rise," and the rain to descend (Matt. 5:45). He "maketh grass to grow upon the mountains." "He giveth snow like wool: he scattereth the hoarfrost like ashes. He casteth forth his ice like morsels. . . . He sendeth out his word, and melteth them: he causeth his wind to blow, and the waters flow" (Ps. 147:8, 16-18). "He maketh lightnings for the rain; he bringeth the wind out of his treasuries" (Ps. 135:7).

These words of Holy Writ say nothing of the independent laws of nature. God furnishes the matter and the properties with which to carry out His plans. He employs His agencies that vegetation may flourish. He sends the dew and the rain and the sunshine, that verdure may spring forth, and spread its carpet over the earth; that the shrubs and fruit trees may bud and blossom and bring forth. It is not to be supposed that a law is set in motion for the seed to work itself, that the leaf appears because it must do so of itself. God has laws that He has instituted, but they are only the servants through which He effects results. It is through the immediate agency of God that every tiny seed breaks through the earth, and springs into life. Every leaf grows, every flower blooms, by the power of God.

The physical organism of man is under the supervision of God; but it is not like a clock, which is set in operation, and must go of itself. The heart beats, pulse succeeds pulse, breath succeeds breath, but the entire being is under the supervision of God. "Ye are God's husbandry, ye are God's building" (1 Cor. 3:9). In God we live and move and have our being. Each heartbeat, each breath, is the inspiration of Him who breathed into the nostrils of Adam the breath of life—the inspiration of the ever-present God, the great I AM.

The ancient philosophers prided themselves on their superior knowledge. Let us read the inspired apostle's understanding of the matter. "Professing themselves to be wise," he says, "they became fools, and changed the glory of the uncorruptible God into an image made like to corruptible man, and to birds, and fourfooted beasts, and creeping things. . . . Who changed the truth of God into a lie, and worshipped and served the creature more than the Creator" (Rom. 1:22-25). In its human wisdom the world cannot know God. Its wise men gather an imperfect knowledge of God from His created works, and then in their foolishness they exalt nature and the laws of nature above nature's God. Those who have not a knowledge of God through an acceptance of the revelation He has made of Himself in Christ, will obtain only an imperfect knowledge of Him in nature; and this knowledge, so far from giving elevated conceptions of God, and bringing the whole being into conformity to His will, will make men idolaters. Professing themselves to be wise, they will become fools.

Those who think they can obtain a knowledge of God aside from His Representative, whom the Word declares is "the express image of his person" (Heb. 1:3), will need to become fools in their own estimation before they can be wise. It is impossible to gain a perfect knowledge of God from nature alone; for nature itself is imperfect. In its imperfection it cannot represent God, it cannot reveal the character of God in its moral perfection. But Christ came as a personal Saviour to the world. He represented a personal God. As a personal Saviour, He ascended on high; and He will come again as He ascended to heaven—a personal Saviour. He is the express image of the Father's person. "In him dwelleth all the fulness of the Godhead bodily" (Col. 2:9).

43.

*Christ the Life-giver**

"In the beginning was the Word, and the Word was with God, and the Word was God. The same was in the beginning with God. All things were made by him; and without him was not any thing made that was made. In him was life; and the life was the light of men. And the light shineth in darkness; and the darkness comprehended it not" (John 1:1-5). The world did not see divinity in the humble Man of Nazareth. The only-begotten Son of the infinite God was in the world, and men knew Him not in His true character.

"In him was life; and the life was the light of men" (John 1:4). It is not physical life that is here specified, but immortality, the life which is exclusively the property of God. The Word, who was with God, and who was God, had this life. Physical life is something which each individual receives. It is not eternal or immortal; for God, the Life-giver, takes it again. Man has no control over his life. But the life of Christ was unborrowed. No one can take this life from Him. "I lay it down of myself" (John 10: 18), He said. In Him was life, original, unborrowed, underived. This life is not inherent in man. He can possess

---

* This article appeared in *The Signs of the Times,* April 8, 1897.

it only through Christ. He cannot earn it; it is given him as a free gift if he will believe in Christ as His personal Saviour. "This is life eternal, that they might know thee the only true God, and Jesus Christ, whom thou hast sent" (John 17:3). This is the open fountain of life for the world.

Giving his charge to Timothy, Paul says, "But thou, O man of God, flee these things; and follow after righteousness, godliness, faith, love, patience, meekness. Fight the good fight of faith, lay hold on eternal life, whereunto thou art also called, and hast professed a good profession before many witnesses. I give thee charge in the sight of God, who quickeneth all things, and before Christ Jesus, who before Pontius Pilate witnessed a good confession; that thou keep this commandment without spot, unrebukeable, until the appearing of our Lord Jesus Christ: which in his times he shall shew, who is the blessed and only Potentate, the King of kings, the Lord of lords; who only hath immortality, dwelling in the light which no man can approach unto; whom no man hath seen, nor can see: to whom be honour and power everlasting" (1 Tim. 6:11-16).

Writing again, Paul says: "This is a faithful saying, and worthy of all acceptation, that Christ Jesus came into the world to save sinners; of whom I am chief. Howbeit for this cause I obtained mercy, that in me first Jesus Christ might shew forth all longsuffering, for a pattern to them which should hereafter believe on him to life everlasting. Now unto the King eternal, immortal, invisible, the only wise God, be honour and glory for ever and ever" (1 Tim. 1:15-17).

Immortality Brought by Christ

Christ "brought life and immortality to light through the gospel" (2 Tim. 1:10). No man can have an independent spiritual life apart from Him. The sinner is not immortal; for God has said, "The soul that sinneth, it shall die" (Eze. 18:4). This means all that it expresses. It reaches farther than the death which is common to all; it means the second death. Men start back at this, saying, Would you make man no more than a beast? This is thought to be degrading. But what is it that elevates man in the sight of God? Is it his accumulation of money?— No; for God declares, The gold and the silver are mine. If man abuses his entrusted treasures, God can scatter faster than man can gather. Man may have brilliant intellect; he may be rich in the possession of natural endowments. But these are all given him by God, his Maker. God can remove the gift of reason, and in a moment man will become as Nebuchadnezzar, degraded to the level of the beasts of the field. This God does because man acts as though his wisdom and power had been gotten independently of Him.

Man is only mortal, and while he feels himself too wise to accept Jesus, he will remain only mortal. Men have done wonderful things in the intellectual world, but who gave them power to do this?—The Lord God of hosts. If in their fancied efficiency men triumph because of their own power, and glorify themselves, following the example of the antediluvian world, they will perish. The imagination of that long-lived race was only evil, and that continually. They were wise to do evil, and the earth was corrupted under the inhabitants thereof. Had they connected themselves with the One who is infinite in wisdom, they could have done marvelous things with their God-given ability and talents. But, turning from God, they chose to follow Satan's lead, as many today are doing; and the Lord swept them from the earth, with all their boasted knowledge.

Humanity may be exalted by the world for what it has done. But man can lower himself very fast in God's sight by misapplying and misappropriating his entrusted talents, which, if rightly used, would elevate him. While the Lord is long-suffering and not willing that any shall perish, He will by no means clear the guilty. Let all take heed to the words of the Lord: "Wherefore kick ye at my sacrifice and at mine offering, which I have commanded in my habitation; and honourest thy sons above me, to make yourselves fat with the chiefest of all the offerings of Israel my people? Wherefore the Lord God of Israel saith, I said indeed that thy house, and the house of thy father, should walk before me for ever: but now the Lord saith, Be it far from me; for them that honour me I will honour, and they that despise me shall be lightly esteemed" (1 Sam. 2:29, 30).

God honors those who obey Him. "The Lord rewarded me according to my righteousness," said David; "according to the cleanness of my hands hath he recompensed me. For I have kept the ways of the Lord, and have not wickedly departed from my God. For all his judgments were before me, and I did not put away his statutes from me" (Ps. 18: 20-22).

How to Obtain Everlasting Life

Only the believer in Christ can receive life everlasting. Only by continually feeding on Christ's flesh and blood can we have the assurance that we are partakers of the divine nature. No one should be indifferent on this subject, saying, If we are honest, it is no matter what we believe. You cannot with safety surrender any seed of vital truth in order to please yourself or anybody else. Do not seek to avoid the cross. If we receive no light from the Sun of Righteousness, we have no connection with the Source of all light; and if this life and light do not abide in us, we can never be saved.

God has made every provision that His purpose in the creation of man shall not be frustrated by Satan. After Adam and Eve brought death into the world by their disobedience, a costly sacrifice was provided for the human race. A higher value than that they originally possessed was placed upon them. By giving Christ, His only-begotten Son, as a ransom for the world, God gave all heaven.

The acceptance of Christ gives value to the human being. His sacrifice carries life and light to all who take Christ as their personal Saviour. The love of God through Jesus Christ is shed abroad in the heart of every member of His body, carrying with it the vitality of the law of God the Father. Thus God may dwell with man, and man may dwell with God. Paul declared, "I am crucified with Christ: nevertheless I live; yet not I, but Christ liveth in me: and the life which I now live in the flesh I live by the faith of the Son of God, who loved me, and gave himself for me" (Gal. 2:20).

If through faith man becomes one with Christ, he can win life everlasting. God loves those who are redeemed through Christ, even as He loves His Son. What a thought! Can God love the sinner as He loves His own Son?—Yes; Christ has said it, and He means just what He says. He will honor all our drafts if we will grasp His promise by living faith, and put our trust in Him. Look to Him, and live. All who obey God are embraced in the prayer which Christ offered to His Father, "I have declared unto them thy name, and will declare it: that the love wherewith thou hast loved me may be in them, and I in them" (John 17:26). Wonderful truth, too difficult for humanity to comprehend!

Christ declares: "I am the bread of life: he that cometh to me shall never hunger; and he that believeth on me shall never thirst" (John 6:35). "And this is the will of him that sent me, that every one which seeth the Son, and believeth on him, may have everlasting life: and I will raise him up at the last day" (John 6:40). "Verily, verily, I say unto you, He that believeth on me hath everlasting life" (John 6:47). "Except ye eat the flesh of the Son of man, and drink his blood, ye have no life in you. Whoso eateth my flesh, and drinketh my blood, hath eternal life; and I will raise him up at the last day. For my flesh is meat indeed, and my blood is drink indeed. He that eateth my flesh, and drinketh my blood, dwelleth in me, and I in him. As the living Father hath sent me, and I live by the Father: so he that eateth me, even he shall live by me. This is that bread which came down from heaven: not as your fathers did eat manna, and are dead: he that eateth of this bread shall live for ever" (John 6:53-58). "It is the spirit that quickeneth; the flesh profiteth nothing: the words that I speak unto you, they are spirit, and they are life" (John 6:63).

44.

*The Risen Saviour**

"I am the resurrection, and the life" (John 11:25). He who had said, "I lay down my life, that I might take it again" (John 10:17), came forth from the grave to life that was in Himself. Humanity died; divinity did not die. In His divinity, Christ possessed the power to break the bonds of death. He declares that He has life in Himself to quicken whom He will.

All created beings live by the will and power of God. They are recipients of the life of the Son of God. However able and talented, however large their capacities, they are replenished with life from the Source of all life. He is the spring, the fountain, of life. Only He who alone hath immortality, dwelling in light and life, should say, "I have power to lay it [my life] down, and I have power to take it again" (John 10:18).

The words of Christ, "I am the resurrection, and the life" (John 11:25), were distinctly heard by the Roman guard. The whole army of Satan heard them. And we understand them when we hear. Christ had come to give His life a ransom for many. As the Good Shepherd, He had laid down His life for the sheep. It was the righteous-

---

* This article appeared in *The Youth's Instructor*, Aug. 4, 1898.

ness of God to maintain His law by inflicting the penalty. This was the only way in which the law could be maintained, and pronounced holy, and just, and good. It was the only way by which sin could be made to appear exceeding sinful, and the honor and majesty of divine authority be maintained.

The law of God's government was to be magnified by the death of God's only-begotten Son. Christ bore the guilt of the sins of the world. Our sufficiency is found only in the incarnation and death of the Son of God. He could suffer, because sustained by divinity. He could endure, because He was without one taint of disloyalty or sin. Christ triumphed in man's behalf in thus bearing the justice of punishment. He secured eternal life to men, while He exalted the law, and made it honorable.

Christ was invested with the right to give immortality. The life which He had laid down in humanity, He again took up and gave to humanity. "I am come," He says, "that they might have life, and that they might have it more abundantly" (John 10:10). "Whoso eateth my flesh, and drinketh my blood, hath eternal life; and I will raise him up at the last day" (John 6:54). "Whosoever drinketh of the water that I shall give him shall never thirst; but the water that I shall give him shall be in him a well of water springing up into everlasting life" (John 4:14).

All who are one with Christ through faith in Him gain an experience which is life unto eternal life. "As the living Father hath sent me, and I live by the Father: so he that eateth me, even he shall live by me" (John 6:57). He "dwelleth in me, and I in him" (John 6:56). "I will raise him up at the last day" (John 6:54). "Because I live, ye shall live also" (John 14:19).

Christ became one with humanity, that humanity might become one in spirit and life with Him. By virtue of this union in obedience to the Word of God, His life becomes their life. He says to the penitent, "I am the resurrection, and the life" (John 11:25). Death is looked upon by Christ as sleep—silence, darkness, sleep. He speaks of it as if it were of little moment. "Whosoever liveth and

believeth in me," He says, "shall never die" (John 11:26).
"If a man keep my saying, he shall never taste of death"
(John 8:52). "He shall never see death" (John 8:51).
And to the believing one, death is but a small matter.
With him to die is but to sleep. "Them also which sleep
in Jesus will God bring with him" (1 Thess. 4:14).

While the women were making known their message
as witnesses of the risen Saviour, and while Jesus was preparing to reveal Himself to a large number of His followers,
another scene was taking place. The Roman guard had
been enabled to view the mighty angel who sang the song
of triumph at the birth of Christ, and hear the angels who
now sang the song of redeeming love. At the wonderful
scene which they were permitted to behold, they had
fainted and become as dead men. When the heavenly train
was hidden from their sight, they arose to their feet, and
made their way to the gate of the garden as quickly as their
tottering limbs would carry them. Staggering like blind or
drunken men, their faces pale as the dead, they told those
they met of the wonderful scenes they had witnessed. Messengers preceded them quickly to the chief priests and
rulers, declaring, as best they could, the remarkable inci-
dents that had taken place.

The guards were making their way first to Pilate, but
the priests and rulers sent word for them to be brought
into their presence. These hardened soldiers presented a
strange appearance, as they bore testimony to the resurrection of Christ and also of the multitude whom He brought
forth with Him. They told the chief priests what they had
seen at the sepulcher. They had not time to think or speak
anything but the truth. But the rulers were displeased with
the report. They knew that great publicity had been given
to the trial of Christ, by holding it at the time of the Pass-
over. They knew that the wonderful events which had
taken place—the supernatural darkness, the mighty earthquake—could not be without effect, and they at once
planned how they might deceive the people. The soldiers
were bribed to report a falsehood.

45.

*The First Fruits**

When Christ cried out while upon the cross, "It is finished" (John 19:30), there was a mighty earthquake, that rent open the graves of many who had been faithful and loyal, bearing their testimony against every evil work, and magnifying the Lord of hosts. As the Life-giver came forth from the sepulcher, proclaiming, "I am the resurrection, and the life" (John 11:25), He summoned these saints from the grave. When alive, they had borne their testimony unflinchingly for the truth; now, they were to be witnesses to Him who had raised them from the dead. These, said Christ, are no longer the captives of Satan. I have redeemed them; I have brought them from the grave as the first fruits of My power, to be with Me where I am, nevermore to see death or experience sorrow.

During His ministry, Jesus raised the dead to life. He raised the son of the widow of Nain, the daughter of Jairus, and Lazarus; but these were not clothed with immortality. After they were raised, they continued to be subject to death. But those who came forth from the grave at Christ's resurrection were raised to everlasting

* This article appeared in the *The Youth's Instructor*, Aug. 11, 1898, under the title "The Risen Saviour—Part 2."

life. They were the multitude of captives that ascended with Him as trophies of His victory over death and the grave.

After His resurrection, Christ did not show Himself to any save His followers; but testimony in regard to His resurrection was not wanting. Those who were raised with Christ "appeared unto many" (Matt. 27:53), declaring, Christ has risen from the dead, and we are risen with Him. They bore testimony in the city to the fulfillment of the scripture, "Thy dead men shall live, together with my dead body shall they arise. Awake and sing, ye that dwell in dust: for thy dew is as the dew of herbs, and the earth shall cast out the dead" (Isa. 26:19). These saints contradicted the lie which the Roman guard had been hired to circulate—that the disciples had come by night and stolen Him away. This testimony could not be silenced.

Christ was the first fruits of them that slept. It was to the glory of God that the Prince of life should be the first fruits, the antitype of the wave sheaf. "For whom he did foreknow, he also did predestinate to be conformed to the image of his Son, that he might be the firstborn among many brethren" (Rom. 8:29). This very scene, the resurrection of Christ from the dead, had been celebrated in type by the Jews. When the first heads of grain ripened in the field, they were carefully gathered; and when the people went up to Jerusalem, these were presented to the Lord as a thank offering. The people waved the ripened sheaf before God, acknowledging Him as the Lord of the harvest. After this ceremony the sickle could be put to the wheat, and the harvest gathered.

So those who had been raised were to be presented to the universe as a pledge of the resurrection of all who believe in Christ as their personal Saviour. The same power that raised Christ from the dead will raise His church, and glorify it with Christ, as His bride, above all principalities, above all powers, above every name that is named, not only in this world, but also in the heavenly courts, the world above. The victory of the sleeping saints will be glorious on the morning of the resurrection. Satan's triumph will end, while Christ will triumph in glory and honor. The Life-giver will crown with immortality all who come forth from the grave.

The Ascension of Christ

The work of the Saviour on earth was finished. The time had come for Him to return to His heavenly home. "And he led them [the disciples] out as far as to Bethany, and he lifted up his hands, and blessed them. And it came to pass, while he blessed them, he was parted from them, and carried up into heaven" (Luke 24:50, 51).

As Christ ascends while in the act of blessing His disciples, an army of angels encircle Him as a cloud. Christ takes with Him the multitude of captives. He will Himself bring to the Father the first fruits of them that slept, as an evidence that He is conqueror of death and the grave. At the portals of the city of God, an innumerable company of angels await His coming. As they approach, the escorting angels address the company at the gate in triumphant tones:—

> "Lift up your heads, O ye gates;
> And be ye lift up, ye everlasting doors;
> And the King of glory shall come in."

"Who is this King of glory?" the waiting angels inquire.

> "The Lord strong and mighty,
> The Lord mighty in battle.
> Lift up your heads, O ye gates;
> Even lift them up, ye everlasting doors;
> And the King of glory shall come in."

Again the waiting angels ask, "Who is this King of glory?" and the escorting angels reply, in melodious strains, "The Lord of hosts, he is the King of glory" (Ps. 24: 7-10). Then the portals of the city of God are opened wide, and the angelic throng sweep through.

There is the throne, and around it the rainbow of promise. There are seraphim and cherubim. The angels circle round Him, but Christ waves them back. He enters into the presence of His Father. He points to His triumph in this antitype of Himself—the wave sheaf—those raised with Him, the representatives of the captive dead who shall come forth from their graves when the trump shall sound. He approaches the Father, and if there is joy in heaven over one sinner that repents, if the Father rejoices over one with singing, let the imagination take in this scene. Christ says: Father, it is finished. I have done Thy will, O My God. I have completed the work of redemption. If Thy justice is satisfied, "I will that they also, whom thou hast given me, be with me where I am" (John 17: 24). And the voice of God is heard; justice is satisfied; Satan is vanquished. "Mercy and truth have met together; righteousness and peace have kissed each other" (Ps. 85: 10). The arms of the Father encircle the Son, and His voice is heard, saying, "Let all the angels of God worship him" (Heb. 1:6).

46.

*A Divine Sin Bearer**

Through disobedience Adam fell. The law of God had been broken. The divine government had been dishonored, and justice demanded that the penalty of transgression be paid.

To save the race from eternal death, the Son of God volunteered to bear the punishment of disobedience. Only by the humiliation of the Prince of heaven could the dishonor be removed, justice be satisfied, and man be restored to that which he had forfeited by disobedience. There was no other way. For an angel to come to this earth, to pass over the ground where Adam stumbled and fell, would not have sufficed. This could not have removed one stain of sin, or brought to man one hour of probation.

Christ, equal with God, the brightness of the Father's "glory, and the express image of his person" (Heb. 1:3), clothed His divinity with humanity, and came to this earth to suffer and die for sinners. The only-begotten Son of God humbled Himself, and became obedient unto death, even the death of the cross. By bearing in His body the curse of sin, He placed happiness and immortality within the reach of all.

---

* This article appeared in *The Signs of the Times,* Sept. 30, 1903.

One honored of all heaven came to this world to stand in human nature at the head of humanity, testifying to the fallen angels and to the inhabitants of the unfallen worlds that through the divine help which has been provided, every one may walk in the path of obedience to God's commands. The Son of God died for those who had no claim on His love. For us He suffered all that Satan could bring against Him.

Wonderful—almost too wonderful for man to comprehend—is the Saviour's sacrifice in our behalf, shadowed forth in all the sacrifices of the past, in all the services of the typical sanctuary. And this sacrifice was called for. When we realize that His suffering was necessary in order to secure our eternal well-being, our hearts are touched and melted. He pledged Himself to accomplish our full salvation in a way satisfactory to the demands of God's justice, and consistent with the exalted holiness of His law.

No one less holy than the Only Begotten of the Father, could have offered a sacrifice that would be efficacious to cleanse all—even the most sinful and degraded—who accept the Saviour as their atonement and become obedient to Heaven's law. Nothing less could have reinstated man in God's favor.

What right had Christ to take the captives out of the enemy's hands?—The right of having made a sacrifice that satisfies the principles of justice by which the kingdom of heaven is governed. He came to this earth as the Redeemer of the lost race, to conquer the wily foe, and, by His steadfast allegiance to right, to save all who accept Him as their Saviour. On the cross of Calvary He paid the redemption price of the race. And thus He gained the right to take the captives from the grasp of the great deceiver, who, by a lie, framed against the government of God, caused the fall of man, and thus forfeited all claim to be called a loyal subject of God's glorious everlasting kingdom.

Our ransom has been paid by our Saviour. No one need be enslaved by Satan. Christ stands before us as our all-powerful helper. "In all things it behoved him to be made like unto his brethren, that he might be a merciful and faithful high priest in things pertaining to God, to make reconciliation for the sins of the people. For in that he himself hath suffered being tempted, he is able to succour them that are tempted" (Heb. 2:17, 18).

"He came unto his own, and his own received him not. But as many as received him, to them gave he power to become the sons of God, even to them that believe on his name. . . . And the Word was made flesh, and dwelt among us, . . . full of grace and truth. . . . And of his fulness have all we received, and grace for grace" (John 1:11-16).

Those who are adopted into the family of God are transformed by His Spirit. Self-indulgence and supreme love for self are changed for self-denial and supreme love for God. No man inherits holiness as a birthright, nor can he, by any methods that he can devise, become loyal to God. "Without me," Christ says, "ye can do nothing" (John 15:5). Human righteousness is as "filthy rags." But with God all things are possible. In the strength of the Redeemer, weak, erring man can become more than conqueror over the evil that besets him.

47.

*The Truth as It Is in Jesus**

In giving His only-begotten Son to die for sinners, God has manifested to fallen man love that is without a parallel. We have full faith in the scripture that says, "God is love" (1 John 4:8); and yet many have shamefully perverted this word, and have fallen into dangerous error because of a false interpretation of its meaning. God's holy law is the only standard by which we can estimate divine affection. If we do not accept the law of God as our standard, we set up a standard of our own. God has given us precious promises of His love, but we are not to ascribe to Jehovah a tenderness that will lead Him to pass over guilt and wink at iniquity.

The Creator loves His creatures, but he who loves sin more than righteousness, error more than truth, perpetuates the transgression that brought woe into our world, and cannot be regarded with favor by the God of truth. The way of truth and righteousness involves a cross. Many misinterpret the requirements of God, and make them mean anything that will not disturb their consciences or inconvenience them in their business relations; but truth is the only sanctifying medium.

---

* This article appeared in *The Review and Herald*, June 17, 1890.

The love of God as manifested in Jesus, will lead us to the true conception of the character of God. As we behold Christ, pierced for our sins, we shall see that we cannot break the law of God and remain in His favor; we shall feel that as sinners we must lay hold of the merits of Christ and cease to sin. Then we are drawing nigh to God. As soon as we have a correct view of the love of God, we shall have no disposition to abuse it.

The cross of Christ testifies to the immutability of the law of God—testifies that God so loved us that He gave His Son to die for our sins; but Christ came not to destroy but to fulfill the law. Not one jot or tittle of God's moral standard could be changed to meet man in his fallen condition. Jesus died that He might ascribe unto the repenting sinner His own righteousness, and make it possible for man to keep the law.

The love of God is infinite, and yet the sinner could not be forgiven save through the plan of redemption that involved the shame, reproach, ignominy, and death of the Son of God. This fact should banish from reasoning minds the idea advanced by many who claim sanctification, that His death put an end to obedience to the law of God. We are to learn daily of the great plan of redemption, in the school of Christ. When we cease to learn, we cease to be pupils in Christ's school. But if we are scholars under the divine Master, our understanding will be opened, and we shall learn wondrous things out of God's law.

Let us walk carefully before the Lord; let us think how often we have broken our vows and marred our best resolutions, how often in the face of great light we have turned from God and sought our idols. It is highly proper for us to humble ourselves under the mighty hand of God.

Mature in Christian Experience

It is natural for us to think more highly of ourselves than we ought to think; but although it is painful for us to know ourselves as we really are, yet we should pray that God will reveal us to ourselves, even as He sees us. But we should not cease to pray when we have simply asked for a revelation of ourselves; we should pray that Jesus may be revealed to us as a sin-pardoning Saviour. When we see Jesus as He is, earnest desires should awaken in our hearts to be rid of self, that we may be filled with all the fullness of Christ. When this is our experience, we shall do good to one another, and use all the means within our reach to attain unto godliness. We must cleanse our souls from all filthiness of the flesh and spirit, and perfect holiness in the fear of God.

The love of a holy God is an amazing principle, which can stir the universe in our behalf during the hours of our probation and trial. But after the season of our probation, if we are found transgressors of God's law, the God of love will be found a minister of vengeance. God makes no compromise with sin. The disobedient will be punished. The wrath of God fell upon His beloved Son as Christ hung upon the cross of Calvary in the transgressor's place. The love of God now reaches out to embrace the lowest, vilest sinner that will come to Christ with contrition. It reaches out to transform the sinner into an obedient, faithful child of God; but not a soul can be saved if he continues in sin.

Sin is the transgression of the law, and the arm that is now mighty to save will be strong to punish when the transgressor passes the bounds that limit divine forbearance. He who refuses to seek for life, who will not search the Scriptures to see what is truth, lest he should be condemned in his practices, will be left to blindness of mind and to the deceptions of Satan. To the same degree that the penitent and obedient are shielded by God's love, the impenitent and disobedient will be left to the result of their own ignorance and hardness of heart, because they receive not the love of the truth that they may be saved.

There are many who profess Christ, but who never become mature Christians. They admit that man is fallen, that his faculties are weakened, that he is unfitted for moral achievement, but they say that Christ has borne all the burden, all the suffering, all the self-denial, and they are willing to let Him bear it. They say that there is nothing for them to do but to believe; but Christ said, "If any man will come after me, let him deny himself, and take up his cross, and follow me" (Matt. 16:24). Jesus kept the commandments of God. The Pharisees declared that He broke the fourth commandment because He made a man every whit whole on the Sabbath day; but Jesus turned to the accusing Pharisees, and asked, "Is it lawful on the sabbath days to do good, or to do evil? to save life, or to destroy it? And looking round about upon them all, he said unto the man, Stretch forth thy hand. And he did so: and his hand was restored whole as the other. And they were filled with madness; and communed one with another what they might do to Jesus" (Luke 6:9-11).

This miracle, instead of convincing the Pharisees that Jesus was the Son of God, filled them with rage, because many who witnessed the miracle glorified God. Jesus declared that His work of mercy was lawful on the Sabbath day. The Pharisees declared that it was not lawful. Which shall we believe? Christ said, "I have kept my Father's commandments, and abide in his love" (John 15:10). Then it is certainly safe for us to follow the way of Christ, and keep the commandments. God has given us faculties which should be constantly exercised in cooperating with Jesus, in working out our own salvation with fear and trembling, for it is God that worketh in us to will and to do of His good pleasure.

Advancement Not to Cease

We are never to rest in a satisfied condition, and cease to make advancement, saying, "I am saved." When this idea is entertained, the motives for watchfulness, for prayer, for earnest endeavor to press onward to higher attainments, cease to exist. No sanctified tongue will be found uttering these words till Christ shall come, and we enter in through the gates into the city of God. Then, with the utmost propriety, we may give glory to God and to the Lamb for eternal deliverance. As long as man is full of weakness—for of himself he cannot save his soul—he should never dare to say, "I am saved."

It is not he that putteth on the armor that can boast of the victory; for he has the battle to fight and the victory to win. It is he that endureth unto the end that shall be saved. The Lord says, "If any man draw back, my soul shall have no pleasure in him" (Heb. 10:38). If we do not go forward from victory to victory, the soul will draw back to perdition. We should raise no human standard whereby to measure character. We have seen enough of what men call perfection here below. God's holy law is the only thing by which we can determine whether we are keeping His way or not. If we are disobedient, our characters are out of harmony with God's moral rule of government, and it is stating a falsehood to say, "I am saved." No one is saved who is a transgressor of the law of God, which is the foundation of His government in heaven and in earth.

Those who ignorantly join the ranks of the enemy, and echo the words of their religious teachers, in the desk, that the law of God is no longer binding upon the human family, will have light to discover their errors, if they will accept the evidence of God's Word. Jesus was the angel enshrouded in the pillar of cloud by day and the pillar of fire by night, and He gave special direction that the Hebrews should teach the law of God, given when the foundation of the earth was laid, when the morning stars sang together and all the sons of God shouted for joy.

The same law was proclaimed in grandeur by His own voice from Sinai. He said: "And these words, which I command thee this day, shall be in thine heart: and thou shalt teach them diligently unto thy children, and shalt talk of them when thou sittest in thine house, and when thou walkest by the way, and when thou liest down, and when thou risest up. And thou shalt bind them for a sign upon thine hand, and they shall be as frontlets between thine eyes" (Deut. 6:6-8). How impatient the transgressors of God's law become when the law is mentioned; they are irritated to have it spoken of.

The Word of God is made of none effect by falsehoods and traditions. Satan has presented his version of God's law to the world, and it has been accepted before a plain "Thus saith the Lord." The controversy begun in heaven over the law of God, has been kept up upon the earth ever since Satan's expulsion from heaven.

We must ever be learning our great need, in order to appreciate our Saviour, and to make Him known to others. We can learn the depths of our transgression only by the length of the chain let down to draw us up. We should put our mental powers to the task to understand the fearful ruin to which sin has brought us, and we should seek to understand the divine plan by which we may be restored to the favor of God. That God's dear Son should have to come to our world to fight our battles for us that we might have strength to conquer in His name, should ever humble our proud hearts. If we look to the cross of Calvary, every boast will die upon our lips, and we shall cry, "Unclean, unworthy of so great suffering, of so rich a price paid for my redemption."

Ignorance and self-sufficiency go hand in hand. The law of God has been given for the regulation of our conduct, and it is far reaching in its principles. There is no sin, no work of unrighteousness, that escapes the condemnation of the law. The great statute book is truth, and truth only; for it delineates with unerring accuracy the history of Satan's deception, and the ruin of his followers. Satan claimed to be able to present laws which were better than God's statutes and judgments, and he was expelled from heaven. He has made a similar attempt upon earth. Ever since his fall he has put forth efforts to deceive the world, to lead men to ruin, that he might be revenged upon God because he was overcome and thrust down from heaven. His efforts to put himself and his devices where God should be, are most persevering and persistent. He has taken the world captive in his snare, and many even of the people of God are ignorant of his devices, and they give him all the opportunity he asks to work the ruin of souls. They do not manifest a burning zeal to lift up Jesus, and proclaim to the perishing multitudes, "Behold the Lamb of God, which taketh away the sin of the world" (John 1:29).

Those who are unacquainted with the laws of God's

government as expounded upon the mount, are unacquainted with the truth as it is in Jesus. Christ revealed the far-reaching principles of the law; He expounded every precept, and exhibited every demand in His example. He that knows the truth as it is in the law, knows the truth as it is in Jesus; and if through faith in Christ he renders obedience to the commandments of God, his life is hid with Christ in God.

The knowledge of the claims of the law would crush out the last ray of hope from the soul if there were no Saviour provided for man; but the truth as it is in Jesus, is a savor of life unto life. God's dear Son died that He might impute unto man His own righteousness, and not that he might be at liberty to break God's holy law, as Satan tries to make men believe. Through faith in Christ, man may be in possession of moral power to resist evil.

Sanctification the Work of a Lifetime

The work of sanctification is the work of a lifetime; it must go on continually; but this work cannot go on in the heart while the light on any part of the truth is rejected or neglected. The sanctified soul will not be content to remain in ignorance, but will desire to walk in the light and to seek for greater light. As a miner digs for gold and silver, so the follower of Christ will seek for truth as for hidden treasures, and will press from light to a greater light, ever increasing in knowledge. He will continually grow in grace and in the knowledge of the truth. Self must be overcome. Every defect of character must be discerned in God's great mirror. We may discover whether or not we are condemned by God's standard of character.

If you are condemned, there is but one course for you to pursue: you must repent toward God because of the transgression of His law, and have faith toward our Lord Jesus Christ as the one who only can cleanse from sin. If we would obtain heaven, we must be obedient to God's holy requirements. Those who strive lawfully will not strive in vain. Only believe the truth as it is in Jesus, and you will be strengthened for the battle with the powers of darkness. The wrestlers of old strove to obtain a perishable crown, and should we not strive to win the crown that fadeth not away?

Every art and device of Satan will be used to accomplish our ruin. If you sit down with the ease-loving ones, with the words on your lips, "I am saved," and disregard the commandments of God, you will be eternally lost. There is truth in Jesus that is terrible to the ease-loving, do-nothing ones. There is truth in Jesus that is full of soothing joy to the obedient. It is the joy of the Holy Ghost. Be persuaded, then, to open the mind and heart, that you may see every ray of light shining from the throne of God.

This is no time to be indifferent and careless and pleasure loving. Christ is coming with power and great glory. Are you ready? Are you putting away your sins? Are you becoming sanctified through the truth in answer to the prayer of Christ? He prayed concerning His disciples, "Sanctify them through thy truth: thy word is truth" (John 17:17).

Parents should bring up their children in the nurture and admonition of the Lord, educating them to love to do the will of God. It is impossible for us to overestimate the advantages of youthful piety. The impressions received in youth are to many as enduring as eternity. It is in youth that the statutes and commandments of God are most easily inscribed on the tablets of the soul. The instruction of children has been greatly neglected; the righteousness of Christ has not been presented to them as it should have been.

The time of probation is given us that we may perfect a character fit for eternity. How solemn is the thought, parents, that your children are in your hands to educate and train that they may develop characters which God will approve, or characters which Satan and his angels can play upon as they choose! Jesus spoke from the pillar of cloud and of fire, and bade His people instruct their children diligently concerning the commandments of God. Who are obeying this instruction? Who are seeking to make their children such as God will approve? Who keep the thought in mind that all the talents and gifts of their children belong to God, and should be wholly consecrated to His service?

Hannah dedicated Samuel to the Lord, and God revealed Himself to him in his childhood and youth. We must labor far more for our children and for the youth; for God will accept them to do great things in His name in teaching the truth to those in foreign lands, to those who are in the darkness of error and superstition. If you indulge your children, gratifying their selfish wishes; if you encourage in them the love of dress, and develop vanity and pride, you will do a work that will disappoint Jesus, who has paid an infinite price for their redemption. He desires that the children shall serve Him with undivided affection.

Parents, there is a great work for you to do for Jesus, who has done everything for you. Take Him as your guide and helper. God has not withheld from you the very best gift He had to give—His only-begotten Son. Children and youth should not be hindered in coming to Jesus. Satan seeks to bind the children to himself as with bands of steel, and you can attain success in bringing them to Jesus only through determined personal effort. Children and youth should receive more earnest labor, for they are the hope of the church. Joseph, Daniel and his fellows, Samuel, David, John, and Timothy are shining examples that testify to the fact that "the fear of the Lord is the beginning of wisdom" (Prov. 9:10).

We must make more earnest, decided efforts, if we would have the Lord Jesus abide with us as a counselor and helper. The light that shines from the Son of God on Calvary can lead every wanderer home. There is power in Him to purify the heart and transform the character. Let every true Christian work for the children and youth, presenting before them the matchless loveliness of Jesus. Then the attractions and the illusions of the world will be eclipsed, and they will see no advantage to be gained in the path of disobedience.

48.

The Divine Standard *

The commandments of God are comprehensive and far reaching; in a few words they unfold the whole duty of man. "Thou shalt love the Lord thy God with all thy heart, and with all thy soul, and with all thy mind, and with all thy strength. . . . Thou shalt love thy neighbour as thyself" (Mark 12:30, 31). In these words the length and breadth, the depth and height, of the law of God is comprehended; for Paul declares, "Love is the fulfilling of the law" (Rom. 13:10). The only definition we find in the Bible for sin is that "sin is the transgression of the law" (1 John 3:4). The Word of God declares, "All have sinned, and come short of the glory of God" (Rom. 3:23). "There is none that doeth good, no, not one" (Rom. 3:12). Many are deceived concerning the condition of their hearts. They do not realize that the natural heart is deceitful above all things, and desperately wicked. They wrap themselves about with their own righteousness, and are satisfied in reaching their own human standard of character; but how fatally they fail when they do not reach the divine standard, and of themselves they cannot meet the requirements of God.

---

* This article appeared in *The Signs of the Times,* Dec. 5, 1892.

We may measure ourselves by ourselves, we may compare ourselves among ourselves, we may say we do as well as this one or that one, but the question to which the judgment will call for an answer is, Do we meet the claims of high heaven? Do we reach the divine standard? Are our hearts in harmony with the God of heaven?

The human family have all transgressed the law of God, and as transgressors of the law, man is hopelessly ruined; for he is the enemy of God, without strength to do any good thing. "The carnal mind is enmity against God: for it is not subject to the law of God, neither indeed can be" (Rom. 8:7). Looking into the moral mirror—God's holy law—man sees himself a sinner, and is convicted of his state of evil, his hopeless doom under the just penalty of the law. But he has not been left in a state of hopeless distress in which sin has plunged him; for it was to save the transgressor from ruin that He who was equal with God offered up His life on Calvary. "God so loved the world, that he gave his only begotten Son, that whosoever believeth in him should not perish, but have everlasting life" (John 3:16).

Our Atoning Sacrifice

Jesus was the majesty of heaven, the beloved commander of the angels, who delighted to do His pleasure. He was one with God, "in the bosom of the Father" (John 1:18), yet He thought it not a thing to be desired to be equal with God while man was lost in sin and misery. He stepped down from His throne, He left His crown and royal scepter, and clothed His divinity with humanity. He humbled Himself even to the death of the cross, that man might be exalted to a seat with Him upon His throne. In Him we have a complete offering, an infinite sacrifice, a mighty Saviour, who is able to save unto the uttermost all that come unto God by Him. In love He comes to reveal the Father, to reconcile man to God, to make him a new creature renewed after the image of Him who created him.

Jesus is our atoning sacrifice. We can make no atonement for ourselves; but by faith we can accept the atonement that has been made. "For Christ also hath once suffered for sins, the just for the unjust, that he might bring us to God" (1 Peter 3:18). "Ye were not redeemed with corruptible things, . . . but with the precious blood of Christ, as of a lamb without blemish and without spot" (1 Peter 1:18, 19). It was through infinite sacrifice and inexpressible suffering that our Redeemer placed redemption within our reach. He was in this world unhonored and unknown, that, through His wonderful condescension and humiliation, He might exalt man to receive eternal honors and immortal joys in the heavenly courts. During His thirty years of life on earth His heart was wrung with inconceivable anguish. The path from the manger to Calvary was shadowed by grief and sorrow. He was a man of sorrows, and acquainted with grief, enduring such heartache as no human language can portray. He could have said in truth, "Behold, and see if there be any sorrow like unto my sorrow" (Lam. 1:12). Hating sin with a perfect hatred, He yet gathered to His soul the sins of the whole world. Guiltless, He bore the punishment of the guilty. Innocent, yet offering Himself as a substitute for the transgressor. The guilt of every sin pressed its weight upon the divine soul of the world's Redeemer. The evil thoughts, the evil words, the evil deeds of every son and daughter of Adam, called for retribution upon Himself; for He had become man's substitute. Though the guilt of sin was not His, His spirit was torn and bruised by the transgressions of men, and He who knew no sin became sin for us, that we might be made the righteousness of God in Him.

Voluntarily our divine Substitute bared His soul to the sword of justice, that we might not perish but have everlasting life. Said Christ, "I lay down my life, that I might take it again. No man taketh it from me, but I lay it down of myself. I have power to lay it down, and I have power to take it again" (John 10:17, 18). No man of earth or angel of heaven could have paid the penalty for sin. Jesus was the only one who could save rebellious man. In Him divinity and humanity were combined, and this was what gave efficiency to the offering on Calvary's cross. At the cross mercy and truth met together, righteousness and peace kissed each other.

As the sinner looks upon the Saviour dying on Calvary, and realizes that the sufferer is divine, he asks why this great sacrifice was made, and the cross points to the holy law of God which has been transgressed. The death of Christ is an unanswerable argument as to the immutability and righteousness of the law. In prophesying of Christ, Isaiah says, "He will magnify the law, and make it honourable" (Isa. 42:21). The law has no power to pardon the evildoer. Its office is to point out his defects, that he may realize his need of One who is mighty to save, his need of One who will become his substitute, his surety, his righteousness. Jesus meets the need of the sinner; for He has taken upon Him the sins of the transgressor. "He was wounded for our transgressions, he was bruised for our iniquities: the chastisement of our peace was upon him; and with his stripes we are healed" (Isa. 53:5). The Lord could have cut off the sinner, and utterly destroyed him; but the costlier plan was chosen. In His great love He provides hope for the hopeless, giving His only-begotten Son to bear the sins of the world. And since He has poured out all heaven in that one rich gift, He will withhold from man no needed aid that he may take the cup of salvation, and become an heir of God, joint heir with Christ.

A Revelation of God's Love

Christ came to manifest the love of God to the world, to draw the hearts of all men to Himself. He said, "And I, if I be lifted up from the earth, will draw all men unto me" (John 12:32). The first step toward salvation is to respond to the drawing of the love of Christ. God sends message after message to men, entreating them to repentance, that He may forgive, and write pardon against their names. Shall there be no repentance? Shall His appeals be unheeded? Shall His overtures of mercy be ignored, and His love utterly rejected? Oh, then man will cut himself off from the medium through which he may

gain life eternal; for God only pardons the penitent! By
the manifestation of His love, by the entreating of His
Spirit, He woos men to repentance; for repentance is the
gift of God, and whom He pardons He first makes penitent. The sweetest joy comes to man through his sincere
repentance toward God for the transgression of His law,
and through faith in Christ as the sinner's Redeemer and
Advocate. It is that men may understand the joy of forgiveness, the peace of God, that Christ draws them through
the manifestation of His love. If they respond to His drawing, yielding their hearts to His grace, He will lead them
on step by step, to a full knowledge of Himself, and this is
life eternal.

Christ came to reveal to the sinner the justice and love
of God, that He might give repentance to Israel and remission of sins. When the sinner beholds Jesus lifted up
upon the cross, suffering the guilt of the transgressor, bearing the penalty of sin; when he beholds God's abhorrence
of evil in the fearful manifestation of the death of the cross,
and His love for fallen man, he is led to repentance
toward God because of his transgression of the law which
is holy, and just, and good. He exercises faith in Christ, because the divine Saviour has become his substitute, his
surety, and advocate, the one in whom his very life is
centered. To the repenting sinner God can show His
mercy and truth, and bestow upon him His forgiveness
and love.

But Satan will not permit a soul to escape from the
captivity of sin if by any means he can prevent it. Though
all heaven has been poured out in one rich gift—for when
God gave His Son, He gave the choicest gift of heaven,
and the treasures of heaven are at our command—yet to the
repenting soul the enemy will seek to represent God as
stern and inexorable, unwilling to pardon the transgressor. At different times letters have come to me from persons who were in despair over their sins. One and another
have written: "I fear I am past all help. Is there any hope
for me?" To these poor souls the message has been given:
"Hope in God. The Father has bread enough and to

spare. Arise, and go to your Father. He will meet you a great way off. He will give you His love and compassion."

When the enemy comes in like a flood, and seeks to overwhelm you with the thought of your sin, tell him: "I know I am a sinner. If I were not, I could not go to the Saviour; for He says, 'I came not to call the righteous, but sinners to repentance' (Mark 2:17). And because I am a sinner I am entitled to come to Christ. I am sinful and polluted, but He suffered humiliation and death, and exhausted the curse that belongs to me. I come. I believe. I claim His sure promise, 'Whosoever believeth in him should not perish, but have everlasting life' (John 3:16)."

Will such a plea made in contrition of soul be turned away?—No, never. By the suffering and death of Christ is proven His boundless love to man. He is willing and able to save to the uttermost all that come unto God by Him.

Then as a little child, come to God, presenting yourself as suppliant at His feet; for we need not ascend into the heavens to bring Jesus down; nor into the earth to bring Him up; for He is ever near us. He says, "Behold, I stand at the door, and knock: if any man hear my voice, and open the door, I will come in to him, and will sup with him, and he with me" (Rev. 3:20). How willing is Christ to take possession of the soul temple if we will let Him! He is represented as waiting and knocking at the door of the heart. Then why does He not enter? It is because the love of sin has closed the door of the heart. As soon as we consent to give sin up, to acknowledge our guilt, the barrier is removed between the soul and the Saviour.

49.

Surrender and Confession *

But in repenting of sin we need not go into a cell, as did Luther, imposing penances upon ourselves to expiate our iniquity, thinking by so doing to gain the favor of God. The question is asked: "Shall I give my firstborn for my transgression, the fruit of my body for the sin of my soul? He hath shewed thee, O man, what is good; and what doth the Lord require of thee, but to do justly, and to love mercy, and to walk humbly with thy God?" (Micah 6:7, 8). The psalmist says, "A broken and a contrite heart, O God, thou wilt not despise" (Ps. 51:17). John writes, "If we confess our sins, he is faithful and just to forgive us our sins" (1 John 1:9). The only reason that we have not remission of sin is that we have not acknowledged to Him whom we have wounded by our transgressions, whom we have pierced by our sins, that we are at fault, and in need of mercy. The confession that is the outpouring of the inmost soul will find its way to the heart of infinite pity; for the Lord is nigh unto him that is of a broken heart, and saveth such as be of a contrite spirit.

How mistaken are those who imagine that confession of sin will detract from their dignity, and lessen their in-

---

* This article appeared in *The Signs of the Times*, Dec. 12, 1892.

fluence among their fellow men. Clinging to this erroneous idea, though seeing their faults, many fail to confess them, but rather pass by the wrongs they have done others, so embittering their own lives, and shadowing the lives of others. It will not hurt your dignity to confess your sins. Away with this false dignity. Fall on the Rock and be broken, and Christ will give you the true and heavenly dignity. Let not pride, self-esteem, or self-righteousness keep anyone from confessing his sin, that he may claim the promise. "He that covereth his sins shall not prosper: but whoso confesseth and forsaketh them shall have mercy" (Prov. 28:13). Keep nothing back from God, and neglect not the confession of your faults to your brethren. "Confess your faults one to another, and pray one for another, that ye may be healed" (James 5:16). Many a sin is left unconfessed to confront the sinner in the day of final account; better far to confront your sins now, to confess them and put them away, while the atoning Sacrifice pleads in your behalf. Do not fail to learn the will of God on this subject. The health of your soul and the salvation of others depends upon the course you pursue in this matter. "Humble yourselves therefore under the mighty hand of God, that he may exalt you in due time: casting all your care upon him; for he careth for you" (1 Peter 5:6, 7). The humble and broken heart can appreciate something of the love of God and the cross of Calvary. Ample will be the blessing experienced by him who meets the condition by which he may become a partaker of the favor of God.

Call for Surrender

We are to surrender our hearts to God, that He may renew and sanctify us, and fit us for His heavenly court. We are not to wait for some special time, but today we are to give ourselves to Him, refusing to be the servants of sin. Do you imagine you can leave off sin a little at a time? Oh, leave the accursed thing at once! Hate the things that Christ hates, love the things that Christ loves. Has He not by His death and suffering made provision for your cleansing from sin? When we begin to realize that we are sinners, and fall on the Rock to be broken, the everlasting arms are placed about us, and we are brought close to the heart of Jesus. Then we shall be charmed with His loveliness, and disgusted with our own righteousness. We need to come close to the foot of the cross. The more we humble ourselves there, the more exalted will God's love appear. The grace and righteousness of Christ will not avail for him who feels whole, for him who thinks he is reasonably good, who is contented with his own condition. There is no room for Christ in the heart of him who does not realize his need of divine light and aid.

Jesus says, "Blessed are the poor in spirit: for theirs is the kingdom of heaven" (Matt. 5:3). There is fullness of grace in God, and we may have His spirit and power in large measure. Do not feed on the husks of self-righteousness, but go to the Lord. He has the best robe to put upon you, and His arms are open to receive. Christ will say, "Take away the filthy garments from him, and clothe him with a change of raiment."

Come as a Repentant Sinner

But shall we wait till we feel that we are cleansed?—No; Christ has promised that "if we confess our sins, he is faithful and just to forgive us our sins, and to cleanse us from all unrighteousness" (1 John 1:9). You are proved of God through the Word of God. You are not to wait for wonderful emotions before you believe that God has heard you; feeling is not to be your criterion, for emotions are as changeable as the clouds. You must have something solid for the foundation of your faith. The word of the Lord is a word of infinite power, upon which you may rely, and He has said, "Ask, and ye shall receive." Look to Calvary. Has not Jesus said that He is your advocate? Has He not said that if you ask anything in His name you shall receive? You are not to depend on your own goodness or good works. You are to come depending upon the Sun of Righteousness, believing that Christ has taken away your sins and imputed to you His righteousness.

You are to come to God as a repenting sinner, through

the name of Jesus, the divine Advocate, to a merciful, forgiving Father, believing that He will do just as He has promised. Let those who desire the blessing of God knock, and wait at the throne of mercy, with firm assurance, saying, "For thou, O Lord, hast said, 'For everyone that asketh receiveth; and he that seeketh findeth, and to him that knocketh it shall be opened.'" The Lord longs to have those who seek after God believe in Him who is able to do all things.

The Lord has sought to show us how ready is God to hear and answer our request by the use of a most familiar and commonplace occurrence. He said: "What man is there of you, whom if his son ask bread, will he give him a stone? Or if he ask a fish, will he give him a serpent? If ye then, being evil, know how to give good gifts unto your children, how much more shall your Father which is in heaven give good things to them that ask him?" (Matt. 7: 9-11). Christ made an appeal to us concerning the willingness of God to help, arguing from the natural love of the parent to his offspring. What father could turn from his son who asks bread? Should anyone dishonor God by imagining that He will not respond to the call of His children? Would we think a parent capable of trifling with his child, and tantalizing him by raising his expectation only to disappoint him? Will a father promise to give good and nourishing food to his child and then give him a stone? If ye then, being human and evil, give good gifts to your children, how much more shall your Father which is in heaven give good things to them that ask Him? The Lord assures those that ask Him that He will give them the Holy Spirit.

With the confession of the repenting, believing sinner, Christ mingles His own righteousness, that the prayer of fallen man may go up as fragrant incense before the Father, and the grace of God be imparted to the believing soul. Jesus says to the trembling, repenting soul: "Let him take hold of my strength, that he may make peace with me; and he shall make peace with me" (Isa. 27:5). "Come now, and let us reason together, saith the Lord: though your sins be as scarlet, they shall be as white as snow; though they be red like crimson, they shall be as wool" (Isa. 1:18). Will you let Him reason with you? Will you commit to Him the keeping of your soul as unto a faithful Creator? Come then, and let us live in the light of His countenance, and pray, as did David, "Purge me with hyssop, and I shall be clean: wash me, and I shall be whiter than snow" (Ps. 51:7). By faith apply the blood of Christ to your heart, for that alone can make you whiter than snow. But you say, "This surrender of all my idols will break my heart." This giving up of all for God is represented by your falling upon the Rock and being broken. Then give up all for Him; for unless you are broken, you are worthless.

When you turn away from the broken cisterns that can hold no water, and in the name of Jesus your Advocate come directly to God, asking for the things you need, the righteousness of Christ will be revealed as your righteousness, the virtue of Christ as your virtue. You will then understand that justification will come alone through faith in Christ; for in Jesus is revealed the perfection of the character of God; in His life is manifested the outworking of the principles of holiness. Through the atoning blood of Christ the sinner is set free from bondage and condemnation; through the perfection of the sinless Substitute and Surety, he may run in the race of humble obedience to all of God's commandments. Without Christ he is under the condemnation of the law, always a sinner, but through faith in Christ he is made just before God.

50.

Come and Seek and Find*

It is impossible for man to save himself. He may deceive himself in regard to this matter, but he cannot save himself. Christ's righteousness alone can avail for his salvation, and this is the gift of God. This is the wedding garment in which you may appear as a welcome guest at the marriage supper of the Lamb. Let faith take hold of Christ without delay, and you will be a new creature in Jesus, a light to the world.

Christ is called "the Lord our righteousness," and through faith each one should say, "The Lord my righteousness." When faith lays hold upon this gift of God, the praise of God will be upon our lips, and we shall be able to say to others, "Behold the Lamb of God, which taketh away the sin of the world" (John 1:29). We shall then be able to tell the lost concerning the plan of salvation, that while the world was lying under the curse of sin, the Lord presented terms of mercy to the fallen and hopeless sinner, and revealed the value and meaning of His grace. Grace is unmerited favor. The angels, who know nothing of sin, do not understand what it is to have grace exercised toward them; but our sinful-

---

* This article appeared in *The Signs of the Times*, Dec. 19, 1892.

ness calls for the exercise of grace from a merciful God. It was grace that sent our Saviour to seek us as wanderers and bring us back to the fold.

Have you a sense of want in your soul? Do you hunger and thirst after righteousness? Then this is an evidence that Christ has wrought upon your heart, and created this sense of need, in order that He may be sought after to do those things for you through the endowment of His Holy Spirit which it is impossible for you to do for yourself. The Lord specifies no conditions except that you hunger for His mercy, desiring His counsel, and long for His love. "Ask!" The asking makes it manifest that you realize your necessity, and if you ask in faith, you will receive. The Lord has pledged His word, and it cannot fail. That you feel and know that you are a sinner is sufficient argument in asking for His mercy and compassion. The condition upon which you may come to God is not that you shall be holy, but that you shall ask God to cleanse you from all sin and purify you from all iniquity. Then why wait longer? Why not take God at His word, and say:

> "Here, Lord, I give myself to Thee,
> 'Tis all that I can do"?

If Satan comes to cast his shadow between you and God, accusing you of sin, tempting you to distrust God and doubt His mercy, say: I cannot allow my weakness to come between me and God; for He is my strength. My sins, which are many, are laid upon Jesus, my divine Substitute and Sacrifice.

> "Nothing in my hand I bring.
> Simply to thy cross I cling."

No man can look within himself and find anything in his character that will recommend him to God, or make his acceptance sure. It is only through Jesus, whom the Father gave for the life of the world, that the sinner may find access to God. Jesus alone is our Redeemer, our Advocate and Mediator; in Him is our only hope for pardon, peace, and righteousness. It is by virtue of the blood of Christ that the sin-stricken soul can be restored to soundness. Christ is the fragrance, the holy incense which makes your petition acceptable to the Father. Then can you not say:

> "Just as I am, without one plea,
> But that Thy blood was shed for me,
> And that Thou bid'st me come to Thee,
> O Lamb of God, I come."

Coming to Christ does not require severe mental effort and agony; it is simply accepting the terms of salvation that God has made plain in His Word. The blessing is free to all. The invitation is, "Ho, every one that thirsteth, come ye to the waters, and he that hath no money; come ye, buy, and eat; yea, come, buy wine and milk without money and without price. Wherefore do ye spend money for that which is not bread? and your labour for that which satisfieth not? hearken diligently unto me, and eat ye that which is good, and let your soul delight itself in fatness" (Isa. 55:1, 2).

Righteousness Found in Christ

Then come, and seek, and find. The reservoir of power is open, is full and free. Come with humble hearts, not thinking that you must do some good work to merit the favor of God, or that you must make yourself better before you can come to Christ. You are powerless to do good, and cannot better your condition. Apart from Christ we have no merit, no righteousness. Our sinfulness, our weakness, our human imperfection make it impossible that we should appear before God unless we are clothed in Christ's spotless righteousness. We are to be found in Him not having our own righteousness, but the righteousness which is in Christ. Then in the name that is above every name, the only name given among men whereby men can be saved, claim the promise of God, saying, "Lord, forgive my sin; I put my hands into Thy hand for help, and I must have it, or perish. I now believe." The Saviour says to the repenting sinner, "No man cometh unto the Father, but by me" (John 14:6), "and him that cometh to me I will in no wise cast out" (John 6:37). "I am thy salvation" (Ps. 35:3).

When you respond to the drawing of Christ, and join yourself to Him, you manifest saving faith. To talk of religious things in a casual way, to pray for spiritual blessings without real soul hunger and living faith, avails little. The wondering crowd that pressed close about Jesus realized no accession of vital power from the contact. But when the poor, suffering woman, who for twelve years had been an invalid, in her great need put forth her hand and touched the hem of His garment, she felt the healing virtue. Hers was the touch of faith, and Christ recognized that touch. He knew that virtue had gone out from Him, and turning about in the throng, He asked, "Who touched me?" (Luke 8:45). Surprised at such a question, the disciples answered, "Master, the multitude throng thee, . . . and sayest thou, Who touched me? And Jesus said, Somebody hath touched me: for I perceive that virtue is gone out of me. And when the woman saw that she was not hid, she came trembling, and falling down before him, she declared unto him before all the people for what cause she had touched him, and how she was healed immediately. And he said unto her, Daughter, be of good comfort: thy faith hath made thee whole; go in peace" (Luke 8:45-48). The faith which avails to bring us in vital contact with Christ expresses on our part supreme preference, perfect reliance, entire consecration. This faith works by love and purifies the soul. It works in the life of the follower of Christ true obedience to God's commandments; for love to God and love to man will be the result of vital connection with Christ. "If any man have not the Spirit of Christ, he is none of his" (Rom. 8:9).

Jesus says, "I am the vine, ye are the branches" (John 15:5). Can we conceive of a more intimate relation than this implies? The fibers of the branch are identical with those of the vine. The communication of life, strength, and nourishment from the trunk to the branches is unobstructed and constant. The root sends its nourishment through the branches. Such is the believer's relation to Christ, if he abides in Christ and draws his nourishment from Him. But this spiritual relation between Christ and the soul can be established only through the exercise of personal faith. "Without faith it is impossible to please him" (Heb. 11:6); for it is faith that connects us with the power of heaven, and brings us strength for coping with the powers of darkness. "This is the victory that overcometh the world, even our faith" (1 John 5:4). Faith familiarizes the soul with the existence and presence of God, and, living with an eye single to the glory of God, more and more we discern the beauty of His character, the excellence of His grace. Our souls become strong in spiritual power; for we are breathing the atmosphere of heaven, and realizing that God is at our right hand, that we shall not be moved. We are rising above the world, beholding Him who is the chief among ten thousand, the one altogether lovely, and by beholding we are to become changed into His image.

51.

*United With the Living Vine**

"If any man be in Christ, he is a new creature: old things are passed away; behold, all things are become new" (2 Cor. 5:17). Nothing but divine power can regenerate the human heart and imbue souls with the love of Christ, which will ever manifest itself with love for those for whom He died. The fruit of the Spirit is love, joy, peace, long-suffering, goodness, faith, meekness, temperance. When a man is converted to God, a new moral taste is supplied, a new motive power is given, and he loves the things that God loves; for his life is bound up by the golden chain of the immutable promises to the life of Jesus. Love, joy, peace, and inexpressible gratitude will pervade the soul, and the language of him who is blessed will be, "Thy gentleness hath made me great" (Ps. 18: 35).

But those who are waiting to behold a magical change in their characters without determined effort on their part to overcome sin, will be disappointed. We have no reason to fear while looking to Jesus, no reason to doubt but that He is able to save to the uttermost all that come unto Him; but we may constantly fear lest our old

---

* This article appeared in *The Signs of the Times,* Dec. 26, 1892.

nature will again obtain the supremacy, that the enemy shall devise some snare whereby we shall again become his captives. We are to work out our own salvation with fear and trembling, for it is God that worketh in you to will and to do of His good pleasure. With our limited powers we are to be as holy in our sphere as God is holy in His sphere. To the extent of our ability, we are to make manifest the truth and love and excellence of the divine character. As wax takes the impression of the seal, so the soul is to take the impression of the Spirit of God and retain the image of Christ.

We are to grow daily in spiritual loveliness. We shall fail often in our efforts to copy the divine pattern. We shall often have to bow down to weep at the feet of Jesus, because of our shortcomings and mistakes; but we are not to be discouraged; we are to pray more fervently, believe more fully, and try again with more steadfastness to grow into the likeness of our Lord. As we distrust our own power, we shall trust the power of our Redeemer, and render praise to God, who is the health of our countenance, and our God.

Wherever there is union with Christ there is love. Whatever other fruits we may bear, if love be missing, they profit nothing. Love to God and our neighbor is the very essence of our religion. No one can love Christ and not love His children. When we are united to Christ, we have the mind of Christ. Purity and love shine forth in the character, meekness and truth control the life. The very expression of the countenance is changed. Christ abiding in the soul exerts a transforming power, and the outward aspect bears witness to the peace and joy that reign within. We drink in the love of Christ, as the branch draws nourishment from the vine. If we are grafted in Christ, if fiber by fiber we have been united with the Living Vine, we shall give evidence of the fact by bearing rich clusters of living fruit. If we are connected with the Light, we shall be channels of light, and in our words and works we shall reflect light to the world. Those who are truly Christians are bound with the chain of love which links earth to heaven, which binds finite man to the infinite God. The light that shines in the face of Jesus Christ shines in the hearts of His followers, to the glory of God.

By beholding we are to become changed; and as we meditate upon the perfections of the divine Model, we shall desire to become wholly transformed, and renewed in the image of His purity. It is by faith in the Son of God that transformation takes place in the character, and the child of wrath becomes the child of God. He passes from death unto life; he becomes spiritual and discerns spiritual things. The wisdom of God enlightens his mind, and he beholds wondrous things out of His law. As a man is converted by the truth, the work of transformation of character goes on. He has an increased measure of understanding. In becoming a man of obedience to God, he has the mind of Christ, and the will of God becomes his will.

He who places himself unreservedly under the guidance of the Spirit of God, will find that his mind expands and develops. He obtains an education in the service of God which is not one-sided and deficient, developing a one-sided character, but one which results in symmetry and completeness. Weaknesses that have been manifested in a vacillating will and powerless character, are overcome, for continual devotion and piety bring the man in such close relation to Christ that he has the mind of Christ. He is one with Christ, having soundness and strength of principle. His perception is clear, and he manifests that wisdom which comes from God. Says James, "Who is a wise man and endued with knowledge among you? let him shew out of a good conversation his works with meekness of wisdom" (James 3:13). "The wisdom that is from above is first pure, then peaceable, gentle, and easy to be intreated, full of mercy and good fruits, without partiality, and without hypocrisy. And the fruit of righteousness is sown in peace of them that make peace" (James 3:17, 18). This will be the wisdom manifested by him who takes the cup of salvation and calls upon the name of the Lord. This salvation, which offers pardon to the transgressor, presents to him the righteousness that will bear the scrutiny of the Omniscient One, gives victory over the powerful enemy of God and man, provides eternal life and joy for its receiver, and may well be a theme of rejoicing to the humble, who hear thereof and are glad.

The Parable of the Lost Sheep

The beautiful parable that Christ gave of the one lost sheep, of the shepherd that left the ninety and nine to go in search of that which was lost, illustrates the work of Christ, the sinner's condition, and the rejoicing of the universe over the salvation of the soul. The shepherd did not look carelessly over the sheep, and say, "I have ninety and nine, and it will cost me too much trouble to go in search of the straying one; let him come back, and I will open the door of the sheepfold that he may come in; but I cannot go after him." No; no sooner does the sheep go astray than the countenance of the shepherd is filled with grief and anxiety. He counts and recounts the flock, and when he is certain that one sheep is lost, he slumbers not. He leaves the ninety and nine within the fold, and, however dark and tempestuous the night, however perilous and unpleasant the way, however long and tedious the service, he does not weary, he does not falter, until the lost is found. And when it is found, he lays the weary, exhausted sheep on his shoulder, and, with cheerful gratitude that his search has not been in vain, he bears back the wanderer to the fold. His gratitude finds expression in the melodious songs of rejoicing, and he calls upon his friends and neighbors, saying unto them, "Rejoice with me; for I have found my sheep which was lost" (Luke 15:6). So when a wanderer is found by the Great Shepherd of the sheep, heavenly angels respond to the Shepherd's note of joy. When the lost is found, heaven and earth unite in thanksgiving and rejoicing. "Joy shall be in heaven over one sinner that repenteth, more than over ninety and nine just persons, which need no repentance" (Luke 15:7).

52.

*Christform Our High Priest**

Justice demands that sin be not merely pardoned, but the death penalty must be executed. God, in the gift of His only-begotten Son, met both these requirements. By dying in man's stead, Christ exhausted the penalty and provided a pardon.

Man through sin has been severed from the life of God. His soul is palsied through the machinations of Satan, the author of sin. Of himself he is incapable of sensing sin, incapable of appreciating and appropriating the divine nature. Were it brought within his reach there is nothing in it that his natural heart would desire it. The bewitching power of Satan is upon him. All the ingenious subterfuges the devil can suggest are presented to his mind to prevent every good impulse. Every faculty and power given him of God has been used as a weapon against the divine Benefactor. So, although He loves him, God cannot safely impart to him the gifts and blessings He desires to bestow.

But God will not be defeated by Satan. He sent His Son into the world, that through His taking the human form and nature, humanity and divinity combined in Him would elevate man in the scale of moral value with God.

---

* Manuscript 50, 1900.

There is no other way for man's salvation. "Without me," says Christ, "ye can do nothing" (John 15:5). Through Christ, and Christ alone, the springs of life can vitalize man's nature, transform his tastes, and set his affections flowing toward heaven. Through the union of the divine with the human nature Christ could enlighten the understanding and infuse His life-giving properties through the soul dead in trespasses and sins.

When the mind is drawn to the cross of Calvary, Christ by imperfect sight is discerned on the shameful cross. Why did He die? In consequence of sin. What is sin? The transgression of the law. Then the eyes are open to see the character of sin. The law is broken but cannot pardon the transgressor. It is our schoolmaster, condemning to punishment. Where is the remedy? The law drives us to Christ, who was hanged upon the cross that He might be able to impart His righteousness to fallen, sinful man and thus present men to His Father in His righteous character.

Christ on the cross not only draws men to repentance toward God for the transgression of His law—for whom God pardons He first makes penitent—but Christ has satisfied Justice; He has proffered Himself as an atonement. His gushing blood, His broken body, satisfy the claims of the broken law, and thus He bridges the gulf which sin has made. He suffered in the flesh, that with His bruised and broken body He might cover the defenseless sinner. The victory gained at His death on Calvary broke forever the accusing power of Satan over the universe and silenced his charges that self-denial was impossible with God and therefore not essential in the human family.

Satan's position in heaven had been next to the Son of God. He was first among the angels. His power had been debasing, but God could not reveal it in its true light and carry all heaven in harmony with Him in removing him with his evil influences. His power was increasing, but the evil was yet unrecognized. It was a deadly power to the universe, but for the security of the worlds and the government of heaven, it was necessary that it should develop and be revealed in its true light.

Self-denial With God

In carrying out his enmity to Christ until He hung upon the cross of Calvary, with wounded, bruised body and broken heart, Satan completely uprooted himself from the affections of the universe. It was then seen that God had in His Son denied Himself, giving Himself for the sins of the world, because He loved mankind. The Creator was revealed in the Son of the infinite God. Here the question, "Can there be self-denial with God?" was forever answered. Christ was God, and condescending to be made flesh, He assumed humanity and became obedient unto death, that He might undergo infinite sacrifice.

Whatever sacrifice a human being could undergo Christ endured, notwithstanding Satan put forth every effort to seduce Him with temptations; but the greater the temptation, the more perfect was the sacrifice. All that was possible for man to endure in the conflict with Satan, Christ endured in His human and divine nature combined. Obedient, sinless to the last, He died for man, his substitute and surety, enduring all that men ever endure from the deceiving tempter, that man may overcome by being a partaker of the divine nature.

Pure truth was found to be a match for falsehood, honesty and integrity for subtlety and intrigue, in everyone who is, like Christ, willing to sacrifice all, even life itself, for the truth's sake. To resist Satan's desires is no easy task. It demands a firm hold of the divine nature from beginning to end, or it cannot be done. Christ, in the victories achieved in His death on Calvary's cross, plainly lays open the way for man, and thus makes it possible for him to keep the law of God through the Way, the Truth, and the Life. There is no other way.

The righteousness of Christ is presented as a free gift to the sinner if he will accept it. He has nothing of his own but what is tainted and corrupted, polluted with sin, utterly repulsive to a pure and holy God. Only through the righteous character of Jesus Christ can man come nigh to God.

Christ as high priest within the veil so immortalized Calvary that though He liveth unto God, He dies continually to sin, and thus if any man sin, he has an advocate with the Father.

He arose from the tomb enshrouded with a cloud of angels in wondrous power and glory—the Deity and humanity combined. He took in His grasp the world over which Satan claimed to preside as his lawful territory, and by His wonderful work in giving His life, He restored the whole race of men to favor with God. . . .

Let no one take the limited, narrow position that any of the works of man can help in the least possible way to liquidate the debt of his transgression. This is a fatal deception. If you would understand it, you must cease haggling over your pet ideas, and with humble hearts survey the atonement. This matter is so dimly comprehended that thousands upon thousands claiming to be sons of God are children of the wicked one, because they will depend on their own works. God always demanded good works, the law demands it, but because man placed himself in sin where his good works were valueless, Jesus' righteousness alone can avail. Christ is able to save to the uttermost because He ever liveth to make intercession for us. All that man can possibly do toward his own salvation is to accept the invitation, "Whosoever will, let him take the water of life freely" (Rev. 22:17). No sin can be committed by man for which satisfaction has not been met on Calvary. Thus the cross, in earnest appeals, continually proffers to the sinner a thorough expiation.

Repentance and Pardon

As you near the cross of Calvary there is seen love that is without a parallel. As you by faith grasp the meaning of the sacrifice, you see yourself a sinner, condemned by a broken law. This is repentance. As you come with humble heart, you find pardon, for Christ Jesus is represented as continually standing at the altar, momentarily offering up the sacrifice for the sins of the world. He is a minister of the true tabernacle which the Lord pitched and not man.

The typical shadows of the Jewish tabernacle no longer possess any virtue. A daily and yearly typical atonement is no longer to be made, but the atoning sacrifice through a mediator is essential because of the constant commission of sin. Jesus is officiating in the presence of God, offering up His shed blood, as it had been a lamb slain. Jesus presents the oblation offered for every offense and every shortcoming of the sinner.

Christ, our Mediator, and the Holy Spirit are constantly interceding in man's behalf, but the Spirit pleads not for us as does Christ, who presents His blood, shed from the foundation of the world; the Spirit works upon our hearts, drawing out prayers and penitence, praise and thanksgiving. The gratitude which flows from our lips is the result of the Spirit's striking the cords of the soul in holy memories, awakening the music of the heart.

The religious services, the prayers, the praise, the penitent confession of sin ascend from true believers as incense to the heavenly sanctuary, but passing through the corrupt channels of humanity, they are so defiled that unless purified by blood, they can never be of value with God. They ascend not in spotless purity, and unless the Intercessor, who is at God's right hand, presents and purifies all by His righteousness, it is not acceptable to God. All incense from earthly tabernacles must be moist with the cleansing drops of the blood of Christ. He holds before the Father the censer of His own merits, in which there is no taint of earthly corruption. He gathers into this censer the prayers, the praise, and the confessions of His people, and with these He puts His own spotless righteousness. Then, perfumed with the merits of Christ's propitiation, the incense comes up before God wholly and entirely acceptable. Then gracious answers are returned.

Oh, that all may see that everything in obedience, in penitence, in praise and thanksgiving, must be placed upon the glowing fire of the righteousness of Christ. The fragrance of this righteousness ascends like a cloud around the mercy seat.

53.

*Transformation Through Faith and Obedience**

The teaching of Christ in the gospel is in perfect harmony with the teaching of Christ through the prophets in the Old Testament. The prophets spoke through the messengers of Christ in the Old Testament as much as the apostles voiced His messages in the New Testament, and there is no contradiction between their teachings. But Satan has ever worked and is still working with all deceivableness of unrighteousness to make the Word of God of none effect. He seeks to make mysterious that which is simple and plain. He has had long experience in this work. He knows the character of God, and through his subtlety he has captivated the world. It was through making the word of God of none effect that sin was brought into the world. Adam believed the falsehood of Satan, and through his misrepresentation of the character of God, Adam's life was changed and marred. He disobeyed the commandment of God, and did the very thing the Lord told him not to do. Through disobedience Adam fell; but had he endured the test, and been loyal to God, the flood-

---

* This article appeared in *The Signs of the Times,* June 5, 1893.

gates of woe would not have been opened upon our world.

Through belief in Satan's misrepresentation of God, man's character and destiny were changed, but if men will believe in the Word of God, they will be transformed in mind and character, and fitted for eternal life. To believe that "God so loved the world, that he gave his only begotten Son, that whosoever believeth in him should not perish, but have everlasting life" (John 3:16), will change the heart, and reproduce in man the image of God.

As many are today, so (before his conversion) Paul was very confident in an hereditary piety; but his confidence was founded on falsehood. It was faith out of Christ, for he trusted in forms and ceremonies. His zeal for the law was disconnected from Christ and was valueless. His boast was that he was blameless in his performance of the deeds of the law; but the Christ who made the law of any value he refused. He was confident that he was right. He says: "I verily thought with myself, that I ought to do many things contrary to the name of Jesus of Nazareth. Which thing I also did in Jerusalem: and many of the saints did I shut up in prison, having received authority from the chief priests; and when they were put to death, I gave my voice against them" (Acts 26:9, 10). For a time Paul did a very cruel work, thinking that he was doing God service; for he says, "I did it ignorantly in unbelief" (1 Tim. 1:13). But his sincerity did not justify his work, or make error truth.

Faith is the medium through which truth or error finds a lodging place in the mind. It is by the same act of mind that truth or error is received, but it makes a decided difference whether we believe the Word of God or the sayings of men. When Christ revealed Himself to Paul, and he was convinced that he was persecuting Jesus in the person of His saints, he accepted the truth as it is in Jesus. A transforming power was manifested on mind and character, and he became a new man in Christ Jesus. He received the truth so fully that neither earth nor hell could shake his faith.

There are many who cry, "Believe, only believe." Ask them what you are to believe. Are you to believe the lies forged by Satan against God's holy, just, and good law? God does not use His great and precious grace to make of none effect His law, but to establish His law. What is the decision of Paul? He says: "What shall we say then? Is the law sin? God forbid. Nay, I had not known sin, but by the law. . . . For I was alive without the law once: but when the commandment came, sin revived, and [the commandment then ended?—No.] I [Paul] died. . . . Wherefore the law is [standing directly in the way of my having liberty and peace?—No.] holy, and the commandment holy, and just, and good" (Rom. 7:7-12).

The Law Cannot Pardon

Paul learned that there was no power in the law to pardon the transgressor of law. "By the deeds of the law there shall no flesh be justified" (Rom. 3:20). "For what the law could not do, in that it was weak through the flesh, God sending his own Son in the likeness of sinful flesh, and for sin, condemned sin in the flesh: that the righteousness of the law might be fulfilled in us, who walk not after the flesh, but after the Spirit" (Rom. 8:3, 4).

The Lord saw our fallen condition; He saw our need of grace, and because He loved our souls, He has given us grace and peace. Grace means favor to one who is undeserving, to one who is lost. The fact that we are sinners, instead of shutting us away from the mercy and love of God, makes the exercise of His love to us a positive necessity in order that we may be saved. Christ says, "Ye have not chosen me, but I have chosen you, and ordained you, that ye should go and bring forth fruit, and that your fruit should remain" (John 15:16).

When Adam fell, provision was made for his restoration. In due time Jesus, the Prince of life, came to our world to enter into controversy with the powers of darkness. In this world Satan had an opportunity to exhibit the result of the working out of his principles of freedom from all law, and Christ, by His unswerving obedience to His

Father's commandments, made manifest the result of practicing the principles of righteousness. In accordance with his principles of evil, Satan harassed the Son of God with fierce temptations, and finally brought Him to the judgment hall, that He might be condemned to death without cause. The confederacy of evil moved upon the hearts of men to work out the principles of evil. Christ and Barabbas were presented before the multitude. Barabbas was a notable robber and murderer; Christ was the Son of God. Pilate looked upon the two, and thought there would be no hesitation in the choice of Jesus. The marks of nobility, intelligence, and purity were plainly revealed in His countenance, in marked contrast to the coarse features of Barabbas. He asked, "Whether of the twain will ye that I release unto you?" (Matt. 27:21). And the hoarse cry of the infuriated mob was heard, calling, "Barabbas." "Pilate saith unto them, What shall I do then with Jesus which is called Christ? They all say unto him, Let him be crucified. And the governor said, Why, what evil hath he done? But they cried out the more, saying, Let him be crucified" (Matt. 27:22, 23).

Satan Defeated by Christ's Death

In this choice the principles of Satan were made manifest; and the hosts of heaven, and all the worlds that God had created, judged that Satan was an accuser of the brethren, a liar, and a murderer. In heaven and among the unfallen worlds the question of Satan's deceiving power, of his malignant principles, was settled, and the perfect purity and holiness of Christ, who was bearing the test and trial in behalf of fallen man, was forever proved. Through the development of Satan's character and principles, he was forever uprooted from the affection of the unfallen worlds, and the controversy concerning his claims and the claims of Christ was forever settled in heaven. The righteousness manifested in the character of Christ was forever to be the anchor, the saving hope, of the world. Every soul who chooses Christ can say with faith, "The Lord my righteousness."

Christ was "despised and rejected of men; a man of sorrows, and acquainted with grief: and we hid as it were our faces from him; he was despised, and we esteemed him not. Surely he hath borne our griefs, and carried our sorrows: yet we did esteem him stricken, smitten of God, and afflicted. But he was wounded for our transgressions, he was bruised for our iniquities: the chastisement of our peace was upon him; and with his stripes we are healed" (Isa. 53:3-5).

The grace of Christ and the law of God are inseparable. In Jesus mercy and truth are met together, righteousness and peace have kissed each other. In His life and character He not only reveals the character of God, but the possibility of man. He was the representative of God and the exemplar of humanity. He presented to the world what humanity might become when united by faith with divinity. The only-begotten Son of God took upon Him the nature of man, and established His cross between earth and heaven. Through the cross, man was drawn to God, and God to man. Justice moved from its high and awful position, and the heavenly hosts, the armies of holiness, drew near to the cross, bowing with reverence; for at the cross justice was satisfied. Through the cross the sinner was drawn from the stronghold of sin, from the confederacy of evil, and at every approach to the cross his heart relents and in penitence he cries, "It was my sins that crucified the Son of God." At the cross he leaves his sins, and through the grace of Christ his character is transformed. The Redeemer raises the sinner from the dust, and places him under the guidance of the Holy Spirit. As the sinner looks upon the Redeemer, he finds hope, assurance, and joy. Faith takes hold of Christ in love. Faith works by love, and purifies the soul.

54.

The Subject Presented in 1883[*]

"If we confess our sins, he is faithful and just to forgive us our sins, and to cleanse us from all unrighteousness" (1 John 1:9).

God requires that we confess our sins, and humble our hearts before Him; but at the same time we should have confidence in Him as a tender Father, who will not forsake those who put their trust in Him. Many of us walk by sight, and not by faith. We believe the things that are seen, but do not appreciate the precious promises given us in God's Word; and yet we cannot dishonor God more decidedly than by showing that we distrust what He says, and question whether the Lord is in earnest with us or is deceiving us.

God does not give us up because of our sins. We may make mistakes, and grieve His Spirit; but when we repent, and come to Him with contrite hearts, He will not turn us away. There are hindrances to be removed. Wrong feelings have been cherished, and there have been pride, self-sufficiency, impatience, and murmurings. All these separate us from God. Sins must be confessed; there must be a deeper

---

* Morning talk to the ministers assembled at the General Conference, Battle Creek, Michigan, November, 1883. Published in *Gospel Workers* (1892 ed.), pp. 411-415, under the title "Christ Our Righteousness."

work of grace in the heart. Those who feel weak and discouraged may become strong men of God, and do noble work for the Master. But they must work from a high standpoint; they must be influenced by no selfish motives.

Merits of Christ Our Only Hope

We must learn in the school of Christ. Nothing but His righteousness can entitle us to one of the blessings of the covenant of grace. We have long desired and tried to obtain these blessings, but have not received them because we have cherished the idea that we could do something to make ourselves worthy of them. We have not looked away from ourselves, believing that Jesus is a living Saviour. We must not think that our own grace and merits will save us; the grace of Christ is our only hope of salvation. Through His prophet the Lord promises, "Let the wicked forsake his way, and the unrighteous man his thoughts: and let him return unto the Lord, and he will have mercy upon him; and to our God, for he will abundantly pardon" (Isa. 55:7). We must believe the naked promise, and not accept feeling for faith. When we trust God fully, when we rely upon the merits of Jesus as a sin-pardoning Saviour, we shall receive all the help that we can desire.

We look to self, as though we had power to save ourselves; but Jesus died for us because we are helpless to do this. In Him is our hope, our justification, our righteousness. We should not despond, and fear that we have no Saviour, or that He has no thoughts of mercy toward us. At this very time He is carrying on His work in our behalf, inviting us to come to Him in our helplessness and be saved. We dishonor Him by our unbelief. It is astonishing how we treat our very best Friend, how little confidence we repose in Him who is able to save to the uttermost, and who has given us every evidence of His great love.

My brethren, are you expecting that your merit will recommend you to the favor of God, thinking that you must be free from sin before you trust His power to save? If this is the struggle going on in your mind, I fear you will gain no strength, and will finally become discouraged.

Look and Live

In the wilderness, when the Lord permitted poisonous serpents to sting the rebellious Israelites, Moses was directed to lift up a brazen serpent and bid all the wounded look to it and live. But many saw no help in this Heaven-appointed remedy. The dead and dying were all around them, and they knew that without divine help their fate was certain; but they would lament their wounds, their pains, their sure death, until their strength was gone, and their eyes were glazed, when they might have had instant healing.

"As Moses lifted up the serpent in the wilderness," even so was "the Son of man . . . lifted up: that whosoever believeth in him should not perish, but have eternal life" (John 3:14, 15). If you are conscious of your sins, do not devote all your powers to mourning over them, but look and live. Jesus is our only Saviour; and although millions who need to be healed will reject His offered mercy, not one who trusts in His merits will be left to perish. While we realize our helpless condition without Christ, we must not be discouraged; we must rely upon a crucified and risen Saviour. Poor, sin-sick, discouraged soul, look and live. Jesus has pledged His word; He will save all who come unto Him.

Come to Jesus, and receive rest and peace. You may have the blessing even now. Satan suggests that you are helpless, and cannot bless yourself. It is true; you are helpless. But lift up Jesus before him: "I have a risen Saviour. In Him I trust, and He will never suffer me to be confounded. In His name I triumph. He is my righteousness, and my crown of rejoicing." Let no one here feel that his case is hopeless; for it is not. You may see that you are sinful and undone; but it is just on this account that you need a Saviour. If you have sins to confess, lose no time. These moments are golden. "If we confess our sins, he is faithful and just to forgive us our sins, and to cleanse us from all unrighteousness" (1 John 1:9). Those who hunger and thirst after righteousness will be filled;

for Jesus has promised it. Precious Saviour! His arms are open to receive us, and His great heart of love is waiting to bless us.

Some seem to feel that they must be on probation and must prove to the Lord that they are reformed, before they can claim His blessing. But these dear souls may claim the blessing even now. They must have His grace, the Spirit of Christ, to help their infirmities, or they cannot form a Christian character. Jesus loves to have us come to Him, just as we are—sinful, helpless, dependent.

Repentance a Gift of God

Repentance, as well as forgiveness, is the gift of God through Christ. It is through the influence of the Holy Spirit that we are convicted of sin, and feel our need of pardon. None but the contrite are forgiven; but it is the grace of God that makes the heart penitent. He is acquainted with all our weaknesses and infirmities, and He will help us.

Some who come to God by repentance and confession, and even believe that their sins are forgiven, still fail of claiming, as they should, the promises of God. They do not see that Jesus is an ever-present Saviour; and they are not ready to commit the keeping of their souls to Him, relying upon Him to perfect the work of grace begun in their hearts. While they think they are committing themselves to God, there is a great deal of self-dependence. There are conscientious souls that trust partly to God, and partly to themselves. They do not look to God, to be kept by His power, but depend upon watchfulness against temptation, and the performance of certain duties for acceptance with Him. There are no victories in this kind of faith. Such persons toil to no purpose; their souls are in continual bondage, and they find no rest until their burdens are laid at the feet of Jesus.

There is need of constant watchfulness, and of earnest, loving devotion; but these will come naturally when the soul is kept by the power of God through faith. We can do nothing, absolutely nothing, to commend ourselves to divine favor. We must not trust at all to ourselves nor to our good works; but when as erring, sinful beings we come to Christ, we may find rest in His love. God will accept every one that comes to Him trusting wholly in the merits of a crucified Saviour. Love springs up in the heart. There may be no ecstasy of feeling, but there is an abiding, peaceful trust. Every burden is light; for the yoke which Christ imposes is easy. Duty becomes a delight, and sacrifice a pleasure. The path that before seemed shrouded in darkness becomes bright with beams from the Sun of Righteousness. This is walking in the light as Christ is in the light.

55.

*Presented as Old Truth in New Framework**

At the Kansas meeting my prayer to God was, that the power of the enemy might be broken, and that the people who had been in darkness might open their hearts and minds to the message that God should send them, that they might see the truth, new to many minds, as old truth in new framework. The understanding of the people of God has been blinded, for Satan has misrepresented the character of God. Our good and gracious Lord has been presented before the people clothed in the attributes of Satan, and men and women who have been seeking for truth, have so long regarded God in a false light that it is difficult to dispel the cloud that obscures His glory from their view. Many have been living in an atmosphere of doubt, and it seems almost impossible for them to lay hold on the hope set before them in the gospel of Christ. . . .

On Sabbath, truths were presented that were new to the majority of the congregation. Things new and old were

---

* Report of camp meeting at Ottawa, Kansas, printed in *The Review and Herald*, July 23, 1889.

brought forth from the treasure house of God's Word. Truths were revealed which the people were scarcely able to comprehend and appropriate. Light flashed from the oracles of God in relation to the law and the gospel, in relation to the fact that Christ is our righteousness, which seemed to souls who were hungry for truth, as light too precious to be received.

But the labors of the Sabbath were not in vain. On Sunday morning there was decided evidence that the Spirit of God was working great changes in the moral and spiritual condition of those assembled. There was a surrendering of the mind and heart to God, and precious testimonies were borne by those who had long been in darkness. One brother spoke of the struggle that he had experienced before he could receive the good news that Christ is our righteousness. The conflict was severe, but the Lord was at work with him, and his mind was changed, and his strength renewed. The Lord presented the truth before him in clear lines, revealing the fact that Christ alone is the source of all hope and salvation. "In him was life; and the life was the light of men." "And the Word was made flesh, and dwelt among us, (and we beheld his glory, the glory as of the only begotten of the Father,) full of grace and truth" (John 1:4, 14).

One of our young ministering brethren said that he had enjoyed more of the blessing and love of God during that meeting than in all his life before. Another stated that the trials, perplexities, and conflicts which he had endured in his mind had been of such a character that he had been tempted to give up everything. He had felt that there was no hope for him, unless he could obtain more of the grace of Christ; but through the influence of the meetings he had experienced a change of heart, and had a better knowledge of salvation through faith in Christ. He saw that it was his privilege to be justified by faith; he had peace with God, and with tears confessed what relief and blessing had come to his soul. At every social meeting many testimonies were borne as to the peace, comfort, and joy the people had found in receiving light.

We thank the Lord with all the heart that we have precious light to present before the people, and we rejoice that we have a message for this time which is present truth. The tidings that Christ is our righteousness has brought relief to many, many souls, and God says to His people, "Go forward." The message to the Laodicean church is applicable to our condition. How plainly is pictured the position of those who think they have all the truth, who take pride in their knowledge of the Word of God, while its sanctifying power has not been felt in their lives. The fervor of the love of God is wanting in their hearts, but it is this very fervor of love that makes God's people the light of the world.

The Laodicean Message

The True Witness says of a cold, lifeless, Christless church, "I know thy works, that thou art neither cold nor hot: I would thou wert cold or hot. So then because thou art lukewarm, and neither cold nor hot, I will spue thee out of my mouth" (Rev. 3:15, 16). Mark the following words: "Because thou sayest, I am rich, and increased with goods, and have need of nothing; and *knowest not* that thou art wretched, and miserable, and poor, and blind, and naked" (Rev. 3:17). Here is represented a people who pride themselves in their possession of spiritual knowledge and advantages. But they have not responded to the unmerited blessings that God has bestowed upon them. They have been full of rebellion, ingratitude, and forgetfulness of God; and still He has dealt with them as a loving, forgiving father deals with an ungrateful, wayward son. They have resisted His grace, abused His privileges, slighted His opportunities, and have been satisfied to sink down in contentment, in lamentable ingratitude, hollow formalism, and hypocritical insincerity. With Pharisaic pride they have vaunted themselves till it has been said of them, "Thou sayest, I am rich, and increased with goods, and have need of nothing."

Has not the Lord Jesus sent message after message of

rebuke, of warning, of entreaty to these self-satisfied ones? Have not His counsels been despised and rejected? Have not His delegated messengers been treated with scorn, and their words been received as idle tales? Christ sees that which man does not see. He sees the sins which, if not repented of, will exhaust the patience of a long-suffering God. Christ cannot take up the names of those who are satisfied in their own self-sufficiency. He cannot importune in behalf of a people who feel no need of His help, who claim to know and possess everything.

The great Redeemer represents Himself as a heavenly merchantman, laden with riches, calling from house to house, presenting His priceless goods, and saying, "I counsel thee to buy of me gold tried in the fire, that thou mayest be rich; and white raiment, that thou mayest be clothed, and that the shame of thy nakedness do not appear; and anoint thine eyes with eyesalve, that thou mayest see. As many as I love, I rebuke and chasten: be zealous therefore, and repent. Behold, I stand at the door, and knock: if any man hear my voice, and open the door, I will come in to him, and will sup with him, and he with me" (Rev. 3:18-20).

Let us consider our condition before God; let us heed the counsel of the True Witness. Let none of us be filled with prejudice, as were the Jews, that light may not come into our hearts. Let it not be necessary for Christ to say of us as He did of them, "Ye will not come to me, that ye might have life" (John 5:40).

In every meeting since the General Conference, souls have eagerly accepted the precious message of the righteousness of Christ. We thank God that there are souls who realize that they are in need of something which they do not possess—gold of faith and love, white raiment of Christ's righteousness, eyesalve of spiritual discernment. If you possess these precious gifts, the temple of the human soul will not be like a desecrated shrine. Brethren and sisters, I call upon you in the name of Jesus Christ of Nazareth, to work where God works. Now is the day of gracious opportunity and privilege.

56.

*A Truth Bearing the Divine Credentials**

A Message From God†

The present message—justification by faith—is a message from God; it bears the divine credentials, for its fruit is unto holiness. Some who greatly need the precious truth that was presented before them, we fear did not receive its benefit. They did not open the door of their hearts to welcome Jesus as a heavenly guest, and they have suffered great loss. There is indeed a narrow way in which we must walk; the cross is presented at every step. We must learn to live by faith; then the darkest hours will be brightened by the blessed beams of the Sun of Righteousness.

We are not safe if we neglect to search the Scriptures daily for light and knowledge. Earthly blessings cannot be obtained without toil, and can we expect that spiritual

---

* Items drawn from reports on the reception of the message of righteousness by faith as it was presented following the General Conference held at Minneapolis in 1888.

† Drawn from report of the camp meeting at Rome, New York.

and heavenly blessings will come without earnest effort on our part? The mines of truth are to be worked. Says the psalmist, "The entrance of thy words giveth light; it giveth understanding unto the simple" (Ps. 119:130). The Word of God must not be kept apart from our life. It must be entertained in the mind, welcomed in the heart, and be cherished, loved, and obeyed. We need also much more knowledge; we need to be enlightened in regard to the plan of salvation. There is not one in one hundred who understands for himself the Bible truth on this subject that is so necessary to our present and eternal welfare. When light begins to shine forth to make clear the plan of redemption to the people, the enemy works with all diligence that the light may be shut away from the hearts of men. If we come to the Word of God with a teachable, humble spirit, the rubbish of error will be swept away, and gems of truth, long hidden from our eyes, will be discovered.

There is great need that Christ should be preached as the only hope and salvation. When the doctrine of justification by faith was presented at the Rome meeting, it came to many as water comes to the thirsty traveler. The thought that the righteousness of Christ is imputed to us, not because of any merit on our part, but as a free gift from God, seemed a precious thought.—*The Review and Herald,* Sept. 3, 1889.

No Relish for Sin

When we are clothed with the righteousness of Christ, we shall have no relish for sin; for Christ will be working with us. We may make mistakes, but we will hate the sin that caused the sufferings of the Son of God.—*The Review and Herald,* March 18, 1890.

Extreme Teaching

There are grand truths, long hidden under the rubbish of error, that are to be revealed to the people. The doctrine of justification by faith has been lost sight of by many who have professed to believe the third angel's message. The

Holiness people have gone to great extremes on this point. With great zeal they have taught, "Only believe in Christ, and be saved; but away with the law of God." This is not the teaching of the Word of God. There is no foundation for such a faith. This is not the precious gem of truth that God has given to His people for this time. This doctrine misleads honest souls. The light from the Word of God reveals the fact that the law must be proclaimed. Christ must be lifted up, because He is a Saviour who forgiveth transgression, iniquity, and sin, but will by no means clear the guilty and unrepentant soul.—*The Review and Herald,* Aug. 13, 1889.

The Message Bears Fruit *

We are having most excellent meetings. The spirit that was in the meeting at Minneapolis is not here. All moves off in harmony. There is a large attendance of delegates. Our five o'clock morning meeting is well attended, and the meetings good. All the testimonies to which I have listened have been of an elevating character. They say that the past year has been the best of their life; the light shining forth from the Word of God has been clear and distinct—justification by faith, Christ our righteousness. The experiences have been very interesting.

I have attended all but two morning meetings. At eight o'clock Brother Jones speaks upon the subject of justification by faith, and great interest is manifested. There is a growth in faith and in the knowledge of our Lord and Saviour Jesus Christ. There are quite a number who have not had an opportunity to hear upon this subject before, but they are taking it in, and are being fed with large morsels from the Lord's table. The universal testimony from those

* Ellen G. White report of the fruitage of the message of righteousness by faith observed at the General Conference of 1889 in Battle Creek, Michigan, October 18 to November 5. Reference to the spirit manifest at Minneapolis is to the situation which grew out of an approach to Bible study, at the General Conference of 1888, held in Minneapolis, in an argumentative and debating spirit accompanied on the part of some with criticism and ridicule.—COMPILERS.

who have spoken has been that this message of light and truth which has come to our people is just the truth for this time, and wherever they go among the churches, light, and relief, and the blessing of God is sure to come in.

We have a feast of fat things, and when we see souls grasping the light we are rejoiced, looking unto Jesus who is the author and finisher of our faith. Christ is the great pattern; His character must be our character. All excellence is in Him. Turning from man and every other model, with open face we behold Jesus in all His glory. And their minds are filled with the grand and overpowering ideas of His excellency; every other object sinks into insignificance, and every part of moral discipline is lost which does not promote their likeness to His image. I see heights and depths that we may reach, accepting every ray of light and going forward to a greater light. The end is near, and God forbid that we shall be asleep at this time.

I am so thankful to see with our ministering brethren a disposition to search the Scriptures for themselves. There has been a very great lack of deep searching of the Scriptures, storing the mind with the gems of truth. How much we all lose because we do not put to the tax our minds to search with much prayer for divine enlightenment to understand His Holy Word.

I believe there will be a decided advance among our people, a more earnest endeavor to keep pace with the third angel's message.—Manuscript 10, 1889.

The Beginning of the Loud Cry

Let every one who claims to believe that the Lord is soon coming, search the Scriptures as never before; for Satan is determined to try every device possible to keep souls in darkness, and blind the mind to the perils of the times in which we are living. Let every believer take up his Bible with earnest prayer, that he may be enlightened by the Holy Spirit as to what is truth, that he may know more of God and of Jesus Christ whom He has sent. Search for the truth as for hidden treasures, and disappoint the enemy.

The time of test is just upon us, for the loud cry of the third angel has already begun in the revelation of the righteousness of Christ, the sin-pardoning Redeemer. This is the beginning of the light of the angel whose glory shall fill the whole earth. For it is the work of every one to whom the message of warning has come, to lift up Jesus, to present Him to the world as revealed in types, as shadowed in symbols, as manifested in the revelations of the prophets, as unveiled in the lessons given to His disciples and in the wonderful miracles wrought for the sons of men. Search the Scriptures; for they are they that testify of Him.

If you would stand through the time of trouble, you must know Christ, and appropriate the gift of His righteousness, which He imputes to the repentant sinner.—*The Review and Herald,* Nov. 22, 1892.

Appropriating the Righteousness of Christ

Through Christ, restoration as well as reconciliation is provided for man. The gulf that was made by sin has been spanned by the cross of Calvary. A full, complete ransom has been paid by Jesus, by virtue of which the sinner is pardoned, and the justice of the law is maintained. All who believe that Christ is the atoning sacrifice may come and receive pardon for their sins; for through the merit of Christ, communication has been opened between God and man. God can accept me as His child, and I can claim Him and rejoice in Him as my loving Father. We must center our hopes of heaven upon Christ alone, because He is our substitute and surety.

We have transgressed the law of God, and by the deeds of the law shall no flesh be justified. The best efforts that man in his own strength can make, are valueless to meet the holy and just law that he has transgressed; but through faith in Christ he may claim the righteousness of the Son of God as all-sufficient. Christ satisfied the demands of the law in His human nature. He bore the curse of the law for the sinner, made an atonement for him, that whosoever believeth in Him should not perish, but have everlasting life. Genuine faith appropriates the righteousness of Christ, and the sinner is made an overcomer with Christ; for he is made a partaker of the divine nature, and thus divinity and humanity are combined.

He who is trying to reach heaven by his own works in keeping the law, is attempting an impossibility. Man cannot be saved without obedience, but his works should not be of himself; Christ should work in him to will and to do of His good pleasure. If a man could save himself by his own works, he might have something in himself in which to rejoice. The effort that man makes in his own strength to obtain salvation, is represented by the offering of Cain. All that man can do without Christ is polluted with selfishness and sin; but that which is wrought through faith is acceptable to God. When we seek to gain heaven through the merits of Christ, the soul makes progress. Looking unto Jesus, the author and finisher of our faith, we may go on from strength to strength, from victory to victory; for through Christ the grace of God has worked out our complete salvation.

Without faith it is impossible to please God. Living faith enables its possessor to lay hold on the merits of Christ, enables him to derive great comfort and satisfaction from the plan of salvation.—*The Review and Herald,* July 1, 1890.

57.

*Christ the Way of Life**

"Jesus came into Galilee, preaching the gospel of the kingdom of God, and saying, The time is fulfilled, and the kingdom of God is at hand: repent ye, and believe the gospel" (Mark 1:14, 15).

Repentance is associated with faith, and is urged in the gospel as essential to salvation. Paul preached repentance. He said, "I kept back nothing that was profitable unto you, but have shewed you, and have taught you publickly, and from house to house, testifying both to the Jews and also to the Greeks, repentance toward God, and faith toward our Lord Jesus Christ" (Acts 20:20, 21). There is no salvation without repentance. No impenitent sinner can believe with his heart unto righteousness. Repentance is described by Paul as a godly sorrow for sin, that "worketh repentance to salvation not to be repented of" (2 Cor. 7:10). This repentance has in it nothing of the nature of merit, but it prepares the heart for the acceptance of Christ as the only Saviour, the only hope of the lost sinner.

As the sinner looks to the law, his guilt is made plain to him, and pressed home to his conscience, and he is condemned. His only comfort and hope is found in looking to

* This article appeared in *The Review and Herald*, Nov. 4, 1890.

the cross of Calvary. As he ventures upon the promises, taking God at His word, relief and peace come to his soul. He cries, "Lord, Thou hast promised to save all who come unto Thee in the name of Thy Son. I am a lost, helpless, hopeless soul. Lord, save, or I perish." His faith lays hold on Christ, and he is justified before God.

But while God can be just, and yet justify the sinner through the merits of Christ, no man can cover his soul with the garments of Christ's righteousness while practicing known sins, or neglecting known duties. God requires the entire surrender of the heart, before justification can take place; and in order for man to retain justification, there must be continual obedience, through active, living faith that works by love and purifies the soul.

James writes of Abraham and says, "Was not Abraham our father justified by works, when he had offered Isaac his son upon the altar? Seest thou how faith wrought with his works, and by works was faith made perfect? And the scripture was fulfilled which saith, Abraham believed God, and it was imputed unto him for righteousness: and he was called the Friend of God. Ye see then how that by works a man is justified, and not by faith only" (James 2:21-24). In order for man to be justified by faith, faith must reach a point where it will control the affections and impulses of the heart; and it is by obedience that faith itself is made perfect.

Faith the Condition of Promise

Without the grace of Christ, the sinner is in a hopeless condition; nothing can be done for him; but through divine grace, supernatural power is imparted to the man, and works in mind and heart and character. It is through the impartation of the grace of Christ that sin is discerned in its hateful nature, and finally driven from the soul temple. It is through grace that we are brought into fellowship with Christ, to be associated with Him in the work of salvation. Faith is the condition upon which God has seen fit to promise pardon to sinners; not that there is any virtue in faith whereby salvation is merited, but because faith can lay hold of the merits of Christ, the remedy provided for sin. Faith can present Christ's perfect obedience instead of the sinner's transgression and defection. When the sinner believes that Christ is his personal Saviour, then, according to His unfailing promises, God pardons his sin, and justifies him freely. The repentant soul realizes that his justification comes because Christ, as his substitute and surety, has died for him, is his atonement and righteousness.

"Abraham believed God, and it was counted unto him for righteousness. Now to him that worketh is the reward not reckoned of grace, but of debt. But to him that worketh not, but believeth on him that justifieth the ungodly, his faith is counted for righteousness" (Rom. 4:3-5). Righteousness is obedience to the law. The law demands righteousness, and this the sinner owes to the law; but he is incapable of rendering it. The only way in which he can attain to righteousness is through faith. By faith he can bring to God the merits of Christ, and the Lord places the obedience of His Son to the sinner's account. Christ's righteousness is accepted in place of man's failure, and God receives, pardons, justifies, the repentant, believing soul, treats him as though he were righteous, and loves him as He loves His Son. This is how faith is accounted righteousness; and the pardoned soul goes on from grace to grace, from light to a greater light. He can say with rejoicing, "Not by works of righteousness which we have done, but according to his mercy he saved us, by the washing of regeneration, and renewing of the Holy Ghost; which he shed on us abundantly through Jesus Christ our Saviour; that being justified by his grace, we should be made heirs according to the hope of eternal life" (Titus 3:5-7).

Again: it is written, "But as many as received him, to them gave he power to become the sons of God, even to them that believe on his name: which were born, not of blood, nor of the will of the flesh, nor of the will of man, but of God" (John 1:12, 13). Jesus declared, "Except a man be born again, he cannot see the kingdom of God" (John 3:3). "Except a man be born of water and of the Spirit, he cannot enter into the kingdom of God" (John 3:

5). It is not a low standard that is placed before us; for we are to become the children of God. We are to be saved as individuals; and in the day of test and trial we shall be able to discern between him that serveth God and him that serveth Him not. We are saved as individual believers in the Lord Jesus Christ.

Many are losing the right way, in consequence of thinking that they must climb to heaven, that they must do something to merit the favor of God. They seek to make themselves better by their own unaided efforts. This they can never accomplish. Christ has made the way by dying our sacrifice, by living our example, by becoming our great high priest. He declares, "I am the way, the truth, and the life" (John 14:6). If by any effort of our own we could advance one step toward the ladder, the words of Christ would not be true. But when we accept Christ, good works will appear as fruitful evidence that we are in the way of life, that Christ is our way, and that we are treading the true path that leads to heaven.

He Becomes Our Righteousness

Christ looks at the spirit, and when He sees us carrying our burden with faith, His perfect holiness atones for our shortcomings. When we do our best, He becomes our righteousness. It takes every ray of light that God sends to us to make us the light of the world.—Letter 33, 1889.

58.

"Thou Hast Left Thy First Love" *

I spoke to the people of Otsego from the fourth and fifth verses of the second chapter of Revelation: "I have somewhat against thee, because thou hast left thy first love. Remember therefore from whence thou art fallen, and repent, and do the first works; or else I will come unto thee quickly, and will remove thy candlestick out of his place, except thou repent" (Rev. 2:4, 5). The people to whom these words are addressed have many excellent qualities, which are recognized by the True Witness; "Nevertheless," He says, "I have somewhat against thee, because thou hast left thy first love." Here is a want that will have to be supplied. All the other graces fail to make up the deficiency. The church is counseled to "remember therefore from whence thou art fallen, and repent, and do the first works; or else I will come unto thee quickly, and will remove thy candlestick out of his place, except thou repent. . . . He that hath an ear, let him hear what the Spirit saith unto the churches; To him that overcometh will I give to eat of the

---

* Portion of a sermon at Otsego, Michigan, Oct. 10, 1890, printed in *The Review and Herald*, Feb. 3, 1891.

tree of life, which is in the midst of the paradise of God"
(Rev. 2:4-7).

In these words are warnings, reproofs, threatenings,
promises, from the True Witness, He that holdeth the
seven stars in His right hand. "The seven stars are the angels of the seven churches: and the seven candlesticks
which thou sawest are the seven churches" (Rev. 1:20).

When this church is weighed in the balance of the
sanctuary, it is found wanting, having left its first love. The
True Witness declares, "I know thy works, and thy labour,
and thy patience, and how thou canst not bear them which
are evil: and thou hast tried them which say they are apostles, and are not, and hast found them liars: and hast borne,
and hast patience, and for my name's sake hast laboured,
and hast not fainted" (Rev. 2:2, 3). Notwithstanding all
this, the church is found wanting. What is the fatal deficiency?—"Thou hast left thy first love." Is not this our
case? Our doctrines may be correct; we may hate false
doctrine, and may not receive those who are not true to
principle; we may labor with untiring energy; but even
this is not sufficient. What is our motive? Why are we
called upon to repent?—"Thou hast left thy first love."

Let each member of the church study this important
warning and reproof. Let each one see if in contending for
the truth, if in debating on the theory, he has not lost the
tender love of Christ. Has not Christ been left out of the
sermons, and out of the heart? Is there not danger that
many are going forward with a profession of the truth, doing missionary work, while the love of Christ has not been
woven into the labor? This solemn warning from the True
Witness means much; it demands that you shall remember
from whence you are fallen, and repent, and do the first
works; "or else," says the True Witness, "I will come unto
thee quickly, and will remove thy candlestick out of his
place, except thou repent" (Rev. 2:5). O that the church
might realize its need of its first ardor of love! When this is
wanting, all other excellences are insufficient. The call to
repentance is one that cannot be disregarded without peril.
A belief in the theory of the truth is not enough. To present

this theory to unbelievers does not constitute you a witness for Christ. The light that gladdened your heart when you first understood the message for this time, is an essential element in your experience and labors, and this has been lost out of your heart and life. Christ beholds your lack of zeal, and declares that you have fallen, and are in a perilous position.

Present Love and Law Together

In presenting the binding claims of the law, many have failed to portray the infinite love of Christ. Those who have so great truths, so weighty reforms to present to the people, have not had a realization of the value of the atoning Sacrifice as an expression of God's great love to man. Love for Jesus, and Jesus' love for sinners, have been dropped out of the religious experience of those who have been commissioned to preach the gospel, and self has been exalted instead of the Redeemer of mankind. The law is to be presented to its transgressors, not as something apart from God, but rather as an exponent of His mind and character. As the sunlight cannot be separated from the sun, so God's law cannot be rightly presented to man apart from the divine Author. The messenger should be able to say, "In the law is God's will; come, see for yourselves that the law is what Paul declared it to be—'holy, and just, and good.'" It reproves sin, it condemns the sinner, but it shows him his need of Christ, with whom is plenteous mercy and goodness and truth. Though the law cannot remit the penalty for sin, but charges the sinner with all his debt, Christ has promised abundant pardon to all who repent, and believe in His mercy. The love of God is extended in abundance to the repenting, believing soul. The brand of sin upon the soul can be effaced only through the blood of the atoning Sacrifice. No less an offering was required than the sacrifice of Him who was equal with the Father. The work of Christ—His life, humiliation, death, and intercession for lost man—magnifies the law, and makes it honorable.

Many sermons preached upon the claims of the law have been without Christ, and this lack has made the truth inefficient in converting souls. Without the grace of Christ it is impossible to take one step in obedience to the law of God. Then how necessary that the sinner hear of the love and power of his Redeemer and Friend! While the ambassador for Christ should plainly declare the claims of the law, he should make it understood that none can be justified without the atoning sacrifice of Christ. Without Christ there can be only condemnation and a fearful looking for of fiery indignation, and final separation from the presence of God. But he whose eyes have been opened to see the love of Christ, will behold the character of God as full of love and compassion. God will not appear as a tyrannical, relentless being, but as a father longing to embrace his repenting son. The sinner will cry with the psalmist, "Like as a father pitieth his children, so the Lord pitieth them that fear him" (Ps. 103:13). All despair is swept from the soul when Christ is seen in His true character.

The Third Angel's Message in Verity

Some of our brethren have expressed fears that we shall dwell too much upon the subject of justification by faith, but I hope and pray that none will be needlessly alarmed; for there is no danger in presenting this doctrine as it is set forth in the Scriptures. If there had not been a remissness in the past to properly instruct the people of God, there would not now be a necessity of calling special attention to it. . . . The exceeding great and precious promises given us in the Holy Scriptures have been lost sight of to a great extent, just as the enemy of all righteousness designed that they should be. He has cast his own dark shadow between us and our God, that we may not see the true character of God. The Lord has proclaimed Himself to be "merciful and gracious, long-suffering, and abundant in goodness and truth."

Several have written to me, inquiring if the message of justification by faith is the third angel's message, and I have answered, "It is the third angel's message in verity."— *The Review and Herald,* April 1, 1890.

59.

*Perfect Obedience Through Christ**

"Ye see then how that by works a man is justified, and not by faith only. . . . For as the body without the spirit is dead, so faith without works is dead also" (James 2:24-26). It is essential to have faith in Jesus, and to believe you are saved through Him; but there is danger in taking the position that many do take in saying, "I am saved." Many have said: "You must do good works, and you will live"; but apart from Christ no one can do good works. Many at the present day say, "Believe, only believe, and live." Faith and works go together, believing and doing are blended. The Lord requires no less of the soul now, than He required of Adam in Paradise before he fell—perfect obedience, unblemished righteousness. The requirement of God under the covenant of grace is just as broad as the requirement He made in Paradise—harmony with His law, which is holy, and just, and good. The gospel does not weaken the claims of the law; it exalts the law and makes it honorable. Under the New Testament, no less is required than was required under the Old

---

* This article appeared in *The Review and Herald,* Nov. 1, 1892.

Testament. Let no one take up with the delusion so pleasant to the natural heart, that God will accept of sincerity, no matter what may be the faith, no matter how imperfect may be the life, God requires of His child perfect obedience.

In order to meet the requirements of the law, our faith must grasp the righteousness of Christ, accepting it as our righteousness. Through union with Christ, through acceptance of His righteousness by faith, we may be qualified to work the works of God, to be colaborers with Christ. If you are willing to drift along with the current of evil, and do not cooperate with the heavenly agencies in restraining transgression in your family, and in the church, in order that everlasting righteousness may be brought in, you do not have faith. Faith works by love and purifies the soul. Through faith the Holy Spirit works in the heart to create holiness therein; but this cannot be done unless the human agent will work with Christ. We can be fitted for heaven only through the work of the Holy Spirit upon the heart; for we must have Christ's righteousness as our credentials if we would find access to the Father. In order that we may have the righteousness of Christ, we need daily to be transformed by the influence of the Spirit, to be a partaker of the divine nature. It is the work of the Holy Spirit to elevate the taste, to sanctify the heart, to ennoble the whole man.

Look to Jesus

Let the soul look to Jesus. "Behold the Lamb of God, which taketh away the sin of the world" (John 1:29). No one will be forced to look to Christ; but the voice of invitation is sounding in yearning entreaty, "Look and live." In looking to Christ, we shall see that His love is without a parallel, that He has taken the place of the guilty sinner, and has imputed unto him His spotless righteousness. When the sinner sees his Saviour dying upon the cross under the curse of sin in his stead, beholding His pardoning love, love awakes in his heart. The sinner loves Christ, because Christ has first loved him, and love is the fulfilling of the law. The repenting soul realizes that God "is faithful and just to forgive us our sins, and to cleanse us from all unrighteousness." The Spirit of God works in the believer's soul, enabling him to advance from one line of obedience to another, reaching on from strength to greater strength, from grace to grace in Jesus Christ.

God justly condemns all who do not make Christ their personal Saviour; but He pardons every soul who comes to Him in faith, and enables him to work the works of God, and through faith to be one with Christ. Jesus says of these, "I in them, and thou in me, that they may be made perfect in one [this unity brings perfection of character]; and that the world may know that thou hast sent me, and hast loved them, as thou hast loved me" (John 17:23). The Lord has made every provision whereby man may have full and free salvation, and be complete in Him. God designs that His children shall have the bright beams of the Sun of Righteousness, that all may have the light of truth. God has provided salvation for the world at infinite cost, even through the gift of His only-begotten Son. The apostle asks, "He that spared not his own Son, but delivered him up for us all, how shall he not with him also freely give us all things?" (Rom. 8:32). Then if we are not saved, the fault will not be on the part of God, but on our part, that we have failed to cooperate with the divine agencies. Our will has not coincided with God's will.

The Redeemer of the world clothed His divinity with humanity, that He might reach humanity; for it took the divine and the human to bring into the world the salvation that was needed by fallen man. Divinity needed humanity that humanity might afford a channel of communication between God and man. Man needs a power out of and above himself to restore him to the likeness of God; but because he needs divine aid, it does not make human activity unessential. Faith on the part of man is required; for faith works by love and purifies the soul. Faith lays hold upon the virtue of Christ. The Lord does not design that human power should be paralyzed; but by cooperating with God, the power of man may be efficient for good. God does not design that our will should be destroyed; for it is through this very attribute that we are to accomplish the work He would have us to do both at home and abroad. He has given to every man his work; and every true worker sheds forth light to the world, because he is united with God and Christ and heavenly angels in the grand work of saving the lost. From divine association he becomes more and more intelligent in working the works of God. In working out what divine grace works in, the believer becomes spiritually great. He who works according to his entrusted ability will become a wise builder for the Master; for he is under the apprenticeship to Christ, learning to work the works of God. He will not shun burdens of responsibility, for he will realize that each one must lift in the cause of God to the extent of his ability, and he places himself under the pressure of the work; but Jesus does not leave His willing and obedient servant to be crushed. It is not the man who carries heavy responsibilities in the cause of God who needs your pity, for he is faithful and true in cooperation with God; and through union of divine and human effort, the work is made complete. It is he who shuns responsibilities, who has no realization of the privilege to which he is called, who is an object of pity.

60.

Relation of Faith and Works *

Napier, New Zealand
April 9, 1893

BROTHER A. T. JONES:

I was attending a meeting, and a large congregation were present. In my dream you were presenting the subject of faith and the imputed righteousness of Christ by faith. You repeated several times that works amounted to nothing, that there were no conditions. The matter was presented in that light that I knew minds would be confused, and would not receive the correct impression in reference to faith and works, and I decided to write to you. You state this matter too strongly. There are conditions to our receiving justification and sanctification, and the righteousness of Christ. I know your meaning, but you leave a wrong impression upon many minds. While good works will not save even one soul, yet it is impossible for even one soul to be saved without good works. God saves us under a law, that we must ask if we would receive, seek if we would find, and knock if we would have the door opened unto us.

---

* Appeared in *Notebook Leaflets,* The Church, No. 5.

Christ offers Himself as willing to save unto the uttermost all who come unto Him. He invites all to come to Him. "Him that cometh to me I will in no wise cast out" (John 6:37). You look in reality upon these subjects as I do, yet you make these subjects, through your expressions, confusing to minds. And after you have expressed your mind radically in regard to works, when questions are asked you upon this very subject, it is not lying out in so very clear lines, in your own mind, and you cannot define the correct principles to other minds, and you are yourself unable to make your statements harmonize with your own principles and faith.

The young man came to Jesus with the question, "Good Master, what shall I do, that I may inherit eternal life?" (Mark 10:17). And Christ saith unto him, "Why callest thou me good? there is none good but one, that is, God: but if thou wilt enter into life, keep the commandments." He saith unto Him, "Which?" Jesus quoted several, and the young man said unto Him, "All these things have I kept from my youth up: what lack I yet?" Jesus said unto him, "If thou wilt be perfect, go and sell that thou hast, and give to the poor, and thou shalt have treasure in heaven: and come and follow me." Here are conditions, and the Bible is full of conditions. "But when the young man heard that saying, he went away sorrowful: for he had great possessions" (Matt. 19:17, 20, 21, 22).

Points to Guard

Then when you say there are no conditions, and some expressions are made quite broad, you burden the minds, and some cannot see consistency in your expressions. They cannot see how they can harmonize these expressions with the plain statements of the Word of God. Please guard these points. These strong assertions in regard to works never make our position any stronger. The expressions weaken our position, for there are many who will consider you an extremist, and will lose the rich lessons you have for them upon the very subjects they need to know. . . . My brother, it is hard for the mind to comprehend this point, and do not confuse any mind with ideas that will not harmonize with the Word. Please to consider that under the teaching of Christ many of the disciples were lamentably ignorant; but when the Holy Spirit that Jesus promised came upon them and made the vacillating Peter the champion of faith, what a transformation in his character! But do not lay one pebble, for a soul that is weak in the faith to stumble over, in overwrought presentations or expressions. Be ever consistent, calm, deep, and solid. Do not go to any extreme in anything, but keep your feet on solid rock. O precious, precious Saviour. "He that hath my commandments, and keepeth them, he it is that loveth me: and he that loveth me shall be loved of my Father, and I will love him, and will manifest myself to him" (John 14:21).

This is the true test—the doing of the words of Christ. And it is the evidence of the human agent's love to Jesus, and he that doeth His will giveth to the world the practical evidence of the fruit he manifests in obedience, in purity, and in holiness of character. . . .

O my brother, walk carefully with God. But remember that there are some whose eyes are intently fixed upon you, expecting that you will overreach the mark, and stumble, and fall. But if you keep in humility close to Jesus, all is well. . . .

There is no place in the school of Christ where we graduate. We are to work on the plan of addition, and the Lord will work on the plan of multiplication. It is through constant diligence that we will, through the grace of Christ, live on the plan of addition, making our calling and election sure. . . . "For if ye do these things ye shall never fall: for so an entrance shall be ministered unto you abundantly into the everlasting kingdom of our Lord and Saviour Jesus Christ" (2 Peter 1:10, 11).—Letter 44, 1893.

No Compromise With Sin

Let my brethren be very careful how they present the subject of faith and works before the people, lest minds become confused. The people need to be urged to diligence in good works. They should be shown how to be successful, how to be purified, and their offerings may be fragrant before God. It is by virtue of the blood of Christ. Messages of a decided character must be borne to the people. Men must go forth reproving, rebuking every manner of evil.

If there is given to the angel of any church a commission like unto that given to the angel of the church of Ephesus, let the message be heard through human agents rebuking carelessness, backsliding, and sin, that the people may be brought to repentance and confession of sin. Never seek to cover sin; for in the message of rebuke, Christ is to be proclaimed as the first and the last, He who is all in all to the soul.

His power awaits the demand of those who would overcome. The reprover is to animate his hearers so that they shall strive for the mastery. He is to encourage them to struggle for deliverance from every sinful practice, to be free from every corrupt habit, even if his denial of self is like taking the right eye, or separating the right arm from the body. No concession or compromise is to be made to evil habits or sinful practices.—Manuscript 26a, 1892.

Cooperation With God

Man is to cooperate with God, employing every power according to his God-given ability. He is not to be ignorant as to what are right practices in eating and drinking, and in all the habits of life. The Lord designs that His human agents shall act as rational, accountable beings in every respect. . . .

We cannot afford to neglect one ray of light God has given. To be sluggish in our practice of those things which require diligence is to commit sin. The human agent is to cooperate with God, and keep under those passions which should be in subjection. To do this he must be unwearied in his prayers to God, ever obtaining grace to control his spirit, temper, and actions. Through the imparted grace of

Christ, he may be enabled to overcome. To be an over-comer means more than many suppose it means.

The Spirit of God will answer the cry of every penitent heart; for repentance is the gift of God, and an evidence that Christ is drawing the soul to Himself. We can no more repent of sin without Christ, than we can be par-doned without Christ, and yet it is a humiliation to man with his human passion and pride to go to Jesus straight-way, believing and trusting Him for everything which he needs. . . .

Let no man present the idea that man has little or nothing to do in the great work of overcoming; for God does nothing for man without his cooperation. Neither say that after you have done all you can on your part, Jesus will help you. Christ has said, "Without me ye can do nothing" (John 15:5). From first to last man is to be a laborer together with God. Unless the Holy Spirit works upon the human heart, at every step we shall stumble and fall. Man's efforts alone are nothing but worthlessness; but cooperation with Christ means a victory. Of ourselves we have no power to repent of sin. Unless we accept divine aid we cannot take the first step toward the Saviour. He says, "I am Alpha and Omega, the beginning and the end" (Rev. 21:6) in the salvation of every soul.

But though Christ is everything, we are to inspire every man to unwearied diligence. We are to strive, wrestle, agonize, watch, pray, lest we shall be overcome by the wily foe. For the power and grace with which we can do this comes from God, and all the while we are to trust in Him, who is able to save to the uttermost all who come unto God by Him. Never leave the impression on the mind that there is little or nothing to do on the part of man; but rather teach man to cooperate with God, that he may be successful in overcoming.

Let no one say that your works have nothing to do with your rank and position before God. In the judgment the sentence pronounced is according to what has been done or to what has been left undone (Matt. 25:34-40).

Effort and labor are required on the part of the receiver

of God's grace; for it is the fruit that makes manifest what is the character of the tree. Although the good works of man are of no more value without faith in Jesus than was the offering of Cain, yet covered with the merit of Christ, they testify [to] the worthiness of the doer to inherit eternal life. That which is considered morality in the world does not reach the divine standard and has no more merit before Heaven than had the offering of Cain.—Manuscript 26a, 1892.

While Submitting to the Holy Spirit

Everyone who has a realizing sense of what it means to be a Christian, will purify himself from everything that weakens and defiles. All the habits of his life will be brought into harmony with the requirements of the Word of truth, and he will not only believe, but will work out his own salvation with fear and trembling, while submitting to the molding of the Holy Spirit.—*The Review and Herald,* March 6, 1888.

Jesus Accepts Our Intentions

When it is in the heart to obey God, when efforts are put forth to this end, Jesus accepts this disposition and effort as man's best service, and He makes up for the deficiency with His own divine merit. But He will not accept those who claim to have faith in Him, and yet are disloyal to His Father's commandment. We hear a great deal about faith, but we need to hear a great deal more about works. Many are deceiving their own souls by living an easy-going, accommodating, crossless religion. But Jesus says, "If any man will come after me, let him deny himself, and take up his cross, and follow me."—*The Signs of the Times,* June 16, 1890.

61.

*Christ the Center of the Message**

The third angel's message calls for the presentation of the Sabbath of the fourth commandment, and this truth must be brought before the world; but the great center of attraction, Jesus Christ, must not be left out of the third angel's message. By many who have been engaged in the work for this time, Christ has been made secondary, and theories and arguments have had first place. The glory of God that was revealed to Moses in regard to the divine character has not been made prominent. The Lord said to Moses, "I will make all my goodness pass before thee" (Ex. 33:19). "And the Lord passed by before him, and proclaimed, The Lord, the Lord God, merciful and gracious, longsuffering, and abundant in goodness and truth, keeping mercy for thousands, forgiving iniquity and transgression and sin, and that will by no means clear the guilty" (Ex. 34:6, 7).

A veil has seemed to be before the eyes of many who have labored in the cause, so that when they presented the law, they have not had views of Jesus, and have not

---

* This article appeared in *The Review and Herald,* March 20, 1894.

proclaimed the fact that, where sin abounded, grace doth much more abound. It is at the cross of Calvary that mercy and truth meet together, where righteousness and peace kiss each other. The sinner must ever look toward Calvary; and with the simple faith of a little child, he must rest in the merits of Christ, accepting His righteousness and believing in His mercy. Laborers in the cause of truth should present the righteousness of Christ, not as new light, but as precious light that has for a time been lost sight of by the people. We are to accept Christ as our personal Saviour, and He imputes unto us the righteousness of God in Christ. Let us repeat and make prominent the truth that John has portrayed: "Herein is love, not that we loved God, but that he loved us, and sent his Son to be the propitiation for our sins" (1 John 4:10).

In the love of God has been opened the most marvelous vein of precious truth, and the treasures of the grace of Christ are laid open before the church and the world. "For God so loved the world, that he gave his only begotten Son . . ." (John 3:16). What love is this—what marvelous, unfathomable love—that would lead Christ to die for us while we were yet sinners! What a loss it is to the soul who understands the strong claims of the law, and who yet fails to understand the grace of Christ which doth much more abound! It is true that the law of God reveals the love of God when it is preached as the truth in Jesus; for the gift of Christ to this guilty world must be largely dwelt upon in every discourse. It is no wonder that hearts have not been melted by the truth, when it has been presented in a cold and lifeless manner. No wonder faith has staggered at the promises of God, when ministers and workers have failed to present Jesus in His relation to the law of God. How often should they have assured the people that "He that spared not his own Son, but delivered him up for us all, how shall he not with him also freely give us all things?" (Rom. 8:32).

Satan is determined that men shall not see the love of God, which led Him to give His only-begotten Son to save the lost race; for it is the goodness of God that leads men to repentance. Oh, how shall we succeed in setting forth before the world the deep, precious love of God? In no other way can we compass it than by exclaiming, "Behold, what manner of love the Father hath bestowed upon us, that we should be called the sons of God" (1 John 3:1)! Let us say to sinners, "Behold the Lamb of God, which taketh away the sin of the world" (John 1:29)! By presenting Jesus as the representative of the Father, we shall be able to dispel the shadow that Satan has cast upon our pathway, in order that we shall not see the mercy and love of God's inexpressible love as manifested in Jesus Christ.

Look at the Cross

Look at the cross of Calvary. It is a standing pledge of the boundless love, the measureless mercy, of the heavenly Father. O that all might repent and do their first works. When the churches do this, they will love God supremely and their neighbors as themselves. Ephraim will not envy Judah, and Judah will not vex Ephraim. Divisions will then be healed, the harsh sounds of strife will no more be heard in the borders of Israel. Through the grace freely given them of God, all will seek to answer the prayer of Christ, that His disciples should be one, even as He and the Father are one. Peace, love, mercy, and benevolence will be the abiding principles of the soul. The love of Christ will be the theme of every tongue, and it will no more be said by the True Witness, "I have somewhat against thee, because thou hast left thy first love" (Rev. 2:4). The people of God will be abiding in Christ, the love of Jesus will be revealed, and one Spirit will animate all hearts, regenerating and renewing all in the image of Christ, fashioning all hearts alike. As living branches of the True Vine, all will be united to Christ, the living head. Christ will abide in every heart, guiding, comforting, sanctifying, and presenting to the world the unity of the followers of Jesus, thus bearing testimony that the heavenly credentials are supplied to the remnant church. In the oneness of Christ's church it will be proved that God sent His only-begotten Son into the world.

When God's people are one in the unity of the Spirit, all of Phariseeism, all of self-righteousness, which was the sin of the Jewish nation, will be expelled from all hearts. The mold of Christ will be upon each individual member of His body, and His people will be new bottles into which He can pour His new wine, and the new wine will not break the bottles. God will make known the mystery which hath been hidden for ages. He will make known what are the "riches of the glory of this mystery among the Gentiles; which is Christ in you, the hope of glory" (Col. 1:27) [verses 28, 29 also quoted].

Jesus came to impart to the human soul the Holy Spirit, by which the love of God is shed abroad in the heart; but it is impossible to endow men with the Holy Spirit, who are set in their ideas, whose doctrines are all stereotyped and unchangeable, who are walking after the traditions and commandments of men, as were the Jews in the time of Christ. They were very punctilious in the observances of the church, very rigorous in following their forms, but they were destitute of vitality and religious devotion. They were represented by Christ as like the dry skins which were then used as bottles. The gospel of Christ could not be placed in their hearts; for there was no room to contain it. They could not be the new bottles into which He could pour His new wine. Christ was obliged to seek elsewhere than among the scribes and the Pharisees for bottles for His doctrine of truth and life. He must find men who were willing to have regeneration of heart. He came to give to men new hearts. He said, "A new heart also will I give you." But the self-righteous of that day and of this day feel no need of having a new heart. Jesus passed by the scribes and the Pharisees, for they felt no need of a Saviour. They were wedded to forms and ceremonies. These services had been instituted by Christ; they had been full of vitality and spiritual beauty; but the Jews had lost the spiritual life from their ceremonies, and clung to the dead forms after spiritual life was extinct among them. When they departed from the requirements and commandments of God, they sought to supply the place of that which they had lost, by multiplying their own requirements, and making more rigorous demands than had God; and the more rigid they grew, the less of the love and Spirit of God they manifested. Christ said to the people: "The scribes and the Pharisees sit in Moses' seat: all therefore whatsoever they bid you observe, that observe and do; but do not ye after their works: for they say, and do not. For they bind heavy burdens and grievous to be borne, and lay them on men's shoulders; but they themselves will not move them with one of their fingers. But all their works they do for to be seen of men: they make broad their phylacteries, and enlarge the borders of their garments, and love the uppermost rooms at feasts, and the chief seats in the synagogues, and greetings in the markets, and to be called of men, Rabbi, Rabbi." "Woe unto you, scribes and Pharisees, hypocrites! for ye pay tithe of mint and anise and cummin, and have omitted the weightier matters of the law, judgment, mercy, and faith: these ought ye to have done, and not to leave the other undone" (Matt. 23:2-7, 23).

The remnant church is called to go through an experience similar to that of the Jews; and the True Witness, who walks up and down in the midst of the seven golden candlesticks, has a solemn message to bear to His people. He says, "I have somewhat against thee, because thou hast left thy first love. Remember therefore from whence thou art fallen, and repent, and do the first works; or else I will come unto thee quickly, and will remove thy candlestick out of his place, except thou repent" (Rev. 2:4, 5). The love of God has been waning in the church, and as a result, the love of self has sprung up into new activity. With the loss of love for God there has come the loss of love for the brethren. The church may meet all the description that is given of the Ephesian church, and yet fail in vital godliness. Of them Jesus said, "I know thy works, and thy labour, and thy patience, and how thou canst not bear them which are evil: and thou hast tried them which say they are apostles, and are not, and hast found them liars: and hast borne, and hast patience, and for my name's sake hast laboured, and hast not fainted. Nevertheless I have somewhat against thee, because thou hast left thy first love" (Rev. 2:2-4).

A legal religion has been thought quite the correct religion for this time. But it is a mistake. The rebuke of Christ to the Pharisees is applicable to those who have lost from the heart their first love. A cold, legal religion can never lead souls to Christ; for it is a loveless, Christless religion. When fastings and prayers are practiced in a self-justifying spirit, they are abominable to God. The solemn assembly for worship, the round of religious ceremonies, the external humiliation, the imposed sacrifice— all proclaim to the world the testimony that the doer of these things considers himself righteous. These things call attention to the observer of rigorous duties, saying, This man is entitled to heaven. But it is all a deception. Works will not buy for us an entrance into heaven. The one great Offering that has been made is ample for all who will believe. The love of Christ will animate the believer with new life. He who drinks from the water of the fountain of life, will be filled with the new wine of the kingdom. Faith in Christ will be the means whereby the right spirit and motive will actuate the believer, and all goodness and heavenly-mindedness will proceed from him who looks unto Jesus, the author and finisher of his faith. Look up to God, look not to men. God is your heavenly Father who is willing patiently to bear with your infirmities, and to forgive and heal them. "This is life eternal, that they might know thee the only true God, and Jesus Christ, whom thou hast sent" (John 17:3). By beholding Christ, you will become changed, until you will hate your former pride, your former vanity and self-esteem, your self-righteousness and unbelief. You will cast these sins aside as a worthless burden, and walk humbly, meekly, trustfully, before God. You will practice love, patience, gentleness, goodness, mercy, and every grace that dwells in the child of God, and will at last find a place among the sanctified and holy.

62.

*Justified by Faith**

When God pardons the sinner, remits the punishment he deserves, and treats him as though he had not sinned, He receives him into divine favor, and justifies him through the merits of Christ's righteousness. The sinner can be justified only through faith in the atonement made through God's dear Son, who became a sacrifice for the sins of the guilty world. No one can be justified by any works of his own. He can be delivered from the guilt of sin, from the condemnation of the law, from the penalty of transgression, only by virtue of the suffering, death, and resurrection of Christ. Faith is the only condition upon which justification can be obtained, and faith includes not only belief but trust.

Many have a nominal faith in Christ, but they know nothing of that vital dependence upon Him which appropriates the merits of a crucified and risen Saviour. Of this nominal faith James says: "Thou believest that there is one God; thou doest well: the devils also believe, and tremble. But wilt thou know, O vain man, that faith without works is dead?" (James 2:19, 20). Many concede that Jesus Christ is the Saviour of the world, but at the same

---

* This article appeared in *The Bible Students' Library* series, April, 1893.

time they hold themselves away from Him, and fail to repent of their sins, fail to accept of Jesus as their personal Saviour. Their faith is simply the assent of the mind and judgment to the truth; but the truth is not brought into the heart, that it might sanctify the soul and transform the character. "For whom he did foreknow, he also did predestinate to be conformed to the image of his Son, that he might be the firstborn among many brethren. Moreover whom he did predestinate, them he also called: and whom he called, them he also justified: and whom he justified, them he also glorified" (Rom. 8:29, 30). Calling and justification are not one and the same thing. Calling is the drawing of the sinner to Christ, and it is a work wrought by the Holy Spirit upon the heart, convicting of sin, and inviting to repentance.

Many are confused as to what constitutes the first steps in the work of salvation. Repentance is thought to be a work the sinner must do for himself in order that he may come to Christ. They think that the sinner must procure for himself a fitness in order to obtain the blessing of God's grace. But while it is true that repentance must precede forgiveness, for it is only the broken and contrite heart that is acceptable to God, yet the sinner cannot bring himself to repentance, or prepare himself to come to Christ. Except the sinner repent, he cannot be forgiven; but the question to be decided is as to whether repentance is the work of the sinner or the gift of Christ. Must the sinner wait until he is filled with remorse for his sin before he can come to Christ? The very first step to Christ is taken through the drawing of the Spirit of God; as man responds to this drawing, he advances toward Christ in order that he may repent.

The sinner is represented as a lost sheep, and a lost sheep never returns to the fold unless he is sought after and brought back to the fold by the shepherd. No man of himself can repent, and make himself worthy of the blessing of justification. The Lord Jesus is constantly seeking to impress the sinner's mind and attract him to behold Himself, the Lamb of God, which taketh away the sins of the world.

We cannot take a step toward spiritual life save as Jesus draws and strengthens the soul, and leads us to experience that repentance which needeth not to be repented of.

When before the high priests and Sadducees, Peter clearly presented the fact that repentance is the gift of God. Speaking of Christ, he said, "Him hath God exalted with his right hand to be a Prince and a Saviour, for to give repentance to Israel, and forgiveness of sins" (Acts 5: 31). Repentance is no less the gift of God than are pardon and justification, and it cannot be experienced except as it is given to the soul by Christ. If we are drawn to Christ, it is through His power and virtue. The grace of contrition comes through Him, and from Him comes justification.

The Meaning of Faith

Paul writes: "But the righteousness which is of faith speaketh on this wise, Say not in thine heart, Who shall ascend into heaven? (that is, to bring Christ down from above:) or, Who shall descend into the deep? (that is, to bring up Christ again from the dead.) But what saith it? The word is nigh thee, even in thy mouth, and in thy heart: that is, the word of faith, which we preach; that if thou shalt confess with thy mouth the Lord Jesus, and shalt believe in thine heart that God hath raised him from the dead, thou shalt be saved. For with the heart man believeth unto righteousness; and with the mouth confession is made unto salvation" (Rom. 10:6-10).

The faith that is unto salvation is not a casual faith, it is not the mere consent of the intellect, it is belief rooted in the heart, that embraces Christ as a personal Saviour, assured that He can save unto the uttermost all that come unto God by Him. To believe that He will save others, but will not save you is not genuine faith; but when the soul lays hold upon Christ as the only hope of salvation, then genuine faith is manifested. This faith leads its possessor to place all the affections of the soul upon Christ; his understanding is under the control of the Holy Spirit, and his character is molded after the divine likeness. His faith is not a dead faith, but a faith that works by love, and leads him to behold the beauty of Christ, and to become assimilated to the divine character. [Deut. 30:11-14 quoted.] "And the Lord thy God will circumcise thine heart, and the heart of thy seed, to love the Lord thy God with all thine heart, and with all thy soul, that thou mayest live" (Deut. 30:6).

It is God that circumcises the heart. The whole work is the Lord's from the beginning to the end. The perishing sinner may say: "I am a lost sinner; but Christ came to seek and to save that which was lost. He says, 'I came not to call the righteous, but sinners to repentance' (Mark 2:17). I am a sinner, and He died upon Calvary's cross to save me. I need not remain a moment longer unsaved. He died and rose again for my justification, and He will save me now. I accept the forgiveness He has promised."

Imputed Righteousness

Christ is a risen Saviour; for, though He was dead, He has risen again, and ever liveth to make intercession for us. We are to believe with the heart unto righteousness, and with the mouth make confession unto salvation. Those who are justified by faith will make confession of Christ. "He that heareth my word, and believeth on him that sent me, hath everlasting life, and shall not come into condemnation; but is passed from death unto life" (John 5:24). The great work that is wrought for the sinner who is spotted and stained by evil is the work of justification. By Him who speaketh truth he is declared righteous. The Lord imputes unto the believer the righteousness of Christ and pronounces him righteous before the universe. He transfers his sins to Jesus, the sinner's representative, substitute, and surety. Upon Christ He lays the iniquity of every soul that believeth. "He hath made him to be sin for us, who knew no sin; that we might be made the righteousness of God in him" (2 Cor. 5:21).

Christ made satisfaction for the guilt of the whole world, and all who will come to God in faith, will receive the righteousness of Christ, "who his own self bare our sins in his own body on the tree, that we, being dead to sins, should live unto righteousness: by whose stripes ye were healed" (1 Peter 2:24). Our sin has been expiated, put away, cast into the depths of the sea. Through repentance and faith we are rid of sin, and look unto the Lord our righteousness. Jesus suffered, the just for the unjust.

Although as sinners we are under the condemnation of the law, yet Christ by His obedience rendered to the law, claims for the repentant soul the merit of His own righteousness. In order to obtain the righteousness of Christ, it is necessary for the sinner to know what that repentance is which works a radical change of mind and spirit and action. The work of transformation must begin in the heart, and manifest its power through every faculty of the being; but man is not capable of originating such a repentance as this, and can experience it alone through Christ, who ascended up on high, led captivity captive, and gave gifts unto men.

Who is desirous of becoming truly repentant? What must he do?—He must come to Jesus, just as he is, without delay. He must believe that the word of Christ is true, and, believing the promise, ask, that he may receive. When sincere desire prompts men to pray, they will not pray in vain. The Lord will fulfill His word, and will give the Holy Spirit to lead to repentance toward God and faith toward our Lord Jesus Christ. He will pray and watch, and put away his sins, making manifest his sincerity by the vigor of his endeavor to obey the commandments of God. With prayer he will mingle faith, and not only believe in but obey the precepts of the law. He will announce himself as on Christ's side of the question. He will renounce all habits and associations that tend to draw the heart from God.

He who would become a child of God must receive the truth that repentance and forgiveness are to be obtained through nothing less than the atonement of Christ. Assured of this the sinner must put forth an effort in harmony with the work done for him, and with unwearied entreaty he must supplicate the throne of grace, that the renovating power of God may come into his soul. Christ pardons none but the penitent, but whom He pardons He first makes penitent. The provision made is complete, and the eternal righteousness of Christ is placed to the account of every believing soul. The costly, spotless robe, woven in the loom of heaven, has been provided for the repenting, believing sinner, and he may say: "I will greatly rejoice in the Lord, my soul shall be joyful in my God; for he hath clothed me with the garments of salvation, he hath covered me with the robe of righteousness" (Isa. 61:10).

Abundant grace has been provided that the believing soul may be kept free from sin; for all heaven, with its limitless resources, has been placed at our command. We are to draw from the well of salvation. Christ is the end of law for righteousness to everyone who believeth. In ourselves we are sinners; but in Christ we are righteous. Having made us righteous through the imputed righteousness of Christ, God pronounces us just, and treats us as just. He looks upon us as His dear children. Christ works against the power of sin, and where sin abounded, grace much more abounds. "Therefore being justified by faith, we have peace with God through our Lord Jesus Christ: by whom also we have access by faith into this grace wherein we stand, and rejoice in hope of the glory of God" (Rom. 5:1, 2).

"Being justified freely by his grace through the redemption that is in Christ Jesus: whom God hath set forth to be a propitiation through faith in his blood, to declare his righteousness for the remission of sins that are past, through the forbearance of God; to declare, I say, at this time his righteousness: that he might be just, and the justifier of him which believeth in Jesus" (Rom. 3:24-26). "For by grace are ye saved through faith; and that not of yourselves: it is the gift of God" (Eph. 2:8). [John 1:14-16 quoted.]

The Promise of the Spirit

The Lord would have His people sound in the faith—not ignorant of the great salvation so abundantly provided for them. They are not to look forward, thinking that at some future time a great work is to be done for them; for the work is now complete. The believer is not called upon to make his peace with God; he never has nor ever can do this. He is to accept Christ as his peace, for with Christ is God and peace. Christ made an end of sin, bearing its heavy curse in His own body on the tree, and He hath taken away the curse from all those who believe in Him as a personal Saviour. He makes an end of the controlling power of sin in the heart, and the life and character of the believer testify to the genuine character of the grace of Christ. To those that ask Him, Jesus imparts the Holy Spirit; for it is necessary that every believer should be delivered from pollution, as well as from the curse and condemnation of the law. Through the work of the Holy Spirit, the sanctification of the truth, the believer becomes fitted for the courts of heaven; for Christ works within us, and His righteousness is upon us. Without this no soul will be entitled to heaven. We would not enjoy heaven unless qualified for its holy atmosphere by the influence of the Spirit and the righteousness of Christ.

In order to be candidates for heaven we must meet the requirement of the law: "Thou shalt love the Lord thy God with all thy heart, and with all thy soul, and with all thy strength, and with all thy mind; and thy neighbour as thyself" (Luke 10:27). We can do this only as we grasp by faith the righteousness of Christ. By beholding Jesus we receive a living, expanding principle in the heart, and the Holy Spirit carries on the work, and the believer advances from grace to grace, from strength to strength, from character to character. He conforms to the image of Christ, until in spiritual growth he attains unto the measure of the full stature in Christ Jesus. Thus Christ makes an end of the curse of sin, and sets the believing soul free from its action and effect.

Christ alone is able to do this, for "in all things it behoved him to be made like unto his brethren, that he might be a merciful and faithful high priest in things pertaining to God, to make reconciliation for the sins of the people. For in that he himself hath suffered being

tempted, he is able to succour them that are tempted"
(Heb. 2:17, 18). Reconciliation means that every barrier
between the soul and God is removed, and that the sinner
realizes what the pardoning love of God means. By reason of
the sacrifice made by Christ for fallen men, God can
justly pardon the transgressor who accepts the merits of
Christ. Christ was the channel through which the mercy,
love, and righteousness might flow from the heart of God
to the heart of the sinner. "He is faithful and just to forgive
us our sins, and to cleanse us from all unrighteousness"
(1 John 1:9).

In the prophecy of Daniel it was recorded of Christ
that He shall "make reconciliation for iniquity, and . . .
bring in everlasting righteousness" (Dan. 9:24). Every
soul may say: "By His perfect obedience He has satisfied
the claims of the law, and my only hope is found in
looking to Him as my substitute and surety, who obeyed
the law perfectly for me. By faith in His merits I am free
from the condemnation of the law. He clothes me with His
righteousness, which answers all the demands of the law.
I am complete in Him who brings in everlasting righteousness. He presents me to God in the spotless garment
of which no thread was woven by any human agent. All
is of Christ, and all the glory, honor, and majesty are to be
given to the Lamb of God, which taketh away the sins of
the world."

Many think that they must wait for a special impulse
in order that they may come to Christ; but it is necessary
only to come in sincerity of purpose, deciding to accept
the offers of mercy and grace that have been extended to
us. We are to say: "Christ died to save me. The Lord's
desire is that I should be saved, and I will come to Jesus
just as I am without delay. I will venture upon the
promise. As Christ draws me, I will respond." The apostle
says, "With the heart man believeth unto righteousness"
(Rom. 10:10). No one can believe with the heart unto
righteousness, and obtain justification by faith, while continuing the practice of those things which the Word of God
forbids, or while neglecting any known duty.

Good Works the Fruit of Faith

Genuine faith will be manifested in good works; for good works are the fruits of faith. As God works in the heart, and man surrenders his will to God, and cooperates with God, he works out in the life what God works in by the Holy Spirit, and there is harmony between the purpose of the heart and the practice of the life. Every sin must be renounced as the hateful thing that crucified the Lord of life and glory, and the believer must have a progressive experience by continually doing the works of Christ. It is by continual surrender of the will, by continual obedience, that the blessing of justification is retained.

Those who are justified by faith must have a heart to keep the way of the Lord. It is an evidence that a man is not justified by faith when his works do not correspond to his profession. James says, "Seest thou how faith wrought with his works, and by works was his faith made perfect?" (James 2:22).

The faith that does not produce good works does not justify the soul. "Ye see then how that by works a man is justified, and not by faith only" (James 2:24). "Abraham believed God, and it was counted unto him for righteousness" (Rom. 4:3).

Imputation of the righteousness of Christ comes through justifying faith, and is the justification for which Paul so earnestly contends. He says: "Therefore by the deeds of the law there shall no flesh be justified in his sight: for by the law is the knowledge of sin. But now the righteousness of God without the law is manifested, being witnessed by the law and the prophets; even the righteousness of God which is by faith of Jesus Christ unto all and upon all them that believe: for there is no difference: for all have sinned, and come short of the glory of God; being justified freely by his grace through the redemption that is in Christ Jesus: whom God hath set forth to be a propitiation through faith in his blood, to declare his righteousness for the remission of sins that are past, through the forbearance of God. . . . Do we then make void the law through faith? God forbid: yea, we establish the law" (Rom. 3:20-31).

Grace is unmerited favor, and the believer is justified without any merit of his own, without any claim to offer to God. He is justified through the redemption that is in Christ Jesus, who stands in the courts of heaven as the sinner's substitute and surety. But while he is justified because of the merit of Christ, he is not free to work unrighteousness. Faith works by love and purifies the soul. Faith buds and blossoms and bears a harvest of precious fruit. Where faith is, good works appear. The sick are visited, the poor are cared for, the fatherless and the widows are not neglected, the naked are clothed, the destitute are fed. Christ went about doing good, and when men are united with Him, they love the children of God, and meekness and truth guide their footsteps. The expression of the countenance reveals their experience, and men take knowledge of them that they have been with Jesus and learned of Him. Christ and the believer become one, and His beauty of character is revealed in those who are vitally connected with the Source of power and love. Christ is the great depositary of justifying righteousness and sanctifying grace.

All may come to Him, and receive of His fullness. He says, "Come unto me, all ye that labour and are heavy laden, and I will give you rest" (Matt. 11:28). Then why not cast aside all unbelief and heed the words of Jesus? You want rest; you long for peace. Then say from the heart, "Lord Jesus, I come, because Thou hast given me this invitation." Believe in Him with steadfast faith, and He will save you. Have you been looking unto Jesus, who is the author and finisher of your faith? Have you been beholding Him who is full of truth and grace? Have you accepted the peace which Christ alone can give? If you have not, then yield to Him, and through His grace seek for a character that will be noble and elevated. Seek for a constant, resolute, cheerful spirit. Feed on Christ, who is the bread of life, and you will manifest His loveliness of character and spirit.

63.

The Pearl of Great Price[*]

"God so loved the world, that he gave his only be-gotten Son, that whosoever believeth in him should not perish, but have everlasting life" (John 3:16). He is the same yesterday, today, and forever. The righteousness of Christ, as a pure white pearl, has no defect, no stain, no guilt. This righteousness may be ours. Salvation, with its blood-bought, inestimable treasures, is the pearl of great price. It may be searched for and found. But all who really find it will sell all they have to buy it. They give evidence that they are one with Christ, as He is one with the Father. In the parable the merchantman is represented as selling all that he had to gain possession of one pearl of great price. This is a beautiful representation of those who appreciate the truth so highly that they give up all they have to come into possession of it. They lay hold by faith of the salvation provided for them at the sacrifice of the only-begotten Son of God.

There are some who are seeking, always seeking, for the goodly pearl. But they do not make an entire surrender of their wrong habits. They do not die to self that Christ may live in them. Therefore they do not find the precious

---

[*] This article appeared in *The Review and Herald*, Aug. 8, 1899.

pearl. They have not overcome unholy ambition and their love for worldly attractions. They do not lift the cross, and follow Christ in the path of self-denial and self-sacrifice. They never know what it is to have peace and harmony in the soul; for without entire surrender there is no rest, no joy. Almost Christians, yet not fully Christians, they seem near the kingdom of heaven, but they do not enter therein. Almost but not wholly saved means to be not almost but wholly lost.

A daily consecration to God brings peace and rest. The merchant sold all that he had to possess the pearl. When those who are seeking for salvation refuse to fail or be discouraged, they will find peace and rest in the Lord. Christ will clothe them with His righteousness. He will provide them with a clean heart and a renewed mind. These blessings cost the life of the Son of God, and are freely offered to those for whom the sacrifice was made. But how do many treat the proffered gift?—They turn away, choosing rather the pleasures of this life. Christ says of them, "Ye will not come to me, that ye might have life" (John 5:40).

Sinners are under a fearful deception. They despise and reject the Saviour. They do not realize the value of the pearl offered to them, and cast it away, rendering to their Redeemer only insult and mockery. Many a woman decks herself with rings and bracelets, thinking to gain admiration, but she refuses to accept the pearl of great price, which would secure for her sanctification, honor, and eternal riches. What an infatuation is upon the minds of many! They are more charmed with earthly baubles, which glitter and shine, than with the crown of immortal life, God's reward for loyalty. "Can a maid forget her ornaments, or a bride her attire? yet my people have forgotten me days without number" (Jer. 2:32).

64.

"The Darkness Comprehended It Not" *

"In the beginning was the Word, and the Word was with God, and the Word was God. The same was in the beginning with God. All things were made by him; and without him was not any thing made that was made. In him was life; and the life was the light of men. And the light shineth in darkness; and the darkness comprehended it not. There was a man sent from God, whose name was John. The same came for a witness, to bear witness of the Light, that all men through him might believe. He was not that Light, but was sent to bear witness of that Light. That was the true Light, which lighteth every man that cometh into the world" (John 1:1-9).

The question has been asked me, "Do you think that the Lord has any more light for us as a people?" I answer that He has light that is new to us, and yet it is precious old light that is to shine forth from the Word of truth. We have only the glimmerings of the rays of the light that is yet to come to us. We are not making the most of the light which the Lord has already given us, and thus we

* This article appeared in *The Review and Herald*, June 3, 1890.

fail to receive the increased light; we do not walk in light already shed upon us.

We call ourselves commandment-keeping people, but we do not comprehend the exceeding breadth of the far-reaching principles of the law of God; we do not understand its sacred character. Many who claim to be teachers of the truth, have no real conception of what they are doing in teaching the law of God, because they do not have a living knowledge of the Lord Jesus Christ.

As we read of Luther, Knox, and other noted Reformers, we admire the strength, fortitude, and courage possessed by these faithful servants of God, and we would catch the spirit that animated them. We desire to know from what source they were out of weakness made strong. Although these great men were used as instruments for God, they were not faultless. They were erring men, and made great mistakes. We should seek to imitate their virtues, but we should not make them our criterion. These men possessed rare talents to carry forward the work of the Reformation. They were moved upon by a power above themselves; but it was not the men, the instruments that God used, that should be exalted and honored, but the Lord Jesus who let His light and power come upon them. Let those who love truth and righteousness, who gather up the hereditary trusts given to these standard-bearers, praise God, the Source of all light.

If it should be announced that angel messengers were to open before men the treasures of the knowledge which relate to heavenly things, what a stir would it create in the Christian world! The atmosphere of heaven would be about the messengers, and how eagerly would many listen to the words that should fall from their lips! Men would write books calling attention to the angels' words, but a greater Being than angels has been in our world; the Lord Himself has come to reflect upon men the light of heaven. He has announced Himself as one with the Father, full of grace and truth, God manifest in the flesh.

The Lord Jesus, who is the image of the invisible God, gave His own life to save perishing man, and, oh, what light, what power, He brings with Him! In Him dwells all the fullness of the Godhead, bodily. What a mystery of mysteries! It is difficult for the reason to grasp the majesty of Christ, the mystery of redemption. The shameful cross has been upraised, the nails have been driven through His hands and feet, the cruel spear has pierced to His heart, and the redemption price has been paid for the human race. The spotless Lamb of God bore our sins in His own body upon the tree; He carried our sorrows.

An Inexhaustible Theme

Redemption is an inexhaustible theme, worthy of our closest contemplation. It passes the comprehension of the deepest thought, the stretch of the most vivid imagination. Who by searching can find out God? The treasures of wisdom and knowledge are opened to all men, and were thousands of the most gifted men to devote their whole time to setting forth Jesus always before us, studying how they might portray His matchless charms, they would never exhaust the subject.

Although great and talented authors have made known wonderful truths, and have presented increased light to the people, still in our day we shall find new ideas, and ample fields in which to work, for the theme of salvation is inexhaustible. The work has gone forward from century to century, setting forth the life and character of Christ, and the love of God as manifested in the atoning sacrifice. The theme of redemption will employ the minds of the redeemed through all eternity. There will be new and rich developments made manifest in the plan of salvation throughout eternal ages.

Were Jesus with us today, He would say to us as He did to His disciples, "I have yet many things to say unto you, but ye cannot bear them now" (John 16:12). Jesus longed to open before the minds of His disciples deep and living truths, but their earthliness, their clouded, deficient comprehension made it impossible. They could not be benefited with great, glorious, solemn truths. The want of spiritual growth closes the door to the rich rays of light that shine from Christ. We shall never reach a period when there is no increased light for us. The sayings of Christ were always far-reaching in their import. Those who heard His teachings with their preconceived opinions, could not take in the meaning attached to His utterances. Jesus was the source, the originator of truth.

The great themes of the Old Testament were misapprehended and misinterpreted, and Christ's work was to expound the truth which had not been understood by those to whom they had been given. The prophets had made the statements, but the spiritual import of what they had written, was undiscovered by them. They did not see the meaning of the truth. Jesus reproved His disciples for their slowness of comprehension. Many of His precious lessons were lost to them, because they did not understand the spiritual grandeur of His words. But He promised that the Comforter should come, that the Spirit of truth should recall these lost utterances to their minds. He gave them to understand that He had left with them precious jewels of truth whose value they did not know.

Precious Gems in Mines of Truth

After the crucifixion and the resurrection of Christ, His disciples listened with wonder and amazement to His lessons of truth; for they seemed as new ideas to them; but He told them, "These are the words which I spake unto you, while I was yet with you. . . . Then opened he their understanding, that they might understand the scriptures" (Luke 24:44, 45). The truth is constantly unfolding and presenting new features to different minds. All who dig in the mines of truth, will constantly discover rich and precious gems. We are anxious that all who claim to believe the truth now open before us, and especially those who take the responsibility of teaching the truth to others, should have a clearer conception themselves of the all-important significance of the themes of the Bible.

Those who stand in vindication of the law of God, are in a position where they need much of the Spirit of God. If ministers are wanting in meekness, if they are easily irritated when opposed, it is evident that they need divine enlightenment. Men must manifest the grace of Christ as they labor for souls. The truth as it is in Jesus will have altogether a different influence upon the minds of unbelievers, from that which it has had when presented as a theory or as a controversial subject.

If we do our very best to present the truth in its stirring character, crossing the opinions and ideas of others, it will be misinterpreted, misapplied, and misstated, to those who are entertaining error, in order to make it appear in an objectionable light. There are few to whom you bring the truth, who have not been drinking of the wine of Babylon. It is hard for them to comprehend the truth, therefore the necessity of teaching it as it is in Jesus.

Those who claim to be lovers of truth can afford to be meek and lowly of heart, as was the Great Teacher. Those who have been diligently working in the mines of God's Word, and have discovered the precious ore in the rich veins of truth, in the divine mysteries that have been hidden for ages, will exalt the Lord Jesus, the Source of all truth, by revealing in their characters the sanctifying power of what they believe. Jesus and His grace must be enshrined in the inner sanctuary of the soul. Then He will be revealed in words, in prayer, in exhortation, in the presentation of sacred truth, for this is the great secret of spiritual success.

When self is woven into our labors, then the truth we bear to others does not sanctify, refine, and ennoble our own hearts; it will not testify that we are fit vessels for the Master's use. It is only through fervent prayer that we may hold sweet fellowship with Jesus, and through this blessed communion the words and the spirit are made fragrant with the spirit of Christ. There is not a heart that will not bear watching. Jesus, the precious Saviour, enjoined watchfulness. The oversight of self must not be relaxed for a moment. The heart must be kept with diligence, for out of it are the issues of life. Watch and discipline the thoughts, that you may not sin with your lips.

65.

*How to Meet a Controverted Point of Doctrine**

We want to understand the time in which we live. We do not half understand it. We do not half take it in. My heart trembles in me when I think of what a foe we have to meet, and how poorly we are prepared to meet him. The trials of the children of Israel, and their attitude just before the first coming of Christ, have been presented before me again and again to illustrate the position of the people of God in their experience before the second coming of Christ—how the enemy sought every occasion to take control of the minds of the Jews, and today he is seeking to blind the minds of God's servants, that they may not be able to discern the precious truth.

When Christ came to our world, Satan was on the ground, and disputed every inch of advance in His path from the manger to Calvary. Satan had accused God of requiring self-denial of the angels, when He knew nothing of what it meant Himself, and when He would not Himself make any self-sacrifice for others. This was the ac-

* Morning talk at Battle Creek, Michigan, Jan. 29, 1890, which was printed in *The Review and Herald* of Feb. 18, 1890.

cusation that Satan made against God in heaven; and after the evil one was expelled from heaven, he continually charged the Lord with exacting service which He would not render Himself. Christ came to the world to meet these false accusations, and to reveal the Father. We cannot conceive of the humiliation He endured in taking our nature upon Himself. Not that in itself it was a disgrace to belong to the human race, but He was the Majesty of heaven, the King of glory, and He humbled Himself to become a babe and suffer the wants and woes of mortals. He humbled Himself not to the highest position, to be a man of riches and power, but though He was rich, yet for our sake He became poor, that we through His poverty might be made rich. He took step after step in humiliation. He was driven from city to city; for men would not receive the Light of the world. They were perfectly satisfied with their position.

Christ had given precious gems of truth, but men had bound them up in the rubbish of superstition and error. He had imparted to them the words of life, but they did not live by every word that proceeds out of the mouth of God. He saw that the world could not find the word of God, for it was hidden by the traditions of men. He came to place before the world the relative importance of heaven and earth, and put truth in its own place. Jesus alone could reveal the truth which it was necessary men should know in order that they might obtain salvation. He only could place it in the framework of truth, and it was His work to free it from error and to set it before men in its heavenly light.

Satan was roused to oppose Him, for had he not put forth every effort since the Fall to make light appear darkness, and darkness light? As Christ sought to place truth before the people in its proper relation to their salvation, Satan worked through the Jewish leaders, and inspired them with enmity against the Redeemer of the world. They determined to do all in their power to prevent Him from making an impression upon the people.

O how Christ longed, how His heart burned, to open to the priests the greater treasures of the truth! But their minds had been cast in such a mold that it was next to an impossibility to reveal to them the truths relating to His kingdom. The Scriptures had not been read aright. The Jews had been looking for the advent of the Messiah, but they had thought He must come in all the glory that will attend His second appearing. Because He did not come with all the majesty of a king, they utterly refused Him. But it was not simply because He did not come in splendor that they refused Him. It was because He was the embodiment of purity, and they were impure. He walked the earth a man of spotless integrity. Such a character in the midst of degradation and evil, was out of harmony with their desires, and He was abused and despised. His spotless life flashed light upon the hearts of men, and discovered iniquity to them in its odious character.

The Son of God was assaulted at every step by the powers of darkness. After His baptism He was driven of the Spirit into the wilderness, and suffered temptation for forty days. Letters have been coming in to me, affirming that Christ could not have had the same nature as man, for if He had, He would have fallen under similar temptations. If He did not have man's nature, He could not be our example. If He was not a partaker of our nature, He could not have been tempted as man has been. If it were not possible for Him to yield to temptation, He could not be our helper. It was a solemn reality that Christ came to fight the battles as man, in man's behalf. His temptation and victory tell us that humanity must copy the Pattern; man must become a partaker of the divine nature.

Divinity and Humanity United in Christ

In Christ, divinity and humanity were combined. Divinity was not degraded to humanity; divinity held its place, but humanity by being united to divinity withstood the fiercest test of temptation in the wilderness. The prince of this world came to Christ after His long fast, when He was an hungered, and suggested to Him to command the stones to become bread. But the plan of God, devised for the salvation of man, provided that Christ should know hunger, and poverty, and every phase of man's experience. He withstood the temptation, through the power that man may command. He laid hold on the throne of God, and there is not a man or woman who may not have access to the same help through faith in God. Man may become a partaker of the divine nature; not a soul lives who may not summon the aid of Heaven in temptation and trial. Christ came to reveal the source of His power, that man might never rely on his unaided human capabilities.

Those who would overcome must put to the tax every power of their being. They must agonize on their knees before God for divine power. Christ came to be our example, and to make known to us that we may be partakers of the divine nature. How?—By having escaped the corruptions that are in the world through lust. Satan did not gain the victory over Christ. He did not put his foot upon the soul of the Redeemer. He did not touch the head though he bruised the heel. Christ, by His own example, made it evident that man may stand in integrity. Men may have a power to resist evil—a power that neither earth, nor death, nor hell can master; a power that will place them where they may overcome as Christ overcame. Divinity and humanity may be combined in them.

It was the work of Christ to present the truth in the framework of the gospel, and to reveal the precepts and principles that He had given to fallen man. Every idea He presented was His own. He needed not to borrow thoughts from any, for He was the originator of all truth. He could present the ideas of prophets and philosophers, and preserve His originality; for all wisdom was His; He was the source, the fountain, of all truth. He was in advance of all, and by His teaching He became the spiritual leader for all ages.

It was Christ that spoke through Melchizedek, the priest of the most high God. Melchizedek was not Christ, but he was the voice of God in the world, the representative of the Father. And all through the generations of the past, Christ has spoken; Christ has led His people, and has been the light of the world. When God chose Abraham as a representative of His truth, He took him out of his country, and away from his kindred, and set him apart. He desired to mold him after His own model. He desired to teach him according to His own plan. The mold of the world's teachers was not to be upon him. He was to be taught how to command his children and his household after him, to keep the way of the Lord, to do justice and judgment. This is the work that God would have us do. He would have us understand how to govern our families, how to control our children, how to command our households to keep the way of the Lord.

John Called to a Special Work

John was called to do a special work; he was to prepare the way of the Lord, to make straight His paths. The Lord did not send him to the school of the prophets and rabbis. He took him away from the assemblies of men to the desert, that he might learn of nature and nature's God. God did not desire him to have the mold of the priests and rulers. He was called to do a special work. The Lord gave him his message. Did he go to the priests and rulers and ask if he might proclaim this message?—No, God put him away from them that he might not be influenced by their spirit and teaching. He was the voice of one crying in the wilderness, "Prepare ye the way of the Lord, make straight in the desert a highway for our God. Every valley shall be exalted, and every mountain and hill shall be made low: and the crooked shall be made straight, and the rough places plain; and the glory of the Lord shall be revealed, and all flesh shall see it together: for the mouth of the Lord hath spoken it" (Isa. 40:3-5). This is the very message that must be given to our people; we are near the end of time, and the message is, Clear the King's highway; gather out the stones; raise up a standard for the people. The people must be awakened. It is no time now to cry peace and safety. We are exhorted to "cry aloud, spare not, lift up thy voice like a trumpet, and shew my people their transgression, and the house of Jacob their sins" (Isa. 5:1).

The light of the glory of God shone upon our Representative, and this fact says to us that the glory of God may shine upon us. With His human arm, Jesus encircled the race, and with His divine arm He grasped the throne of the Infinite, connecting man with God, and earth with heaven.

The light of the glory of God must fall upon us. We need the holy unction from on high. However intelligent, however learned a man may be, he is not qualified to teach unless he has a firm hold on the God of Israel. He who is connected with Heaven will do the works of Christ. By faith in God he will have power to move upon humanity. He will seek for the lost sheep of the house of Israel. If divine power does not combine with human effort, I would not give a straw for all that the greatest man could do. The Holy Spirit is wanting in our work. Nothing frightens me more than to see the spirit of variance manifested by our brethren. We are on dangerous ground when we cannot meet together like Christians, and courteously examine controverted points. I feel like fleeing from the place lest I receive the mold of those who cannot candidly investigate the doctrines of the Bible.

Those who cannot impartially examine the evidences of a position that differs from theirs, are not fit to teach in any department of God's cause. What we need is the baptism of the Holy Spirit. Without this, we are no more fitted to go forth to the world than were the disciples after the crucifixion of their Lord. Jesus knew their destitution, and told them to tarry in Jerusalem until they should be endowed with power from on high. Every teacher must be a learner, that his eyes may be anointed to see the evidences of the advancing truth of God. The beams of the Sun of Righteousness must shine into his own heart if he would impart light to others.

No one is able to explain the Scriptures without the aid of the Holy Spirit. But when you take up the Word of God with a humble, teachable heart, the angels of God will be by your side to impress you with evidences of the truth. When the Spirit of God rests upon you, there will be no feeling of envy or jealousy in examining another's position; there will be no spirit of accusation and criticism, such as Satan inspired in the hearts of the Jewish leaders against Christ. As Christ said to Nicodemus, so I say to you, "Ye must be born again." "Except a man be born again, he cannot see the kingdom of God" (John 3:7, 3). You must have the divine mold before you can discern the sacred claims of the truth. Unless the teacher is a learner in the school of Christ, he is not fitted to teach others.

The Special Work of Ellen G. White

We should come into a position where every difference will be melted away. If I think I have light, I shall do my duty in presenting it. Suppose I consulted others concerning the message the Lord would have me give to the people, the door might be closed so that the light might not reach the ones to whom God had sent it. When Jesus rode into Jerusalem, "the whole multitude of the disciples began to rejoice and praise God with a loud voice for all the mighty works that they had seen; saying, Blessed be the King that cometh in the name of the Lord: peace in heaven, and glory in the highest. And some of the Pharisees from among the multitude said unto him, Master, rebuke thy disciples. And he answered and said unto them, I tell you that, if these should hold their peace, the stones would immediately cry out" (Luke 19:37-40).

The Jews tried to stop the proclamation of the message that had been predicted in the Word of God; but prophecy must be fulfilled. The Lord says, "Behold, I will send you Elijah the prophet before the coming of the great and dreadful day of the Lord" (Mal. 4:5). Somebody is to come in the spirit and power of Elijah, and when he appears, men may say, "You are too earnest, you do not interpret the Scriptures in the proper way. Let me tell you how to teach your message."

There are many who cannot distinguish between the work of God and that of man. I shall tell the truth as God gives it to me, and I say now, If you continue to find fault, to have a spirit of variance, you will never know the truth. Jesus said to His disciples, "I have yet many things to say unto you, but ye cannot bear them now" (John 16:12). They were not in a condition to appreciate sacred and eternal things; but Jesus promised to send the Comforter, who would teach them all things, and bring all things to their remembrance, whatsoever He had said unto them. Brethren, we must not put our dependence in man. "Cease ye from man, whose breath is in his nostrils: for wherein is he to be accounted of?" (Isa. 2:22). You must hang your helpless souls upon Jesus. It does not become us to drink from the fountain of the valley, when there is a fountain in the mountain. Let us leave the lower streams; let us come to the higher springs. If there is a point of truth that you do not understand, upon which you do not agree, investigate, compare scripture with scripture, sink the shaft of truth down deep into the mine of God's Word. You must lay yourselves and your opinions on the altar of God, put away your preconceived ideas, and let the Spirit of Heaven guide you into all truth.

My brother said at one time that he would not hear anything concerning the doctrine we hold, for fear he should be convinced. He would not come to the meetings, or listen to the discourses; but he afterward declared that he saw he was as guilty as if he had heard them. God had given him an opportunity to know the truth, and He would hold him responsible for this opportunity. There are many among us who are prejudiced against the doctrines that are now being discussed. They will not come to hear, they will not calmly investigate, but they put forth their objections in the dark. They are perfectly satisfied with their position. "Thou sayest, I am rich, and increased with goods, and have need of nothing; and knowest not that thou art wretched, and miserable, and poor, and blind, and naked: I counsel thee to buy of me gold tried in the fire, that thou mayest be rich; and white raiment, that thou mayest be clothed, and that the shame of thy nakedness do not appear; and anoint thine eyes with eyesalve, that thou mayest see. As many as I love, I rebuke and chasten: be zealous therefore, and repent" (Rev. 3:17-19).

This scripture applies to those who live under the

sound of the message, but who will not come to hear it.
How do you know but that the Lord is giving fresh evidences of His truth, placing it in a new setting, that the
way of the Lord may be prepared? What plans have you
been laying that new light may be infused through the
ranks of God's people? What evidence have you that God
has not sent light to His children? All self-sufficiency, egotism, and pride of opinion must be put away. We must
come to the feet of Jesus, and learn of Him who is meek
and lowly of heart. Jesus did not teach His disciples as the
rabbis taught theirs. Many of the Jews came and listened as
Christ revealed the mysteries of salvation, but they came not
to learn; they came to criticize, to catch Him in some inconsistency, that they might have something with which to
prejudice the people. They were content with their knowledge, but the children of God must know the voice of the
True Shepherd. Is not this a time when it would be highly
proper to fast and pray before God? We are in danger of
variance, in danger of taking sides on a controverted point;
and should we not seek God in earnestness, with humiliation of soul, that we may know what is truth?

Go Under the Fig Tree

Nathanael heard John as he pointed to the Saviour and
said, "Behold the Lamb of God, which taketh away the sin
of the world" (John 1:29)! Nathanael looked at Jesus, but
he was disappointed in the appearance of the world's Redeemer. Could He who bore the marks of toil and proverty
be the Messiah? Jesus was a worker; He had toiled with
humble workingmen, and Nathanael went away. But he
did not form his opinion decidedly as to what the character
of Jesus was. He knelt down under a fig tree, inquiring
of God if indeed this man was the Messiah. While he was
there, Philip came and said, "We have found him, of whom
Moses in the law, and the prophets, did write, Jesus of
Nazareth, the son of Joseph." But the word "Nazareth"
again aroused his unbelief, and he said, "Can there any
good thing come out of Nazareth?" He was full of prejudice, but Philip did not seek to combat his prejudice; he

simply said, "Come and see." When Nathanael came into the presence of Jesus, Jesus said, "Behold an Israelite indeed, in whom is no guile!" Nathanael was amazed. He said, "Whence knowest thou me? Jesus answered and said unto him, Before that Philip called thee, when thou wast under the fig tree, I saw thee" (John 1:45, 46, 47, 48).

Would it not be well for us to go under the fig tree to plead with God as to what is truth? Would not the eye of God be upon us as it was upon Nathanael? Nathanael believed on the Lord, and exclaimed, "Rabbi, thou art the Son of God; thou art the King of Israel. Jesus answered and said unto him, Because I said unto thee, I saw thee under the fig tree, believest thou? thou shalt see greater things than these. And he saith unto him, Verily, verily, I say unto you, Hereafter ye shall see heaven open, and the angels of God ascending and descending upon the Son of man" (John 1:49-51).

This is what we shall see if we are connected with God. God wants us to depend upon Him, and not upon man. He desires us to have a new heart; He would give us revealings of light from the throne of God. We should wrestle with every difficulty, but when some controverted point is presented, are you to go to man to find out his opinion, and then shape your conclusions from his?—No, go to God. Tell Him what you want; take your Bible and search as for hidden treasures.

We Do Not Go Deep Enough

We do not go deep enough in our search for truth. Every soul who believes present truth will be brought where he will be required to give a reason of the hope that is in him. The people of God will be called upon to stand before kings, princes, rulers, and great men of the earth, and they must know that they do know what is truth. They must be converted men and women. God can teach you more in one moment by His Holy Spirit than you could learn from the great men of the earth. The universe is looking upon the controversy that is going on upon the earth. At an infinite cost, God has provided for every man an opportunity to know that which will make him wise unto salvation. How eagerly do angels look to see who will avail himself of this opportunity!

When a message is presented to God's people, they should not rise up in opposition to it; they should go to the Bible, comparing it with the law and the testimony, and if it does not bear this test, it is not true. God wants our minds to expand. He desires to put His grace upon us. We may have a feast of good things every day; for God can open the whole treasure of heaven to us. We are to be one with Christ as He is one with the Father, and the Father will love us as He loves His Son. We may have the same help that Christ had, we may have strength for every emergency; for God will be our front guard and our rearward. He will shut us in on every side, and when we are brought before rulers, before the authorities of the earth, we need not meditate beforehand of what we shall say. God will teach us in the day of our need. Now may God help us to come to the feet of Jesus and learn of Him, before we seek to become teachers of others.

The Bible Our Creed

When God's Word is studied, comprehended, and obeyed, a bright light will be reflected to the world; new truths, received and acted upon, will bind us in strong bonds to Jesus. The Bible, and the Bible alone, is to be our creed, the sole bond of union; all who bow to this Holy Word will be in harmony. Our own views and ideas must not control our efforts. Man is fallible, but God's Word is infallible. Instead of wrangling with one another, let men exalt the Lord. Let us meet all opposition as did our Master, saying, "It is written." Let us lift up the banner on which is inscribed, The Bible our rule of faith and discipline.— *The Review and Herald,* Dec. 15, 1885.

Scripture Index

The following Scripture Index indicates where the author has quoted the passage of Scripture referred to or has said something having a bearing upon it.

General Index

I

U